Cleveland: A Tradition of Reform

EDITED BY
DAVID D. VAN TASSEL
and
JOHN J. GRABOWSKI

Cleveland:
A Tradition of Reform

THE KENT STATE UNIVERSITY PRESS

All photos are used by permission of the Western Reserve Historical Society, Cleveland, Ohio 44106.

The paper in this book meets the guidelines for permanence and durability of the Committee on Production Guidelines for Book Longevity of the Council on Library Resources.

Library of Congress Cataloging-in-Publication Data

Main entry under title:

Cleveland—a tradition of reform.

   Includes bibliographical references and index.
   1. Social movements—Ohio—Cleveland—History—Addresses, essays, lectures.
2. Social reformers—Ohio—Cleveland—History—Addresses, essays, lectures.
3. Cleveland (Ohio)—Social conditions—Addresses, essays, lectures.   4. Cleveland (Ohio)—Politics and government—Addresses, essays, lectures.   I. Van Tassel, David D. (David Dirck), 1928–   . II. Grabowski, John J.
HN80.C6C58   1986   306'.09771'32   85-8165
ISBN 0-87338-322-2

Contents

Preface and Acknowledgments

Cities have personalities; both travelers and chambers of commerce will testify to this. Yet, despite posters and civic propaganda, few people can isolate the essence of individuality in any city, be it San Francisco, Chicago, or Cleveland. Finding the truth behind an urban stereotype and attesting to its correctness or deceptiveness is one of the urban historian's tasks.

The essays in this volume are the result of just such a search for the historical personality of Cleveland, Ohio. The editors, supported generously by the Cleveland Foundation and a number of other local foundations, families, and businesses, have, since 1981, been engaged in the compilation of the *Encyclopedia of Cleveland History*. In the early stages of this larger project, one of the persistent questions was, "What is special about Cleveland?" Typical, traditional responses to this query have centered on the area's geographic location and its New England roots. Neither answer has proved to be wholly correct, though both factors have added measurably to the city's persona. What has emerged, however, is the remarkable consistency of the primacy of reform in all periods of the city's past, and the special nature of reform and philanthropy in Cleveland. Both have been constantly smoothed and ordered throughout the city's history. Rough, radical edges have been removed and a tack has always been set for the conservative middle ground of reform. Given the primacy of reform and its special nature in Cleveland, as well as the enduring concern of historians with reformers and reform as agents of change, we felt that this aspect of local history was sufficiently important and of interest to warrant a separate book. Fortunately, the Cleveland Foundation, itself a late product of the local urge to organize and order philanthropy, concurred in our belief and also lent support to this undertaking. Though the essays in this book do not treat all reform movements in Cleveland and though they are not often comprehensive in their view of a particular reform, they provide an important analysis of a critical part of Cleveland's psyche. We hope, too, that they serve to spur further research into this and other aspects of Cleveland history for, from an academic standpoint, the city remains undeservedly understudied.

We would like to acknowledge the Cleveland Foundation for the funds that made possible the research, writing, and typing of this manuscript, and give particular thanks to Dr. Susan LaJoie, program officer for the Foundation whose enthusiastic support for the idea provided us with constant encouragement. Our authors, too, deserve thanks for the patience they have shown throughout the editorial process. Finally, we owe a great deal to Mary Stavish, Coordinator for the *Encyclopedia of Cleveland History* project and to Betty Tracy. True to her title, Mary managed to keep all the pieces of this work together throughout a long gestation, and Betty showed skill and patience in typing and retyping the manuscript. The errors of omission and commission, not many, we hope, are the responsibility of the editors.

David D. Van Tassel
Professor of History
Case Western Reserve University

John J. Grabowski
Curator of Manuscripts
Western Reserve Historical Society

D A V I D   D .   V A N   T A S S E L

Introduction:
Cleveland and Reform

Book distribution sponsored by Hiram House social settlement in the lower Woodland Avenue neighborhood, ca. 1905

Tradition and reform are, at first glance, terms in apparent opposition: one implies stability while the other popularly connotes change. Arguments over the exact definition of reform not withstanding, there can still be traditions of reform in families, in social groups, or in cities. Such has been the case in Cleveland, Ohio, where participation in reform movements has formed a continuum throughout the city's history. The essays presented in this volume examine that participation. Individually, each essay explores the history of a particular reform movement. Together, they present an overview of the nature of power and leadership in an evolving urban center as well as the ordering and secularization of religious impulses in modern America.

Historians for decades have written about the nature of reform in America, making various efforts at definition and classification. One of the pioneer historians of antebellum reform, Alice Felt Tyler, classified reformers and reforms as conservative or radical in her book *Freedom's Ferment* (1944). Conservative reforms, according to Tyler, were those which made no attempt to change the overall fabric of society, but which sought to improve certain aspects, as was the case with temperance and prison reform. Equal rights for women or the abolition of slavery were, however, considered radical threats to society. Radical political reforms such as socialism and its variations were often considered foreign and doctrinaire, while conservative movements sought to eliminate some of the perceived evils of the political system and return democracy to the people, usually the middle class. Such reforms might seek the elimination of corruption through competitive bidding for municipal contracts, direct primaries, public referendums, or the institution of professional city managers. None of these definitions, however, has withstood much examination, so we have opted for the broadest and most neutral view, that of reform as an effort to correct social or political faults. Within this, some reforms may be perceived as good, some may not, and others are simply incomprehensible.

This volume treats eight reform movements in Cleveland: antebellum benevolence, temperance, abolitionism, the women's movement, black civil rights, educational reform, social reform, and political reform. This is certainly not an exhaustive catalog of those movements which affected Cleveland. Religious reforms such as Shakerism, labor reforms, and sanitary and housing reforms have been consciously omitted. The movements considered in this volume were included for various reasons. Political reform and social reform, for example, were areas in which the city was in the national forefront. Lincoln Steffens's pronouncement that Cleveland was "the best governed city in the United States" is recalled here as is the consolidation of the fiscal support of the area's philanthropic and charitable agencies in the early 1900s.[1] Foremost in the selection of topics, however, was their chronological position in the history of the city. Though several of the movements have continued to the present, each arose at a different period in the nineteenth century. This provides the opportunity to examine the continuity of leadership and motive for a variety of causes over a long period of time.

The background against which each of these movements was played was the evolution of a major, cosmopolitan urban center from a rural, homogeneous village. Cleveland was planned in 1796 by agents of the Connecticut Land Company, a speculative enterprise which had purchased the vast Western Reserve of the state of Connecticut. The agents and their surveyors platted the village site in the image of a New England town and, for many years, it existed as such with a central square, white picket fences, and a Protestant population of Yankees, New Yorkers, and Anglo immigrant stock. Business needs and the New England heritage, both inherent in the city's establishment, remained central to its communal psyche through much of its history and, as noted throughout this volume, colored every reform effort. Though the settlement's position at the mouth of the Cuyahoga River boded well for its eventual commercial success, it was not until 1825, with the completion of the first portion of the Ohio-Erie Canal between Lake Erie and the Ohio River, that any substantial commercial and demographic growth began. Before that time, the area remained rural and somnolent; Cleveland's population in 1820 was only 606. Ten years later it had risen to 1,075, the increase occasioned largely by opportunities generated by the canal.[2]

Demographic growth brought an end to the area's homogeneity.

Irish and German immigrants began arriving in the 1820s, and German Jews in the late 1830s. The religious spectrum of the village suddenly broadened to include Roman Catholics and Jews. Until the Civil War, the city continued to grow as a mercantile center, attracting numerous businesses, a railroad network, and more immigrants from the aforementioned groups. On the eve of that war Cleveland's population stood at 43,417.

The city's nascent industrial base grew vigorously during the war and in the following decades. Major enterprises such as Standard Oil, Warner and Swasey, and Sherwin Williams had their roots in the city during this period. The need for cheap labor and the opening of large-scale immigration from southern and eastern Europe in the latter decades of the nineteenth century attracted a new, diverse element to Cleveland's population. By the end of the mass immigration in the 1920s, over one-third of the population of 796,841 was foreign-born and represented over fifty ethnic groups. This influx challenged the city's services, schools, political structure, and philanthropic agencies. An expansion of the city's black community accompanied this white ethnic immigration. Recruitment of blacks for jobs in wartime industry had expanded the black community from 8,448 in 1910 to 34,451 in 1920.[3] To the casual observer, the only aspects of turn-of-the-century Cleveland that seemed remotely like New England were its central Public Square and the spires of its Protestant churches, though the latter shared the skyline with the domes and towers of Catholicism and Judaism. Like many other urban areas, Cleveland enjoyed the prosperity of the 1920s, suffered through the Depression, boomed again during World War II, and then saw its industrial base and population erode in the 1960s and 1970s. The city's population peaked at 914,808 in 1950, and then receded to its present level of just over five hundred thousand.

In such a volatile situation could reform have any continuity, any tradition, particularly when the concerns of reformers shifted from national and rural themes to focus more on local and urban issues in the late nineteenth century? The most recent scholarly work on reform in America, Ronald Walters's excellent study, *American Reformers, 1815–1860*, indicates that tradition would not be the norm. Walters concludes that "a lack of continuity marks one of the chief characteristics of American reform: Failure, or inability, to build traditions and institutions capable of surviving across generations."[4]

However, while changes in style, in organization, in approaches, and even in goals in a single reform movement occurred during the course of the nineteenth and twentieth centuries, a very distinct tradition of reform developed in Cleveland. It grew, as noted by many historians, out of the Protestant evangelical impulse to perfect man and his society, an impulse that was a latent part of the heritage of the city's founders. The essays here by Michael McTighe, Marian Morton, and Bertram Wyatt-Brown, dealing with antebellum benevolence, temperance, and abolitionism, respectively, show the strong influence of the Protestant base of Cleveland and the Western Reserve on these early reform movements. The church was the focus of these movements, particularly in the cases of benevolence and abolitionism. McTighe's reformers met and distributed aid from their churches, while Wyatt-Brown's abolitionists chose their church according to its degree of commitment to the cause. Even at the turn of the century, when Cleveland was far from its rural Protestant roots, social reform in the guise of settlement houses was very much a result of the evangelical spirit, as evidenced in the essay by John Grabowski. One Cleveland social reformer, Frederick C. Howe, wrote in his autobiography, *Confessions of a Reformer*, that he had rejected religion in college, in fact was resentful of it, but he observed that

> Physical escape from the embraces of evangelical religion did not mean moral escape. . . . It was with difficulty that realism got lodgment in my mind; early assumptions as to virtue and vice, goodness and evil remained in my mind long after I had tried to discard them. This is, I think, the most characteristic influence of my generation. It explains the nature of our reforms, the regulatory legislation in morals and economics, our belief in men rather than institutions and our messages to other people. Missionaries and battleships, anti-saloon leagues and the Ku Klux Klan, Wilson and Santo Domingo, are all a part of that evangelical psychology. . . .[5]

This sense of moral mission is certainly characteristic of reform and reformers in Cleveland.

The reform tradition in Cleveland centers on its leadership. With the exception of the black movement for civil rights, treated in the essay by Christopher Wye, each reform movement drew its leaders from the city's Protestant upper middle and upper classes. The evangelical genesis of reform in Cleveland became a family and class matter. McTighe's essay clearly outlines the religious and social backgrounds of the city's early reformers. Many of the same names, and other names of Anglo-Saxon origin, appear in movements as diverse in time and focus as women's rights and educational reform. Those active in reform were the business, legal, and financial leaders of the city, their spouses, and, very often, their clergy. As a religious people, they sought to do what was right and proper, in an efficient and orderly manner. Leadership in reform, benevolence, and philanthropy in Cleveland continued to be a matter of class throughout the nineteenth century and into the early twentieth. The boards of directors of the city's settlement houses, as noted in the Grabowski essay, were exclusively the well-to-do and business leaders of the community. As described in that same essay, the move to rationalize and order philanthropic affairs in the city arose from a committee of the chamber of commerce. Leaders of political reform in Cleveland may be classified in the same manner; Tom L. Johnson and Newton D. Baker, the major figures in local progressive politics were, respectively, a businessman and a lawyer. As noted in James Richardson's essay, some of the policies espoused by Johnson, and many of those put forth by Baker, were eagerly supported by a business community looking for continuity and order in periods of rapid change.

It is easy to see why reform in Cleveland would have begun as a matter of money and class. Those dispensing aid in the antebellum city needed the resources to do so. Similarly, the involvement of many of these same individuals in the antislavery and temperance movements would have been made possible by their extended leisure time and, perhaps, in some instances, by a broader educational background than the bulk of the citizenry. What is interesting, however, is that many of the same types of individuals and even members of the same families continued to be involved in and lead other reform and philanthropic endeavors well into the next century. In this they were often joined by wealthy community members of a more recent vintage, but usually of the same religious background. So, although leadership formed a continuum in reform in Cleveland, the targets of those reforms changed with the economic and demographic bases of the city.

If one accepts the premise that reform movements in Cleveland emanated from a stable, Protestant, upper middle and upper class, it becomes more than a matter of idle curiosity to identify the targets of the movements. In almost all the cases cited in this volume, the reforms were directed outward, toward groups other than those advocating the reform. Implicit in this is the assumption that reform in Cleveland involved preservation of the status quo or the regaining of a lost or fading societal order.

One of the earliest movements examined here, abolitionism, had to be directed outward for it championed the rights of a group apart from mainstream society. However, in its most rigorous form, abolitionism deeply involved its advocates, for it was viewed by many as a purging of a society that condoned slavery, a matter of expiation on the part of its proponents. But, as noted by Wyatt-Brown in his essay on abolitionism and antislavery in the Western Reserve, Cleveland was a bastion of proponents of antislavery, but a city little tolerant of the extremism of such abolitionists as Theodore Weld and John Brown. Little or no money from Cleveland went to the bloody border forays of the latter, or even to the purchase of "Beecher's Bibles" for the fight over Kansas. Immediatism, fanaticism, and radicalism threatened stability, so strict abolition, that is, immediate emancipation, found a small audience in Cleveland. The city would rather have colonized than freed slaves.

Temperance, another of the early reform movements, seemed originally to have been directed at a diverse group which included its proponents. As shown here by Morton, it was an effort to rid society of a vice that debilitated, destroyed character, and robbed the city of workers and the common wealth they produced. Christianity certainly seemed to characterize those temperance advocates whom Morton depicts signing pledges of total abstinence along with the canalers and Lake Erie sailors. By the 1900s, however, a change in motivation took place as alcohol became largely associated with the newer immigrant groups arriving in the city. The apogee of the movement, reached during the anti-German phobia of World War I, bears out the fact that temperance had become a reform reaching beyond its generative class. Its success at this time owed much to the general unpopularity of those toward whom it was directed.

The good citizens active in the benevolent associations described by McTighe also began work among their peers, caring for their own and for the common good at the same time. With the growth of the village into a city they were overwhelmed by the needs of a burgeoning and increasingly diverse populace. By the eve of the Civil War, people such as Benjamin and Rebecca Rouse were no longer caring for friends or cultural and religious peers, but for strangers who had arrived in the city from all corners of the country. Faced with such demands, those dispensing charity became concerned with identifying the worthy poor and eliminating duplication of effort. They also began to see the close connection between relieving distress and the stability of their own stations in life.

The topics of the reforms evolving in Cleveland after the Civil War seem to have little direct linkage to those groups advocating them. As such these movements fall into the classic category of reforms designed to preserve or re-create a social order. This is not to deny the altruistic or religious motives of individuals active in the areas of educational, political, or social reform in Cleveland, but merely to note the assessment of their actions in a broad historical perspective.

Edward Miggins's review of educational reform in Cleveland comes precisely to this point. Certainly those individuals modernizing and systematizing the Cleveland Public Schools sought to impose a curriculum that would be of greatest benefit in turning children, especially the children of immigrants, into useful citizens with useful careers. However, no matter what the direction chosen, be it the provision of manual training, the establishment of English classes for recent arrivals, or the revision of the classic "three R's" curriculum, these reformers must be seen as acting upon a group who were given little voice in the matter. Indeed, the preservation of a stable, functional society would have been uppermost in the minds of Clevelanders whose city by 1900 was over one-third foreign-born. What is also striking about educational reform in Cleveland is the emphasis placed on efficiency. Not only were the curriculum changes expected to produce a more efficient populace, but the study and analysis of pedagogy, the emphasis on teacher training, and the search for superintendents with broad experience show the melding of reform with the industrial philosophy of Frederick W. Taylor. Taylorism not only guided the industries that drew people to Cleveland at the turn of the century, but now molded the manner in which they and their children were to be educated and assisted.

Perhaps nowhere was the gulf between reformer and subject more apparent than in the establishment of social settlements, a facet of reform examined in John Grabowski's essay. The settlement was, by its nature, an implantation of one cultural group into the neighborhood of another. Again, as Grabowski shows, the roots of the movement were strongly evangelical and the settling of reformers in immigrant communities a genuine expression of neighborliness. In particular, the concept of the settlement was partly a reaction against the growing formality of benevolence through systematization. But in spite of the settlement workers' desire to be a part of their neighborhoods, they always remained separate in terms of religion and class. Even in Goodrich House, the most liberal of the institutions examined in this essay, the workers were considered alien. Frederick Howe, a former worker at Goodrich House, was, as cited above, left with bitter memories of reform, many of which can be traced to the awkwardness he felt during his work at the settlement.

Social reform in Cleveland culminated in the establishment of the Federation for Charity and Philanthropy in 1913. The federation epitomized both the outward nature of reform as well as the move toward efficiency and order. It conducted a unified drive to fund those charities deemed to be nonredundant and credible. Although individual social workers (a term soon to come into vogue) may have had deep personal motives for their service, they were now dependent upon a higher authority for their resources, and that authority, in turn, was oriented only toward the careful marshalling and expenditure of funds. Benevolence in Cleveland had come a long way from the home-to-home visits undertaken by the leading men and true women of McTighe's essay.

It would seem that efficiency was also the watchword for political reform in Cleveland. Though much has been written about progressive political reform originating from a need to preserve and protect urban government from corruption, this goal seems secondary to the striving for efficiency in Cleveland's early move toward political reform, as noted by James Richardson in his essay. Whether achieved by home rule or the city manager, this motive was so strong that it sometimes drove the city's chamber of commerce into alliance with Tom L. Johnson, the almost mythological radical of Cleveland political life, when the chamber saw programs such as the group plan and a housing code as being to the city's advantage. This is not as strange as it might seem, for Johnson was, after all, a businessman and the chamber members his peers. The often mutual interests of business and government continued to prosper under Johnson's political heir, Newton D. Baker, and reached their pinnacle with the adoption of the city manager plan in the 1920s. However, lack of support on the ward and neighborhood level caused the demise of the city manager plan and later the failure to create a regional government.

Two of the movements discussed in this volume—women's rights and black civil rights—do not fit easily into the foregoing analysis because they were championed by groups that were not a part of mainstream society. Yet, in their own way, they are part of the conservative tradition of reform in Cleveland. Lois Scharf's essay on the women's movement in Cleveland shows that the city was certainly not a hotbed for women's rights. The rather late entry of Cleveland women into the movement during the nineteenth century seems to parallel the city's experience with immediate abolitionism. Both movements were directed toward the radical alteration of society, and in such matters Clevelanders, whether male or female, seem to have trod lightly. Scharf notes that "Cleveland women who chose public roles during the nineteenth century preferred benevolent charity and moral suasion to ameliorate the perceived disabilities of women." Then, even upon entry into the movement, Cleveland's women's rights advocates, most of whom were educated, middle-class women, seemed hesitant about the degree to which they should assert themselves. So limited was the radical aspect of the movement that local feminists of the 1960s and 1970s at first felt they had arisen in a historical vacuum. Only through study did they discover the small band of women who had ventured beyond the local, conservative norm over fifty years earlier.

Christopher Wye's essay on black civil rights in Cleveland depicts another movement that remained outside of the mainstream of local reform largely because its leadership was made up of those most affected by the cause being championed and because the movement would engender large-scale social readjustment. Blacks may have had white advocates during the struggle for abolitionism and in more recent civil rights work, but for much of the late nineteenth and early twentieth centuries in Cleveland, they carried the burden of the movement themselves. As was the case with immediate emancipation, the cause of full civil rights for blacks was too radical to attract much white support in Cleveland. A difference in color of reformer, however, does not allow us to place this movement completely outside of local reform tradition. Whether advocating immediatism or gradualism, those blacks working for civil rights from the 1880s to the 1920s were from the upper middle class of the community and, even when advocating the radical Du Bois position, couched their desires in acceptable terms. It is interesting and worth noting that one of the first whites to become involved in black civil rights in Cleveland during this century was Russell Jelliffe, a graduate of Oberlin College and an heir to that institution's very liberal reform tradition. Only during the Depression did the civil rights movement begin to stray beyond a conservative Cleveland line when individuals such as John Holly used the boycott to move the issue of discrimination in hiring to resolution.

Given the stable, monied nature of the leadership of reform in Cleveland, it comes as no surprise that the tradition of reform in the city was one of conservatism and compromise. Stability was the essense of a sound business community. While reform could be accepted, chaos could not. So the reforms of Cleveland were structured and orderly.

Sometimes it is interesting to note the images a city attempts to project in its mottos, because these reflect the self-perception of the city's individual inhabitants as well as its collective consciousness. In the context of this volume they measure the success of reform in ordering the destiny of Cleveland. In 1904, Clevelanders proudly assumed Lincoln Steffens's accolade as a motto for years to come, improving upon it during the short period of the city manager system in the late twenties with billboards pronouncing Cleveland "the best managed city in the world." But as the decades of the twentieth century marched on, a note of desperation crept into the city's slogans, until "Cleveland Now" appeared all over the city during the 1960s; one observer explained that it was "a slogan, a prayer, a bit of chest beating, as well as the name and the concept of the city's major rehabilitative program."[6] Rehabilitative? What had happened? Cleveland had gone from "the best governed city in the United States" to the worst governed; from "the Forest City" and "the best location in the nation" to "the burning river city" or "the mistake on the lake"—from reform to rehabilitation. Something had gone awry. Certainly, the city's reform tradition was still intact by the 1930s, ordered and led by the same types of individuals who had overseen its creation. But while order and stability may have still underpinned local charity and philanthropy in the 1930s, the economic order that, in turn, provided the deepest substrata for that system was being shaken. It would continue to shake and shift for the next fifty years and in doing so would severely test the strength and purpose of Cleveland's tradition of reform.[7]

MICHAEL J. McTIGHE

Leading Men, True Women, Protestant Churches, and the Shape of Antebellum Benevolence

Bank (West 6th) Street headquarters of the Soldier's Aid Society of Northern Ohio, ca. 1864

In 1853 Cleveland's city directory reflected the changes that in less than fifty years had seen the city develop from "silent, forest clad solitude" into "the mart of commerce, the theatre of busy bustling industry, the seat of science, the abode of fashionable wealth; a city of 30,000 souls, graced with all the embellishments of art, and rich in all the refinements of good and evil which characterize modern civilization—all this partakes of the marvelous." That urban and economic development brought evil as well as good came as a disappointment to the city's boosters. Despite the progress symbolized by the railroads and factories, Clevelanders could not help but notice that severe and persistent destitution blighted their "Emerald City of the Lakes."[1]

By the 1850s the situation was undeniable. A letter to the *Plain Dealer* from "God Help the Poor" in 1857 expressed a common sentiment: "There is not a street, alley, or lane within the corporation, inhabited, but you will find destitution in its worst form." Residents complained of "swarms of beggars" and "rowdy" and "rascally" boys infesting their streets. The progress symbolized by the arrival of the Cleveland, Columbus, and Cincinnati railroad in 1851 seemed only to highlight the misfortune and misery. The *Forest City Democrat* thus summarized the anomaly in 1857: "Destitution and ignorance riot in our lanes and alleys, in our most fashionable streets, crawl in filthy rags past the mansions of the rich, past the gorgeous fronts of temples dedicated to a god of mercy."[2]

Economic and urban development, which brought with it growing numbers of poor and needy, forced Clevelanders to look for alternatives to the personal, ad hoc, and small-scale benevolence which had characterized the city since its founding. By the 1850s charity offered by the individuals or mutual aid societies receded in importance as more systematic, institutional, and public efforts became widespread.

13

The shift from religiously based private benevolence to public and institutional benevolence is a familiar theme in accounts of antebellum reform. Yet this gives a misleading portrait, especially of benevolence at the local level where there was more diversity in the relationship between private and public altruism than the conventional descriptions allow. Although there was a decided movement toward more public and institutional projects, the history of antebellum philanthropy would not be complete without taking into account two other trends that marked Cleveland's reforms—the persistence of private, small-scale benevolence and the coexistence and cooperation of public and private efforts. Private efforts persisted throughout the antebellum years in the work of individuals, mutual aid societies, and churches. Private voluntary societies retained a role even in institutional projects, which are usually treated as the archetype of public benevolence. The public benevolence of the local government supplemented rather than replaced private benevolence. Local authorities took up the burden private societies did not have the resources to bear, and the city government cooperated in the funding and operation of institutions which were organized and supervised by private societies.

The persistence of private benevolence, often in alliance with the local government, and the trend toward more public, institutional, and systematic benevolence, can both be attributed to the characteristics of the reformers who presided over antebellum aid-giving. They were a well-connected and Protestant leadership elite. Cleveland's humanitarian reformers were able to strike up a partnership between public authorities and religiously based private societies because the same individuals moved easily in both worlds. As city leaders and as Protestant church members and officers, the city's reformers worried that if they failed to respond to the destitution of the poor or to the rowdy and rascally boys, both city growth and the spread of religion would be threatened.

Relief to the poor was the most prominent antebellum benevolent project. It set the trend toward more public and institutional forms of benevolence, and established a pattern of parallel public and private aid-giving. The earliest forms of poor relief in Cleveland and Ohio City were personal and ad hoc. Thanksgiving, for example, always brought calls for aid to the needy, as did sudden calamities such as fire, injury, disease, or the death of a family member. Unfortunately, these unorganized, occasional, and sporadic efforts are largely lost to view for lack of publicity and institutionalization. Judging from scattered newspaper accounts, they were a substantial element of the benevolent

14

activity of the city, and they remained a permanent feature of antebellum benevolence.[3]

The sporadic aid forthcoming in response to misfortune had a limited scope. This kind of ad hoc benevolence depended on the resources of a few individuals. It required that instances of suffering and destitution be especially dramatic and that they come to the attention of the benevolently inclined.

The associated benevolence of mutual aid societies and churches surmounted some of these limitations. Organized groups had the money and the concerted volunteer help lacking in the more individual and occasional forms of charity. Most churches, fraternal societies, and ethnic and racial groups formed mutual benefit associations whose underlying rationale was the impulse to help one's own. These mutual aid groups took pride in keeping their kin from the humiliation of the public dole. Mayor William B. Castle, speaking to the St. Andrew's Society in 1856, saw as a sign of the efficiency with which they relieved the unfortunate and distressed that among the thousands that had received city poor funds, only one was a Scotchman. The Mona's Relief Society congratulated itself that only one Manxman had been a resident of the poorhouse and insisted that he would have been aided, but he had only revealed his birthplace on his deathbed.[4]

The city's churches assumed some of the functions of mutual aid societies. Virtually all of the churches made provisions to deal with their own members who were poor. Part of the quarterly collection of most churches was earmarked for the poor. Special collections or disbursements met occasional needs, such as when the First Presbyterian Church gave Polly Wright five dollars in 1837 because she was about to move and was indigent.[5] From time to time, a church would make a provision for a "Christian traveler" who needed money.

The mutual aid societies and churches were more permanent and stable than were ad hoc poor relief efforts, yet they, too, had their drawbacks. They were forms of exclusive benevolence, capable of reaching only the members of their own church, lodge, or immigrant group.

Voluntary poor relief societies that had concerns beyond helping their own ethnic or religious group were slow to emerge. It was not until the formation of a women's organization in 1843, the Martha Washington and Dorcas Society (MWDS), that a concerted voluntary effort was made in the area of general poor relief. According to its constitution, the society was organized "for the retarding of intemperance, to which is added, systematic labor for the inevitable result of the vice, namely, poverty of every description." For the term of its existence, the

MWDS was the major provider of poor relief in Cleveland outside the poorhouse. The society's aid was designed to be temporary. As its report for 1847 stated, "our object has been to assist those families, who by long and protracted sickness, are temporarily in distress—and who, with a little help at such time, are soon able to take care of themselves."[6]

The prime mover of the MWDS and its only president was Rebecca Rouse. Rouse often made daily visits to comfort and aid sufferers, providing families with wood, food, medicine, nurses, beds, and bedspreads. The society found jobs for men and widows, and arranged to have children who needed care taken into homes. It also sent clothes to the hospital for cholera victims whose own clothes had to be burned.[7]

The MWDS disbanded after six years of work, largely because Rouse, in the course of her visitations, became concerned with the plight of poor children and turned her energies toward the organization of an orphan asylum. The society had been the lengthened shadow of one woman, and when Rouse left, the organization collapsed. But other factors were also involved in its demise. The *Daily True Democrat* attributed the folding of the MWDS to "the increase of pauperism and the added burden of aiding paupers without assistance from the local government." It was, like many volunteer societies, a group with a narrow base and limited resources faced with a social problem that had grown beyonds its capacities.[8]

The collapse of the MWDS brought a reassessment of how benevolence should be aimed at the poor. The secretary of the society, Catharine (Mrs. J. E.) Lyon, set the terms of the debate in her report for 1849. Who will replace Rouse? she asked. Who would visit? Who would "have our homes besieged at all hours of the day by the sick, the lame, the halt and the blind?" Can we not have some permanent form of relief? Lyon pleaded. All the elements of the benevolence of Cleveland's last antebellum decade are present in Lyon's laments. More public involvement, insistence on a permanent form of relief, a greater reliance on institutions, and a lurking fear of being besieged by the needy were the marks of late antebellum benevolence in Cleveland.[9]

The private and voluntary poor relief societies of the 1850s which followed the MWDS, conscious that the problem of poverty dwarfed their capacities, developed new strategies based on ordered and discriminating giving. The newspapers spoke of "a more systematic assessment" or of "systematic measures." Aid would be targeted to the "deserving," as determined by the dispensers. Terms handy in distinguishing some poor from others, such as the "deserving" poor and the "worthy" poor, became staples of the discussion of relief. Cleveland benevolence rushed toward what one Episcopal minister called "the *substitution of a system* in the dispensation of your charities, for the more promiscuous and consequently less satisfactory mode of alms-giving which must prevail, where a systematic and organized charity like this does not exist."[10]

The private relief societies reflected the calls for a broader-scale, more systematic benevolence. The Society for the Relief of the Poor, soon known as the Relief Association, was formed in 1850 with Rebecca Rouse and her husband Benjamin Rouse as agents. The new association may have had the benefit of the MWDS's Rebecca Rouse, but it represented a decidedly different approach to poor relief. The society was run by men, with women relegated to a Committee on Entertainments. Funding was on a larger basis than had been available for the Martha Washington and Dorcas Society. Where the earlier society had raised much of its money with door-to-door solicitations, the Relief Association depended on large subscriptions from benefactors who formed a "committee of twenty."[11]

On a smaller scale, other poor relief efforts, such as those of the Sons of Malta, the Ladies' Home Missionary Society of the First Methodist Church, and the City Mission of the Euclid Street Presbyterian Church, evidenced the concern of the 1850s for methodical benevolence. The Sons of Malta set up a system using its five hundred members to report cases of need to headquarters, which would then evaluate how best to disburse its limited to resources to needy of the same ethnic background. The Ladies' Home Missionary Society expressed a similar impulse in stating that it was called into existence "to rescue from degradation and crime a class of human beings hitherto beyond the pale of Christian effort in our city, but now brought under the influence of well directed and systematic Christian philanthropy."[12]

Euclid Street Presbyterian Church's City Mission was a visitation program which combined a concern for methodical poor relief with insistent proselytizing. Visitors were to find out how many in each family attended Sunday school or church as well as whether any were in want or in need of employment. Tracts were distributed, families were encouraged to attend church or Sunday school, and nonattenders were offered free seats in church if they were unable to pay pew rents.[13]

The program of visiting allowed potential almsgivers to investigate claims more closely than usual. According to the church's missionary, "Our rules were adopted with a view to securing our absolute knowledge of the moral condition of the families within certain bounds and to ascertain every case of actual want and detect every case of importance by a thorough and continued acquaintance with the people themselves." He cited the example of two families who pretended to be in want, but the visitors were told by neighbors that the families were not in fact needy.[14]

The destitute were relieved from a common church fund, and this would be temporary relief, with strings attached. The trustees resolved that "no continued and permanent relief shall be granted to any family from the Relief Fund that is not or will not become connected with some Protestant Church or Sabbath School or congregation and that in some cases where destitute families are found to be connected with some church or congregation such church will be requested to support and aid such families."[15]

Difficulties remained for private poor relief organizations despite the turn to systematic benevolence. The participants in the Relief Association and the Euclid Street Presbyterian Church's City Mission were uncomfortable with the responsibility of being the major source of poor relief in Cleveland. A notice for a meeting of the association in 1852 reported that the question of whether poor relief would "continue to be done by this and other voluntary Associations, or by a well arranged Municipal Plan" would probably be discussed. Later that month, the association's position was stated clearly: poor relief was an appropriate and necessary city responsibility. When done by the city the "expense and burden of it fall upon all alike, in proportion to their property and means, like any other city expenditure, instead of being drawn from such as, while they are ever ready, should never in justice be *required* to do more than their due share of what is a common and public duty."[16]

The City Mission model of systematic visitation and assessment of need likewise failed as a plan for poor relief because its effort and resources did not match the need for aid. After the mission's agent, Harry C. Luce, resigned in 1860, he catalogued the plan's shortcomings. The church's visitors failed to investigate and monitor the moral condition and needs of the destitute. Even worse, there was not enough money. Luce had $34.87, when not less than one hundred dollars was needed— "this lack of means rendering the agent the prey of a score of needy families who will ruin him for relief and be a constant drain on his family stores." Several members of the church most able to help had evidenced little enthusiasm or generosity. Luce was inclined to believe "that there is too great a lack of zeal in this church to make any organized plan really efficient."[17]

In the calls for city involvement by the Relief Association, and in the complaints about lack of zeal by the Euclid Presbyterian Church missionary, one sees a benevolent community which, although it felt a Christian duty to relieve the suffering of the poor, found the effort and expense burdensome. The natural recourse of the benevolently inclined was to look for others to shoulder the burden. The calls for a "system that will look to permanency for the care of the poor" pointed in the direction of the involvement of the local government, the only antebellum institution with the resources and continuity necessary to sustain a long-term commitment to humanitarianism.[18]

The development of the public poor relief effort paralleled that of the private societies. As urban growth brought not only progress but also deprivation and disorder, initial small-scale efforts gave way to more systematic approaches. Public provisions for the poor centered on the poorhouse throughout the antebellum years. After Cleveland was incorporated in 1836 it used its new powers under the city charter to transfer the control of the township poorhouse to the city's board of health. Funding the poorhouse proved difficult, since some in the city's council claimed that the city did not have the power to lay a tax to support it, and after a two-year attempt at poor relief the city returned administration of the poorhouse to the township. The township poorhouse remained a fixture of poor relief, housing small numbers of poor throughout the antebellum years.[19]

In 1849 the city received the taxing power from the state to support a facility to aid the increasing number of impoverished Clevelanders. The city council authorized a Poor House and Hospital that same year, and the main building was completed in 1855 at a cost of twenty thousand dollars. At the start the Poor House and Hospital, which was by then known as the City Infirmary, had three departments: a hospital, a unit for the insane, and a unit for the indigent and aged poor. The facility was to be controlled and managed by public authorities.[20]

The ordinance which set up the City Infirmary repeated the concern of the decade that poor relief be given only to the deserving and established rules "for the purpose of meeting promptly the wants of meritorious cases, and preventing fraudulent exactions." Directors were to inquire personally about the circumstances of those who applied for aid. Outdoor relief, aid given outside the confines of the building, was a special concern, since it required an unforeseeable outlay of funds, rather than a manageable, firm commitment to the infirmary building and staff. The ordinance set a limit on outdoor relief at five hundred dollars. Only where removal to the infirmary seemed impractical would outdoor relief be given. Outdoor relief would be in the form of food, fuel, clothing, medicine, or medical attendance. No money or orders to be drawn on a store were to be granted. To further tighten the financial strings, the directors had to ask for quarterly appropriations from the city council and were forbidden to spend money without prior authorization.[21]

With the establishment of the City Infirmary by the local government and of the Relief Association and the City Mission by private voluntary groups, the provision of poor relief to the general population assumed a different aspect. The change was not so much a shift from private to public, but rather a shift in the scale of both public and private efforts. Both required larger sums of money than had been spent in the days of the Martha Washington and Dorcas Society and the township poorhouse, and relief at both levels had become larger in scope and more systematic. It had also become, as the concerns about the "worthy" poor and "systematic" benevolence indicate, less personal and more institutional.

Children were the other prominent target of antebellum altruism in Cleveland. Benevolence directed at children optimized the trend toward institutional projects, but of the five children's institutions established in Cleveland before the Civil War, only one was a public facility. Two remained private, church-related facilities, and the other two were joint projects of the local government and religiously based voluntary societies.

Worries about neglected and vagrant children crested in the 1850s, much as did the concern about the growing numbers of poor. Nascent industrial development left many new city dwellers, children and adults alike, without an economic function, carving out a precarious existence on the margins of city life. For children there was the added factor of lack of supervision, often because parents were overworked. Benevolent reformers were worried that failure to incorporate children as productive members of the city, or at least to neutralize their disruptive potential, could undercut the attempt to create a thriving commercial and manufacturing city. Destitute and neglected children, the *Leader* informed its readers, faced the daily temptation to lie, cheat, and steal: "Every hour in the city is a prison which is sealing such young offenders to a life of infamy and disgrace." The paper found "knee beggars" the most annoying of the city's ill-disciplined children. "These urchins, always unwashed and uncombed, open your door, and pop down on their knees, commencing a whining supplication for a loaf of bread, or for something else as the case may be." The *Daily True Democrat* summed up the worries:

> Our cities are nests of corruption for boys without parents, or with parents who cannot control them. Here in Cleveland they may be seen daily.
>
> But nothing is done for them; and all they know of society, of religion of God, is through the fangs of the law, or the abuse of the people. Society pays dearly for its neglect, and as years roll on, and our population increases, it will pay dearer yet.[22]

Private almsgiving, aid from voluntary societies, and mission work were the preferred and familiar approaches to such problems. But aid given to families and individuals by the existing voluntary societies and by private donations was not reaching the knee beggars or the crowds of rascally boys. Common schools and Sunday schools were established in the 1840s and 1850s to reach these urban Huckleberry Finns and Tom Sawyers, yet they, too, failed to deter the "swarms" of beggars. So in the 1850s the city's first benevolent projects aimed especially at children were organized, all as institutions—Catholic and Protestant orphan asylums in 1851 and 1852, the Ragged School in 1853, and the House of Correction in 1857. These drew from what seemed to be an inexhaustible supply of vagrant children.[23]

The founding of the city's children's institutions ran the gamut in terms of the roles played by private societies and the local government. The two Catholic orphan asylums were established directly by the diocese and its bishop, Amadeus Rappe, and they resembled mutual aid organizations in caring for only their own. The Cleveland Orphan Asylum, organized in a meeting at the First Presbyterian Church, differed from its Catholic counterparts in that it was not the direct creation of a single church, but a cooperative endeavor of the members of many Protestant churches. The Ragged School was the project of a single Protestant church, and was organized in 1853 by Rev. Dillon Prosser and other Methodists, primarily from First Methodist Church. The Ladies' Home Missionary Society of that church supervised the school and provided money for it. The Ragged School was a day school which aimed to attract the unchurched, unsupervised children of the city. As the superintendent described it in 1858, the school "is made up of children that are too poor to attend public schools, or too degraded to submit to their rules." The last of the antebellum children's institutions, the House of Correction, was created by the local government as part of an effort to combat the presence of rowdy and rascally boys.[24]

The two Catholic orphan asylums remained private, church-related institutions throughout the antebellum years, and there is no evidence that the city gave any support to them. The Cleveland Orphan Asylum and the Ragged School became quasi-public institutions later in the 1850s. The local government became involved in the Cleveland Orphan Asylum in 1855, when the asylum solicited and received city funds of $150 a year because it took in children from the City Infirmary. The city also agreed to pay $150 that year for the support of a teacher. But the city's role in the asylum was limited to supplementing the work of the private, voluntary, and Protestant benevolent project. The asylum's reports called on the local government to do still more, since private donations were not sufficient to sustain the project. The annual report published in March of 1861 argued that "an institution like an Orphan Asylum, which is an integral part of every Christian city, dare not rely, for its maintenance on alms asked monthly, or yearly, of many whose sympathies are exhausted by minor enterprises."[25]

The city's involvement in the Ragged School was more substantial than the role it played in supporting the Cleveland Orphan Asylum. The school began as a private, voluntary, religious project, and ended as a publicly controlled, privately operated institution known as the Industrial School. The impetus for the shift came in 1855 when the city government appointed a committee to investigate the problem of vagrant, neglected, and disruptive children. The committee reported that the city harbored between two hundred and three hundred children between the ages of six and fifteen who were idle or begging, and who, if not already of vicious habits, soon would be. Destitute children in the city were "subject to no proper control or wholesome moral influences," said the committee. "What they most need is the extension of a friendly hand to guide and direct them." Other cities had established successful industrial schools to educate and train children, concluded the committee, and it recommended the same for Cleveland. The *Plain Dealer* agreed, arguing that city funds spent for an industrial school would be the ounce of prevention that would be better than the pound of cure then being provided by the courts and prisons.[26]

The result was that in 1857 the Ragged School was adopted by the city. The city council assumed control of the school, renamed it the Industrial School, and supported its work out of general city funds. The city paid the salary of the superintendent and three teachers. In one year, the city council made up the difference between the school's expenses and the income it got from private contributions. At other times, the city took responsibility for major improvements or expenses—building an addition, painting, fixing up a basement, or providing for wood and coal. In an address in 1858, John A. Foote, a state as well as a local leader, found city government support appropriate, since the school had a public purpose: "It is changing scholars from dangerous into industrious citizens."[27]

The takeover of the Ragged School by local authorities did not end private fund-raising efforts or the participation of voluntary groups in running the school. The city council approved the formation of a private group, the Children's Aid Society, to serve as the supervisory body for the Industrial School. Voluntary societies associated with Protestant churches continued to sponsor fairs and balls to raise money, and private individuals and businesses still contributed funds to the school.[28]

The House of Correction was unique among the children's institutions in being totally controlled and funded by local authorities. Unlike the Ragged School and the Cleveland Orphan Asylum, it did not engage the interest or efforts of a private voluntary society.

Like poor relief, where public aid assumed a more important role after the founding of the City Infirmary, the balance between public and private involvement in children's institutions was shifting by the close of the antebellum years. In the supplementary aid to the Cleveland Orphan Asylum, the takeover of the Ragged School, and the creation of the House of Correction, local government involvement gradually increased although it did not displace private projects. It played a subsidiary role in supporting one essentially private benevolent effort, the Cleveland Orphan Asylum, and a complementary role in a quasi-public institution, the Industrial School.

Private benevolent efforts directed toward the poor and children persisted and were allied with public efforts in the years before the Civil War because both grew out of the concerns of an essentially Protestant group which functioned as a leadership elite both in voluntary societies and in the city at large. The *Daily True Democrat* captured the source of most of the city's philanthropic efforts in 1850 when it called on Protestants to imitate Catholics by establishing a general orphan asylum. The city had many wealthy men who could see to this, said the paper. If they were unwilling, it could still be done if the city's "true women" would concentrate their energies and if all Protestant churches would unite. "Wealthy men," "true women," and "Protestant churches": these indeed were the initiators of organized benevolence outside of mutual aid societies. They formed the tripod which supported antebellum philanthropy. The city's Catholic, German, Irish, and black residents had neither the resources nor the leisure to reach out a helping hand to others. Only the city's Protestants and wealthy had the economic security, organizational stability, and time to devote themselves in an extensive way to the needs of others.[29]

The first of the three groups the *Daily True Democrat* appealed to was "wealthy men." The fund-raising of benevolent societies brought them into contact with the well-to-do. Wealthy men and businessmen were commonly mentioned targets of charitable project solicitors. Contributions in goods and services from the city's railroads, omnibus lines, business colleges, and merchants helped sustain many of the larger benevolent projects. After one benefit concert the *Plain Dealer* concluded that "all the good looking and benevolent people of the city were there, besides a number of others"; it was "one of the largest and most fashionable looking audiences we have seen in some time past."[30]

The difficulty of establishing the wealth of the city's benevolent community precludes an even firmer linking of wealthy men and philanthropy. The few benevolent society officers located in the 1850 census had substantially more property than the average Clevelander over the age of eighteen, but not enough were located to support anything but a suggestion that wealth and benevolence went hand in hand.

Women were the second leg of the benevolent tripod. Philanthropy gave Cleveland women a socially sanctioned entry into the world outside the home, and a way to translate private piety into social activity. The women organized, staffed, and supervised a wide variety of mission, sewing, maternal, and other benevolent societies. There was hardly a church, Catholic, Jewish, or Protestant, without a ladies' foreign missionary society, a ladies' home missionary society, a ladies' aid society, or a ladies' sewing society. These groups sewed garments and collected provisions and money for distribution to the needy at home and abroad. The Female Baptist Sewing Society associated with the First Baptist Church, for example, gave money to the Baptist Home Missionary Society, made shirts to be sold, and bound shoes for a local shoemaking concern, Seaman and Ranney, both of whose principals were members of the First Baptist Church.[31]

Many of the city's benevolent organizations were run by women officers. The Martha Washington and Dorcas Society and most of the church mission and sewing societies were controlled entirely by women. Other organizations had parallel sets of male and female officers. The Cleveland Orphan Asylum had a popular structure—an all-female board of managers who supervised the facility, combined with an all-male board of managers who offered general guidance and access to money. A history of the women of Cleveland written in 1893 described the general pattern of such organizations. At the founding of the asylum in 1852 at the First Presbyterian Church, "a committee of gentlemen drew up a plan for work, which was handed to a committee of ladies to be executed."[32]

The men and women active in benevolence were the city's leading men and women. The officers of benevolent societies were part of an interlocking network of Cleveland's business, political, educational, and moral reform leaders. Of the eighty-eight male benevolent society officers who served from 1837 to 1860, seventeen (19.3 percent) were officers of businesses, twenty-three (26.1 percent) were government officeholders, twenty-seven (30.7 percent) were political party candidates, twenty-six (29.6 percent) were officers of moral reform societies, and twenty-six (29.6 percent) were administrators or board members in education, or teachers in schools. The male benevolent society officers were especially active in banks, public education, Cleveland government, and temperance. Politically, they were most likely found in the Whig or Republican parties, although a few were Democrats. The activities of the women who were benevolent society officers were not as extensive as was true for the men, but they were active within the sphere in which they were confined, benevolence and moral reform. A few of the women were found in lists of temperance society officers, and there was some crisscrossing of officers among the individual benevolent societies.[33]

The officers of the voluntary benevolent societies also formed a direct link between Protestant churches and private charity aimed at the general population. Half of the men who were officers of benevolent societies in the years from 1837 to 1860 (forty-four out of eighty-eight) were traced to lists of those who joined Cleveland and Ohio City English-speaking Protestant churches through 1860. Had more complete lists been available, it is likely that more than 80 percent of the men active in benevolence would have been found to have joined a Protestant church. The same number of women as men, eighty-eight, were identified as officers of benevolent groups from 1837 to 1860. Tracing women officers of benevolent societies to church lists was more difficult, since many names are listed only by initial. Of the eighty-eight, eighteen (20.4 percent) were found in lists of Protestant church joiners.[34]

In general, Presbyterian churches, led by First and Second Presbyterian churches, were the leaders in attracting benevolent society officers. In addition, some of the officers joined Baptist and Methodist churches, especially the First Baptist Church. The pattern of church joining suggests that benevolence was a preserve of the Protestant community generally, and not just of any single denomination. When the *Daily True Democrat* appealed to the city's Protestant churches to take the lead in charity, it was addressing a sympathetic audience.

Protestantism furnished the impetus and ideology for antebellum charity, as efforts which looked to reach out to the general population were invariably couched in Protestant rhetoric. For evangelical Protestants, benevolence was one of the fruits of conversion—virtually an outward sign of inward grace—since promoting the good of one's fellow creatures advanced the glory of God. Cleveland humanitarianism reflected this evangelical foundation. James A. Thome, minister of Ohio City's First Presbyterian Church, saw "the true idea of Christianity as a union of piety and philanthropy." The Second Presbyterian Church's *Manual* suggested that members ask themselves, "Is my religion merely negative, not doing any harm, or am I positively active in devising and executing schemes of goodness?" Similar sentiments were expressed by Baptist and Episcopal ministers. The statement of purpose of the First Baptist Church's Female Baptist Sewing Society, founded in 1834, makes a convenient summary of the Protestant concerns that sparked benevolence:

> Deeply impressed with the importance of doing all that we can to promote the good of our fellow creatures, and thus ultimately advance the glory of God, and in consideration of the moral destitution around us, and the high claims of God—of the church—and of the world resting upon us, and fully believing that it is "more blessed to give than to receive," and also that the widow's mite is acceptable to God if given with the widow's prayer. . . .[35]

God's claims and the needs of "fellow creatures" blended to form a firm commitment to benevolence by the city's Protestants.

There was a markedly proselytizing tone to almost all charitable efforts, reflecting Thome's description of true Christianity. Thomas Starkey, minister of Trinity Episcopal, in calling for a well-arranged and systematic plan of charity, saw such a project as both "a ministry of mercy to men's bodies" and "a ministry of reconciliation to men's souls." Many of the voluntary societies established with some statement of a benevolent purpose were instead primarily vehicles for evan-

26

gelization, moral reform, and raising money for internal church improvements. This was especially true for the women's sewing and mission societies, while other organizations had similar aims. The Western Seamen's Friend Society was primarily interested in evangelization and sustaining its Bethel Church in Cleveland, although it also served as a mutual aid organization for seamen. The Female Moral Reform Society promoted moral uplift, in addition to aiding women in trouble. The Martha Washington and Dorcas Society, the Cleveland Orphan Asylum, the Ragged School, and the Euclid Street Presbyterian Church's City Mission all had a healthy measure of evangelization.[36] When benevolent reformers extended a helping hand with food and care, the likelihood was that the other hand held a Bible or tract.

The *Plain Dealer*, with its Democratic and presumably less Protestant audience, expressed doubts about the prevailing mixture of benevolence and evangelization. Efforts to improve morals, educate minds, supply Bibles, and save souls were good in their place, the paper agreed, but "it is hard to acquire knowledge on an empty stomach, or to read the Lord's Prayer without 'daily bread,' or to get religion without pork and potatoes. The poor want something to eat, and wherewithal to be clothed. The superfluities of grace will do well as a dessert, but are a poor substitute for the substantial necessaries of life."[37]

There were those who charged that there was an underside to the piety that animated Protestant benevolence—persistent anti-Catholicism. When the MWDS reported in 1848 that fifty-nine of the eighty-two families helped were Catholic, it remarked: "We would not complain of the preponderance of Catholics, if the church to which they belong, manifested a disposition to aid us in proportion to others." A letter to the *Plain Dealer* in 1852 complained that under the Relief Association and its agent, Benjamin Rouse, "the funds for the poor are taking a selfish, sectarian, close communion direction." The letter added that "the Deacon [Benjamin Rouse was a deacon of First Baptist Church] seems to act much like the Priest and Levite who found the man half dead between Jerusalem and Jericho, he passes him by the other side."[38]

Protestant intolerance marked many of the city's public benevolences as well. A letter signed "Constitution" complained in the *Plain Dealer* in 1853 that Catholics were being denied relief by the City Infirmary. "Constitution" reminded the newspaper's readers that public funds, from members of every sect and denomination, financed the

27

poorhouse. When an unfortunate and destitute man knocked on the door it should be open to his relief if he is found worthy, insisted "Constitution,"

> whether he be Jew or Gentile, Catholic or Protestant. But no! he is turned away, not because he is an imposter, for want and distress stand confessed in every garb and feature, but because he is too honest to deny that he worships at an altar different from those public servants having temporary charge of the poor.

"Is this Christianity?" the letter asked. "God forbid."[39]

The officers of Cleveland's antebellum humanitarian societies, then, were Protestant and prominent. Scratch an officer of the Cleveland Orphan Asylum, and one was likely to find an officer of the Children's Aid Society, an elder of Second Presbyterian Church, a temperance activist, and a bank president.[40] The welding of Protestantism with the social interests of this leadership elite set the framework for these societies. First, it smoothed the way for the cooperation between local authorities and private voluntary societies. For people who were conspicuous in government, voluntary societies, and churches, public interests tended to mesh with private ones. When they wore their other hats, benevolent reformers had the experience of evoking public power, and often the influence and leverage to pass legislation to meet what they perceived to be the city's benevolent needs.

Because the same individuals served prominently in both realms, the public benevolence of local authorities and the private benevolence of voluntary societies were not separate and antithetical to reform. Public decisions about supporting charity coincided with the efforts of private voluntary societies were not separate and antithetical approaches to reform. Public decisions about supporting charity coincided with the efforts of private voluntary societies since both were the reflection of the work of a single network of city leaders and Protestant church-joiners.[41] With "leading men," "true women," and Protestant churches blazing the trail, local public officials and religiously based private voluntary societies became allies in creating benevolent projects designed to assure that neither the poor who crawled in filthy rags past the mansions of the rich, nor the rowdy and rascally boys who infested the streets, would hinder the city from becoming a "mart of commerce" and a "theatre of busy bustling industry."

J O H N   J.   G R A B O W S K I

Social Reform
and Philanthropic Order
in Cleveland, 1896–1920

First quarters (141 Orange Avenue) for Hiram House social settlement in Cleveland's lower Woodland Avenue neighborhood, 1896

The city of Cleveland celebrated the centennial of its founding in 1896. Parades, a plaster triumphal arch on Public Square, speeches, and a variety of ceremonial events manifested a feeling of civic pride in the city's progress from a pastoral outpost of New England to a cosmopolitan, industrial metropolis. Particular attention centered on the growth of the city's population from less than 80,000 in 1860 to over 261,000 in 1890. Within four years the population would rise to 381,760 and give cause for further civic self-congratulation.[1]

Yet, while Clevelanders celebrated their city's growth and industrial maturity, they also had to recognize that its roads, sewer system, and health and housing codes were more characteristic of the mercantile town it had been some forty years and three hundred thousand people earlier. The city was overwhelmed by the people who came to it, and polluted by the industries which attracted them. Surveys conducted less than a decade after the centennial found only eighty-three bathtubs serving a population of 7,728 people in one Cleveland ward, and described housing conditions in another as follows: "This house was formerly a barn and is divided into two parts. By the front door of one of the apartments the manure was piled until carried away . . . . The cellar contains a few inches of water and during a rain, a few feet . . . . This house formerly had sixteen men boarders, but the owner says they have all gone back to the old country."[2] Irregular employment, poor working conditions, and low pay characterized many of the new industries in the city. The immigrants, who were largely from southern and eastern Europe, and who were the cause of the city's burgeoning population, bore the brunt of these conditions. Between 1890 and 1900, the foreign-born consistently constituted nearly one-third of Cleveland's population.[3]

The city's charitable and relief agencies were unable to cope effec-

30

tively with the new burdens placed upon them. As immigrant groups established their own agencies for relief and assistance and, particularly, as foreign doctrines such as socialism and anarchism came to be advocated as cures for the causes of urban distress, older agencies searched for more effective means to deal with the problems. By drawing upon the ethical structure of Protestant Christianity and the principles of efficient management, Cleveland was able to meet and ameliorate many of its urban needs and problems in a manner which avoided both systemic disruption and social chaos.

A broad movement toward social reform was one of the most important aspects of the city's efforts to cope with its new problems. Directed toward the elimination of the causes of social and economic inequities, social reform in Cleveland, as elsewhere in the nation, sprang from a new interpretation of the ethical structure of Protestant Christianity. It was unlike other church-directed charitable work, which was often based on the philosophy of good works and which treated symptoms rather than causes. Because social reform represented an extension of the dominant religious system, it was, in most cases, an acceptable process. By the second decade of the twentieth century, it, as well as charitable work, became secularized and institutionalized. And both succumbed to the overriding search for order and efficiency which characterized Cleveland and the nation during the Progressive Era.

Social reform in Cleveland during the Progressive Era grew out of the social gospel movement which originated in the 1870s and was closely associated with men such as Washington Gladden, Josiah Strong, and Walter Rauschenbusch. By the 1880s the gospel had become an important aspect of American Protestant thought and action.[4] Advocates of the social gospel sought to take religion outside of the church edifice and make it a practical standard for daily life. They called for an everyday application of the teachings of Jesus and generally evinced a belief in the inherent goodness of all men. By this recognition, the social gospel helped shift the blame for human misery and failure from the individual to his environment.

It is impossible to say with certainty when the social gospel first came to Cleveland. The beginning of the Salvation Army's work in the city in 1889 is an early example of pragmatic Christianity, for members of General Booth's "army" ministered to the body as well as the soul. The late nineteenth-century activities of the Young Men's and Young Women's Christian Associations were also bound within the confines of the social gospel. A YMCA branch began operating in Cleveland in 1854, but, moribund during the last years of the Civil War, it was reorganized in 1867. The YWCA did not establish a local branch until 1869. The early activities of these organizations showed a parochial concern for the well-being of Protestant youth in the city. Both promoted lectures, worship services, and other activities which were dedicated to the maintenance of a good Christian environment and which were viewed as more suitable alternatives to the other entertainments which might be found in Cleveland. The YMCA, in particular, provided athletic facilities, both to maintain health and to provide an acceptable outlet for the carnal energies of young men confronted by the temptations of the city.[5]

Though the YMCA opened a home for bootblacks and newsboys in 1875, it was not until the 1890s that both agencies also concerned themselves with programs directed toward the people outside of their membership. Lecturers at the YMCA often addressed the social issues of the day and encouraged members to use their Christian training for the good of society. This attitude was particularly evident during the early years when Glen K. Shurtleff served as general secretary of the Cleveland YMCA. Shurtleff was active in many of the social reform organizations of Cleveland and was particularly close to the directors of the city's early social settlement houses.[6]

The YWCA's work outside of its membership was more pronounced than that of its male counterpart. The Cleveland YWCA established boarding homes for working girls in the 1890s. Its interest and work in the area of immigration and immigrant problems led to the establishment of the Cleveland International Institute in 1916. Patterned after similar agencies established by the YWCA throughout the country, the Cleveland Institute was one of the first agencies to use workers of foreign background when dealing with immigrants.[7]

The construction of a new building for the Pilgrim Congregational Church on Jennings Avenue in 1895 provides a more important benchmark of the social gospel movement in Cleveland. Pilgrim was the city's first institutional church, a structure designed not only for religious services, but also for community work. The new Pilgrim Church provided room for community gatherings, recreation, and club work; all of this was integral to the need, as expressed in the social gospel, for the church to minister not only to the religious, but also to the secular needs of the people.[8]

The most important and effective manifestation of the social gospel movement in the United States and in Cleveland was the social settlement house. The settlement served as the primary instrument for the advocacy of social reform measures during the Progressive Era. Settlements have been aptly characterized as "spearheads for reform,"[9] although settlement work did not involve benevolence or charity, per se. Rather than attempting to ameliorate social problems by the provision of material aid, the settlements sought to cure these problems by eliminating their causes. The basic premise of the settlement movement was the actual residence of well-educated settlement workers within depressed areas of the city. By sharing the living conditions of the urban poor, the workers would learn the roots of urban problems. Using their own knowledge and skills, these individuals hoped to eradicate the problems at their sources and to educate the neighborhood residents so that they might overcome their condition. The desire to create an urban village lay at the heart of many settlement efforts. Those involved in the settlement movement believed that urban neighborhoods could overcome their problems if they established the network of mutual aid and sharing considered to typify small-town life.

The movement which began in England quickly spread to the United States. By 1900 there were nearly one hundred settlement houses in the nation, five of which were located in Cleveland.[10] Four of these early enterprises, Hiram House, Goodrich House, Alta House, and the Council Educational Alliance, have left behind them substantial information concerning their origins, supporters, personnel, and policies. This information makes possible a survey of their divergent, yet similar characteristics.

Hiram House, established in July of 1896, is generally considered to have been the first true social settlement in Cleveland. The idea for the settlement originated in a YMCA study class at Hiram College in Hiram, Ohio. Affiliated with the Disciples of Christ Church, the college attracted students with both religious and academic interests. The class chose to study the social settlement movement and, encouraged by lectures from luminaries such as Graham Taylor, founder of the Chicago Commons Settlement, decided to examine the possibility of starting a settlement house in Cleveland, some fifty miles to the north. A visit to the city convinced the students, most of whom were from small towns, that such work would be needed: "We went to Whiskey Isle; there we found saloons, prostitution, open sewers, and all in all everything was not very good. We went back to Hiram College with the report that Cleveland needed a settlement very bad."[11]

Seven members of that class began actual settlement work following graduation in June of 1896. They took up residence in a rented house in the Irish quarter near Whiskey Island on the city's West Side. They began kindergarten classes and started planning for educational classes directed toward all age levels in the neighborhood. Pamphlets issued by the students while at this location emphasized the Christian, social gospel basis of the work and clearly outlined their idealistic goals. The hope of Hiram House, they said, "is to become part of the life of its own ward becoming so by personal helpfulness. In helping the masses, its wish is to help remove the cause of distress, further than this we do not commit ourselves to any social program regarding the vexed industrial and economic problems of the day." Other early publications solicited support from the general public for the work in the name of Christ.[12]

Protestant Christianity could not long prosper in an Irish Catholic neighborhood. By the autumn of 1896 pressure from local priests forced the settlement to relocate. It moved to the Haymarket district on the East Side. This was the center of the city's Jewish community, and despite some early protests by the residents of the area the settlement managed to take root. Its initial locations in this area, a series of rented houses along Orange Avenue, provided Hiram House with enough space to continue and expand its programs. The workers again began a kindergarten to which they added a day nursery, high school classes for older youths, debating clubs, excursions to parks, and a summer camp.[13] Most of these programs were directed toward educating the people of the neighborhood and providing them with the intellectual means to rise above their environment. Other programs, such as camping and excursions, were attempts to physically remove people, especially children, from the crowded conditions and debilitating atmosphere of the inner city.

The staff carried on its work without substantive support from any single institution. Hiram College provided its good wishes and a continuous flow of student volunteers, but no financial support. Funds came primarily from collections taken up in rural churches by one of the original student volunteers, George Bellamy. Initially financial solicitor for the settlement, Bellamy assumed control of all work in 1897 and retained it until his retirement in 1946.[14]

Bellamy came from a religious family of moderate means. He was born in Cascade, Michigan, in 1872, descended on his mother's side from colonists who had arrived in 1620. Several relatives were active in the Disciples of Christ Church, and his older brother, William, a Hiram graduate, served as a minister for that denomination. Bellamy followed his brother into the ministerial course at Hiram, earning all of his college expenses through summer jobs and part-time employment during the school year. His interest in social settlement work was sparked in 1895 by a chance meeting with Graham Taylor while at a Chatauqua lecture. Years later he would credit his conversion to the social gospel to a vision he had had in church while still a youth.[15]

Bellamy's convictions were tested to the limit during his first several years at the settlement. He worked without pay, having given his savings to the settlement. He was often rebuffed when he attempted to solicit funds from the major churches in Cleveland because the enterprise he represented was viewed as socialistic. One church official told Bellamy, "You ought to be ostracized from [for] living among such people. God never intended to save such people. You should shove them off in a corner and let them be there and rot."[16] Fund raising was successful only among small Disciples congregations in the rural towns surrounding the city. They contributed not only money, but flowers as well for distribution in the bleak city neighborhood.

Despite the youthful dedication and idealism committed to the settlement, Hiram House prospered only after Bellamy found a substantial secular source of funds. A meeting in 1898 with a prominent jurist and member of the Disciples of Christ Church, Henry White, paved the way for this change. White contributed money, but more importantly, he formed an executive committee to oversee the affairs of Hiram House. By 1900 the committee had evolved into a board of trustees that consisted primarily of prominent businessmen, most of whom were important enough to be listed in the city's *Blue Book*. The board of trustees served to legitimize Hiram House as an institution worthy of support. Within two years it solicited sufficient funds, including substantial donations from John D. Rockefeller and Samuel Mather, to build and equip a four-story structure for the settlement at East 27th Street and Orange Avenue. The guarantee of support allowed Hiram House's budget to grow from $2,210.31 in 1898 to $6,860.00 in 1900, to $12,745.60 in 1905, and to $20,614.10 in 1910.[17] More importantly, Samuel Mather, perhaps the city's richest citizen, became a member of the board during this period and took an unflagging interest in the work of the settlement.

Having such wherewithal, Bellamy was able to expand programs and activities which he believed would eliminate the problems plaguing his neighborhood. A new publication, *Hiram House Life*, initially offered a forum for studies of local problems. A playground constructed at the rear of the settlement building provided much-needed open space for the neighborhood. The ample structure had rooms which were used by clubs and classes as well as by other organizations, such as the Visiting Nurse Association and a branch of the Cleveland

Public Library. New staff, including a playground director, a director of boys' work and a neighborhood visitor, similarly extended the settlement's work and its utility. By World War I, Hiram House provided play areas for children, meeting rooms for clubs (mainly for children), weekly entertainments, a gymnasium, and vocational education and homemaking classes within its facilities, as well as headquarters for nurses and workers who visited the sick and needy in its surrounding neighborhood.[18]

The ethnic background of Hiram House's clientele was changing, too, during this time. As the Jewish immigrant population prospered and moved out of the Haymarket district, Italian immigrants began moving in, beginning about 1905. They, in turn, were eventually replaced by southern blacks, who began moving to Cleveland in large numbers during the First World War.

Relieved by the successful efforts of his board of trustees from the constant task of soliciting funds, Bellamy became involved in various non-settlement activities directed toward social reform. For example, he made some effort to rid the neighborhood of Harry Bernstein, its corrupt ward boss. He also became an active member of the Cleveland Council of Sociology, an organization comprised of clerics, charity workers, and others, which was devoted to the discussion of the social issues of the day. He served on two committees of the chamber of commerce, both of which were dedicated to the elimination of particular social ills: the chamber's Bath House Committee of 1901 studied the lack of bathing facilities in the inner city and successfully implemented a program for the construction of bathhouses; and its Committee on the Housing Problem of 1903−4 surveyed housing conditions in the city and made recommendations for a revision of the city's housing code.[19]

As late as 1905, Bellamy also remained active in the Disciples of Christ Church. He used a speech at a church convention that year to set forth his strong social gospel idealism and to decry the criticism of reform-minded clerics by the church establishment: "The representatives of the most advanced religious thought, no matter how God-fearing or how conscientious, have by no means passed the period of church discipline or rebuke. This lack of freedom in religious thought and study has hindered a wholesome, righteous growth of religious understanding."[20]

The growth of Hiram House had consequences for both Bellamy's social thought and the institution itself. As it grew, Hiram House drifted away from the concept of "personal helpfulness." Certainly neighborhood residents could meet and work with staff members, but these workers were much less neighbors in themselves. They were professional employees who answered to the demands of an institutional bureaucracy. As early as 1902, Hiram House had eleven different departments directed largely by paid staff rather than by student volunteers. These employees reported to George Bellamy. By 1910 Bellamy was an administrator of an institution removed, for the most part, from close contact with its clientele. As an administrator responsible to a board of trustees he had to ensure that his operation ran smoothly and that its backers were pleased with both its progress and programs. To these ends he devised settlement programs which were popular, and personally abstained from causes or issues which might irritate his supporters. Popular programs drew large numbers of people to the settlement and thus seemed to prove its worth to its patrons. Therefore, by World War I, Hiram House had come to concentrate on recreational programs which would appeal to the children in the neighborhood. It tended to avoid programs which were educational or which were directed at adult immigrants, as the former would be unpopular and the latter dealt with a clientele which was difficult to attract in large numbers.[21]

While Hiram House would come to be characterized as one of the city's most conservative settlement houses, Goodrich House, the second settlement in the city, was perhaps its most liberal. This social settlement evolved from a series of boys' clubs and classes held in Cleveland's First Presbyterian (Old Stone) Church in the mid-1890s. Located on Public Square, the church had one of the city's oldest and most prestigious congregations. The classes and clubs, which attracted children from the congested, run-down neighborhood to the north of the church, were directed by Elizabeth and Edward W. Haines, Elizabeth being the daughter of the church's pastor, Dr. Hiram C. Haydn.[22]

As the work seemed to fill a major need in the neighborhood, the church began planning its expansion. Central to this planning was Flora Stone Mather, a member of the church, the wife of Samuel Mather, and the daughter of Amasa Stone, railroad builder and industrialist and one of the city's most influential men in the immediate post–Civil War period. Wealthy in her own right, Flora Stone's marriage to Samuel Mather allowed her to become the benefactor of a variety of charitable and educational agencies. Goodrich, however, was her most important charitable interest. Upon her death in 1909, her husband noted, "There was nothing she ever did in which she was more interested than Goodrich House."[23]

Originally, Flora Mather proposed that she would construct a parish house in which the church could undertake neighborhood work. However, the lack of land immediately adjacent to the church and a feeling that the scope of such work might soon overwhelm the church led to a reconsideration. Since 1893, Mather had carried on a correspondence with Professor Henry E. Bourne of Western Reserve University in which they discussed social settlement work. Bourne apparently used this correspondence to assist her in understanding settlement work. She had probably first learned of settlement work through a friend, Lucy B. Buell, a former resident of the College Settlement in New York. The physical problems of constructing a parish house and her correspondence with Bourne led Mather to propose the construction of a fully equipped settlement in the general neighborhood of the church. When Goodrich House finally began work in May 1897, it operated out of a new building constructed expressly for it at St. Clair and East Sixth Street. Flora Mather had paid for the structure and for a number of years thereafter underwrote the cost of the settlement's operations.[24]

The programs in the new building were supervised by Starr Cadwallader. Cadwallader, a graduate of Union Theological Seminary in Utica, New York, had worked briefly at Union Settlement before coming to Cleveland. During his five-year tenure at Goodrich House, he directed the agency in many of the standard areas of settlement work. The structure housed a bowling alley, baths, laundry, library, and meeting rooms which were made available to neighborhood residents and to a variety of clubs and social groups. Cadwallader and his staff also attempted to improve neighborhood conditions by lobbying for cleaner streets and encouraging area residents to plant home gardens.[25]

However, quite unlike Hiram House, Goodrich House became known as a public forum for the discussion of social reform issues; records indicate, for example, that a young socialist club met at the facilities. Some of the meetings held at Goodrich House led to the creation of such reform-oriented groups as the Consumers' League of Ohio, and the Legal Aid Society, as well as the creation of a separate, rural boys' farm for housing juvenile offenders.[26] Among the settlement residents who took part in such discussions were Frederick C. Howe and Newton D. Baker, both of whom left the settlement for positions in Tom L. Johnson's mayoral administration.

Goodrich had a board of directors as soon as it had a building. Composed largely of people affiliated with the First Presbyterian Church and their friends, this body did little, if anything, to challenge the somewhat radical events at the settlement. Dr. Haydn presided over the first board, which included Flora and Samuel Mather, Elizabeth and Edward Haines, Professor Bourne, and Lucy Buell. By 1905 Cadwallader, Howe, and Baker, all of whom had left the employ of the settlement, had joined the board. James R. Garfield, son of President Garfield and law partner of Howe, also served on the board during the early years of the settlement.[27]

The tightly knit nature of this board and its ties to the church rather than to business, were probably two factors which allowed Goodrich to pursue a more radical course than Hiram House. That the settlement existed because of Flora Mather's largess is, however, a more important factor. Whereas Bellamy had a number of donors to please, Cadwallader had only Mrs. Mather and his rather small board to consider when directing the settlement. Then, too, Hiram House was Bellamy's creation; its failure would be his failure. Cadwallader could, and did, walk away from Goodrich whenever he pleased. In his case, the social goals he wished to achieve took precedence over loyalty to any particular institution.

Goodrich was an institution from the first day it opened its doors. Its funding, operations, and physical structure grew simultaneously. As such it proved to be both sound and remarkably flexible. When the population of its neighborhood began to decline around 1908, it was easily able to move its operations to a new location at East 31st Street and St. Clair, some twenty-four blocks to the east. Mather had expressly provided for such a contingency when she deeded the settlement to its board:

> I desire the house to be used for a Christian Social Settlement so long as, in the judgment of the trustees, that is a useful and needful work in the neighborhood; but if ever in their judgment there was a time when to continue such work, there would be a waste of energy the trustees may dispose of the property. If it should be deemed wise by the trustees to discontinue the work there I wish them to use the funds, including the proceeds of any sale of the house, to carry on the work in some other downtown locality.[28]

Though the liberal nature of Goodrich could not be written into its articles of incorporation, it nevertheless seemed to be an integral part of the settlement. Cadwallader's work seems to have set the liberal tone for the settlement. Thereafter it would tend to attract new headworkers of a similar mien. Five headworkers followed in rather quick succession when Cadwallader left Goodrich in 1904. The rapid turnover ended in 1917 when Alice Gannett, formerly of Henry Street Settlement in New

York, took the position and held it until 1947. Gannett continued and strengthened Goodrich's liberal reputation. During her career she served as president of the Ohio Consumers' League and the National Federation of Settlements, and was active in the League for Human Rights.[29]

Alta House, which began settlement work in Cleveland's Little Italy district in 1900, provides yet another example of the diversity of the settlement and reform impulse in Cleveland. Sequestered in a compact ethnic neighborhood, it exhibited none of the neighborhood activism which characterized the very early years of Hiram House nor the liberal leanings characteristic of Goodrich and its staff. Nor was Alta the creation of youthful idealism or a church.

Alta House reflected the expressed needs of the neighborhood as acted upon by social gospel idealism. Mothers in the Little Italy district attempted to establish a day nursery in the mid-1890s. Many of them worked in the vineyards in the east of the city and needed day care for their children. They appealed to the Cleveland Day Nursery Association for help. Louise (Mrs. Marius E.) Rawson of the association directed its efforts to assist the Italian mothers. Rawson, a New England-born school teacher, began the nursery in a small cottage which the work soon outgrew. Relocated in a larger structure, the nursery expanded to include boys' clubs, mothers' clubs, and cooking classes, and again strained the capacity of its quarters. At this point, Rawson began to search for funding to provide a permanent, larger building for the work. She approached John D. Rockefeller for that aid.[30]

Rockefeller was a natural choice. He was wealthy and a devoutly religious man. As such, he made his money available to a number of worthy causes in and outside of Cleveland—whether his philanthropy signified a social gospel-like desire to help his fellow men or followed the tradition of benevolence by the wealthy cannot be stated with any certainty.[31] Most important in Rawson's plans was the fact that Rockefeller, when in Cleveland, daily traveled through the Italian district on his way to and from his estate in Forest Hills.

Rockefeller proved amenable to assisting the undertaking. In 1898 he agreed to build a structure for the work being carried on by Rawson. During the discussion and construction phases, the work projected for the new building grew well beyond the confines of a nursery and evolved into a settlement.[32]

Rockefeller's hopes for the settlement were in the best tradition of the social gospel movement. He expressed them as follows in a letter he sent to the dedication ceremony for the building in 1900: "May the spirit of the Christ Child dwell within this house, built primarily for the children, and may that same spirit of love go out with each one who passes through its doors and be broadly disseminated in the surrounding homes." While Rockefeller's letter spelled out the Christian foundations of the endeavor, a second letter from his daughter, Alta Rockefeller Prentice (after whom the settlement was named), explicitly stated its purpose: "The work for which it stands, namely that of helping to educate your children mentally, morally, and physically, and through them aiding in every effort to elevate and purify home life and the life of the neighborhood is very dear to me."[33]

Katherine E. Smith, formerly of the Rivington Street Settlement in New York, came to Cleveland to head the work at Alta House. Work in the new structure focused primarily on child-oriented activities. It included a day nursery, a kindergarten, boys' clubs, girls' classes in sewing, millinery, and cooking, a school for eighteen crippled children, and a gymnasium. In addition, a medical dispensary, a resident visiting nurse, public baths, a public laundry, and a playground were provided.[34]

Smith answered to a board of trustees which included J. G. W. Cowles, a real estate dealer who lived in the Heights area just above the settlement; Paul L. Feiss, one of the officers of the Joseph and Feiss clothing company; John D. Rockefeller, Jr.; Alta Rockefeller Prentice; Professor Matoon M. Curtis of neighboring Western Reserve University; Belle Sherwin, daughter of a prominent family and a leading figure in various reform movements; Maude O. (Mrs. William) Truesdale, the wife of an assistant professor at Western Reserve University; and Louise Rawson.[35] The board certainly did not represent the religious element, nor, excepting the Rockefeller contingent, did it lean particularly on the wealthiest families of the city. The presence of Rawson and Truesdale, neither of whom represented money or social status, was unusual, but was an acknowledgment of the Day Nursery Association's role in the creation of Alta House, as well as of Truesdale's strong educational programming.

Alta House had no need to combat social evils such as poor housing, overcrowding, or open sewers. The housing stock of the neighborhood was largely new, having been erected by the Italian immigrants during the last decades of the nineteenth century. It was almost a rural area, five miles from the center of the city. Its only industries were a streetcar carbarn and the monument works of Joseph Carabelli. The settlement's task, therefore, naturally centered on the social, academic, civic, and sanitary education of the immigrants. Smith may have chafed at

these apparently pedestrian duties. Her first annual report, for example, indicated an interest in starting a social reform club for young
boys. The record does not indicate if she accomplished this.[36] However,
classes in English, sewing, cooking, and hygiene, as well as physical
education programs, were still strong, if indirect, means of social reform for they seemed to guarantee the training of useful, healthy future
citizens who would be assets to the community.

The Rockefeller family continued to support Alta House until 1921,
at which time John D. Rockefeller, Jr., asked to be relieved of its annual costs.[37] Because of the long-term interest of the Rockefellers and
the insular nature of the Little Italy neighborhood, Alta House was
quite dissimilar from either Hiram House or Goodrich House. Yet it
still shared the Christian seed of these organizations as well as their
dedication to social reform in one guise or another.

A fourth major settlement in the city, the Council Educational Alliance, began operating in 1899. Though established by the Cleveland
branch of the Council of Jewish Women, its principles were largely the
same as those set forth in the social gospel and shared by the Christian
settlements in the city. The Council Educational Alliance grew out of
programs sponsored by the Jewish women's branch. These included
clubs, homemaking classes, and a free synagogue, all directed toward
the residents of the lower Woodland Avenue district who were mostly
poor, recent Jewish immigrants of the eastern European Orthodox
background.[38]

In direct contrast to the area's residents, the council's membership
consisted mostly of well-to-do women of German or Hungarian Jewish background. Some represented families that had been in Cleveland
since the 1840s. All were well assimilated into American and local civic
life, a fact underscored by their synagogue affiliations. The council
women were members of the Temple (Tifereth Israel Congregation) or
the Scovill Avenue Temple (Anshe Chesed Congregation), the two
oldest Jewish religious bodies in the city. By the turn of the century,
both were in the forefront of American Reform Judaism. The Temple,
in particular, moved in the liberal direction under the leadership of
Rabbi Moses Gries. It became an open temple, with services open to the
general public. Music, sermons on topics of general social concern,
and a lack of Hebrew used in these services made them akin to those in
Protestant churches. Gries's move of his services to the Christian Sabbath completed the resemblance.[39]

When the council decided in 1897 to formalize its operations on lower Woodland by building a home for Jewish organizations in which its programs would be housed, they used the Temple as a forum to build support for the plan. Jane Addams and Washington Gladden were among the figures invited to speak at the Temple. Their remarks, plus the example of local settlement efforts, particularly at Goodrich House, caused the women to redefine their project as the creation of a Jewish settlement. Ironically, while the council admired the work of and the ideas behind the Christian settlement houses, they espoused their cause partly in an effort to provide a Jewish alternative for Jewish children attending Christian agencies.[40] With the donation of the former home of Moritz Joseph at Perry (East 22nd) Street and Woodland in 1899, the council finally acquired a site for settlement work.

Initial work at the Council Educational Alliance lacked true settlement character since none of the workers resided at the location. However, its programs, which included clubs, academic classes, lectures on current topics, and a playground, paralleled those of other settlements. Only the provision of a free synagogue and Hebrew classes betrayed a difference in religious origin.[41]

Despite the common religious background of the sponsors and clientele of the Council Educational Alliance, all did not go smoothly at first. The institution's operations on the Jewish Sabbath offended the neighborhood population, while the conservative supporters of the settlement objected to the discussion of labor-oriented topics at the agency. The alliance, however, eventually evolved into an agency which shared its neighborhood's culture and outlook. The employment of Isaac Spectorsky, a New Yorker of eastern European Jewish background, as director in the early 1900s helped place the alliance in a more acceptable position. By 1905 the settlement hosted the meetings of Zionist clubs, and by World War I it had become a center for Yiddish cultural activity—even while it maintained standard settlement programs and Americanization work.[42]

Though the Council Educational Alliance was eventually considered as one of the city's most prominent Jewish institutions, its roots derived from the social gospel philosophy. The Council of Jewish Women began the work in an effort to help their coreligionists escape their debilitating environment. Such action, obviously not based on a reading of the New Testament, certainly emulated contemporary Christian attempts to deal with the problems of the urban poor. While many of the council women may have been motivated by a desire to make the Orthodox Jews acceptable to the Christian community in

43

which the Reform Jews held a position of relative esteem, they nevertheless viewed their enterprise as being on a par with that of Jane Addams or Flora Stone Mather.

Alta, Goodrich, Hiram, and the Council Educational Alliance were four of the five social settlements in Cleveland at the turn of the century. Though these agencies, through their devotion to the creation of a better living environment, were the major forces working for social reform, they were not the only organizations attempting to solve the problems of the industrial city. Over fifty additional charitable and benevolent organizations operated in Cleveland. Many, like the YMCA, the YWCA, and the Associated Charities had served the city for a number of years. Many others, however, were much newer, born of the increased needs of the expanding city.

Each agency in the city solicited funds for its own operation. This was accomplished by door-to-door canvassing, usually in the wealthier neighborhoods, and through charitable balls and carnivals. By the 1890s some donors, particularly businessmen and the well-to-do, were finding themselves inundated by requests for funds. Similarly, the existence of such a vast array of charitable agencies raised questions about the need for and trustworthiness of many of the endeavors. Certainly the rebuffs delivered to George Bellamy indicated that a portion of the citizenry had strong doubts about some of the new enterprises in the city.

One of the hallmarks of the Progressive Era was a passion for order, for the elimination of unnecessary expenditures of time, energy, or money. The doctrine of efficient management reaped benefits in terms of profit and productivity when applied in business and industry. Its application in charitable and even in reform-oriented enterprises was, as has been shown in the case of Hiram House, a natural second step. Not surprisingly, the movement to regulate and streamline Cleveland's benevolent organizations began in the city's chamber of commerce, which represented its business and industrial interests. Confronted by the multiplicity of charities in the city, the chamber created a special Committee on Benevolent Associations in 1900. Chaired by Martin A. Marks, a prominent Jewish insurance executive, the committee consisted of six businessmen, an officer of the Brotherhood of Locomotive Engineers, and a doctor. Many of the members, such as James Barnett, president of the Associated Charities (the city's major private benevolent organization), were active in various benevolent organizations.[43]

The committee initially set out to determine which of the city's charities were legitimate and worthy of support. They accomplished this by sending a questionnaire to each agency. The form included questions concerning the purpose of the agency, the nature and size of its staff, its administrative and board structure, and the specific nature of the services provided. Agencies which did not reply, or which sent questionable responses received a follow-up visit from a committee member.[44] Most agencies chose to reply, for they were probably aware of the purpose of the committee's work—the compilation of a list of endorsed charities. The committee would, if it found no fault with a charity, issue its solicitor a card indicating its endorsement of the group.

During the committee's first year of operation it received responses from sixty-six agencies. It endorsed fifty-one of these, but denied its imprimatur to five others, including the Newsboys and Working Boys Home, and the Army of Truth and Inspiration. Ten additional agencies, operated primarily by immigrant groups, were considered to be outside of the committee's jurisdiction. Within three years of its establishment, the committee's endorsement program had become a major factor in Cleveland philanthropy. The endorsement card became a coveted possession for charitable agencies, since most potential donors refused to consider supporting any agency lacking it.[45] It was at this point that the next step in the fiscal control of the city's philanthropic agencies occurred.

The city's Jewish community pioneered in this area of philanthropic order, the unified solicitation of funds. Plagued by a proliferation of fiscal demands and agencies, many created to serve the large numbers of newly arrived eastern European Jews, leaders of the city's Jewish community decided in 1904 to create a Federation of Jewish Charities. Headed by Martin Marks and Charles Eisenman, the federation undertook a single fund drive for all of its member agencies and then distributed the funds according to agency need. This was the fourth such unified fund drive undertaken among Jewish charitable agencies in the United States.[46]

Surprisingly, Marks did not use his position as chairman of the Committee on Benevolent Associations to advocate a unified fund drive for all charities in the city. The suggestion for such work apparently came instead from Howard Strong. The son of Josiah Strong, he had taken a position as special secretary to the committee in 1904. In 1906 he suggested that the committee consider a unified fund drive for Cleveland.[47] During the next several years the committee made tentative inquiries to see if the city's charities would support such a drive. Little negative comment was received and the committee proceeded with its plan.

In 1913 a special subcommittee of the Committee on Benevolent Associations drew up a plan for a federated fund drive. Among the members of the subcommittee were Newton D. Baker, former Goodrich House worker and now the mayor of Cleveland; Samuel Mather; Starr Cadwallader, another Goodrich alumnus; and Homer H. Johnson, president of the chamber of commerce. They advocated implementation of the federated plan for two reasons: federated giving would allow for a more equitable division of the available monies, and a well-coordinated solicitation campaign would increase the total sum donated as well as elicit donations from people who had not supported charitable work in the past.[48]

After a final consultation with various charitable organizations and their governing boards, the committee proceeded to create the Federation for Charity and Philanthropy on March 1, 1913. Among the agencies participating in the federated program were two social settlements, Hiram House and the Central Friendly Inn. Charles Whiting Williams became the full-time head of the federation. A graduate of Oberlin College, Williams initially entered the ministry, but changed course for a more lucrative career in business. Prior to coming to the federation he had been assistant to the president of Oberlin College, in which capacity he was responsible for the solicitation of funds.[49]

Williams conducted the federation's first fund drive in June 1913. Though the drive fell $37,000 short of its goal of $250,000, the money received represented contributions from a greater number of donors than had previously given to the city's charities.[50] Through the use of effective speaking and publicity campaigns, which included the publication of booklets graphically illustrating the needs of the city's charities, Williams ensured that future fund drives would meet their goals.

The move toward coordination of the city's charitable monies was paralleled by efforts to direct the services offered by such agencies. In 1907, at the suggestion of the Associated Charities, eight agencies combined to form a Committee on Cooperation. This committee worked to eliminate duplication of service, particularly among agencies which provided direct relief to families. The committee's first act was the creation in 1909 of a Charities Clearing House whose primary purpose was the preparation of an index of all persons and families receiving aid from private agencies, such as the Associated Charities, the Humane Society, the Visiting Nurse Association, the Deaconess Home, and the

Salvation Army, as well as governmental assistance from the Department of Public Charities. The Committee on Benevolent Associations felt this work to be most important to its own efforts and soon made membership in the Clearing House a prerequisite for endorsement on the part of certain types of charities.[51]

Supported largely by the Associated Charities, the Committee on Cooperation proceeded in 1910 and 1914 to publish guides to the philanthropic, educational, and religious resources of the city. And by 1911 the committee had also assumed the role of arbiter in disputes concerning the responsibilities of various agencies. In this capacity it attempted to eliminate duplication of services and, in some instances, apparently tried to direct certain agencies into new areas of work.[52]

The Committee on Cooperation also played a role in the professionalization of social work in Cleveland. The Associated Charities by 1910 had an in-house training program for its staff and volunteers, and with that example in mind, the committee began a survey of similar training programs in the city in 1914, in order to obtain an overview of the techniques and methods being employed. It planned to affiliate with Western Reserve University for the purpose of establishing a professional training program for social workers. Professor James E. Cutler, chairman of the university's sociology department, was a member of the committee and also of the new newly formed Federation for Charity and Philanthropy. This connection accounted, in part, for the establishment of the School of Applied Social Sciences at the university in 1917.[53]

In 1914, following Cleveland's receipt of a new city charter and the creation of the city Department of Public Welfare, the Committee on Cooperation became the Welfare Council, a "voluntary combination of social and civic bodies to cooperate with the newly created Department of Public Welfare."[54] Unfunded, with membership voluntary for charitable agencies, the council served as a forum in which issues of concern to both public and private welfare agencies could be discussed.

Three years later, in 1917, the final step in the coordination of the city's charitable work took place when the functions of the Federation for Charity and Philanthropy and the Welfare Council were combined in the Welfare Federation of Cleveland. The federation oversaw the solicitation of funds for charitable and reform work, allocated those funds to its member agencies, and, most importantly, determined the general direction of charitable and reform work in Cleveland.

The unity of these functions did not survive the World War I period.

The extraordinary fiscal demands of agencies such as the YMCA, the YWCA, and the Red Cross during the war years dictated that a separate, special fund-raising drive again be instituted in Cleveland. The Victory Chest campaign, first held in 1917, supported not only the operations of war-oriented organizations, but also those affiliated with the Welfare Federation. Spurred by patriotic fervor and a high-pressure solicitation campaign, Cleveland's citizens donated over ten million dollars to the campaign in 1918. The success of such a campaign resulted in the removal of the fund-raising function from the Welfare Federation after the war and its assignment to a new organization, the Cleveland Community Fund, in 1919. With periodic changes in responsibility for the allocation of funds, this dual ordering of the welfare needs of Cleveland has continued to the present day.[55]

By 1919 the population of Cleveland had risen to over seven hundred thousand people, almost a twofold increase since 1900. Its streets were paved or being paved, its sewer and water systems had been adequately expanded, and its program of reform and philanthropy had been institutionalized. Eighty-eight agencies, both public and private, were now affiliated with the Welfare Federation. Sixty-six received their funds from the Community Fund.[56] Of the eleven settlement houses then operating in Cleveland, over half received support from the Community Fund and, within a decade or two, all would be dependent on the fund.

Staffing of the settlements was largely professional. Students from the training courses at Western Reserve University and other schools supplemented many staffs during the busy summer season. Though Christian impulse may have motivated many of the staff members and students in their choice of vocation, it seemed hidden beneath their professional demeanor. Nowhere was the change in the settlement, in the social reform impulse, better exemplified than in University Neighborhood Centers, the last settlement established in Cleveland. Begun in 1926 on the city's southeast side, University Neighborhood Centers was a creation of the School of Applied Sciences of Western Reserve University and an experimental center established for the training of its students. The Polish immigrant neighborhood it served had seen little outside philanthropic work prior to this time. It therefore provided a pristine testing ground for social work techniques, as well as a site for in-service training. Eventually University Neighborhood Centers became independent of Western Reserve University and, in 1936, began to draw its funding from the Welfare Federation.[57]

By the time Cleveland reached its 125th anniversary in 1921, it seemed well able to cope with the problems created by its industrial and demographic metamorphosis. Settlement houses, originally agencies of unique purpose and outlook, had by then become only another segment of a controlled, logical system of public and private philanthropy directed toward meeting the needs of the city's less fortunate citizens. The same forces of order and efficiency which had transformed Cleveland from a village to an industrial city had come to control its philanthropic agencies. Whereas independent Christian altruism had characterized benevolent work and social reform at the turn of the century, benevolence and reform had become, some two decades later, merely another aspect of the secular corporate order.

MARIAN   J.   MORTON

Temperance Reform in the "Providential Environment," Cleveland, 1830–1934

John Brodnik's saloon, located in Cleveland's St. Clair Avenue Slovenian immigrant community, ca. 1910

In 1852 Cleveland's population of 25,670 boasted a Marine Total Abstinence Society, with a roll "many fathoms in length" upon which both mariners and gentlemen signed the pledge to abstain; a Sons of Temperance Lodge, with a secret ritual but public meetings at its headquarters at Ontario Street, near Public Square; a Father Mathew Mutual Benevolent Total Abstinence Society, established when the famous Irish priest visited the city the preceding year; a Cuyahoga County Total Abstinence Society, originally formed in 1830 by a "large and respectable" group of citizens and an offshoot of the oldest national temperance body, the American Temperance Society; and a Ladies' Temperance Union, only two years old but with fourteen hundred members.[1]

These groups illustrate the wide appeal and the remarkable diversity which characterized the temperance movement from the first quarter of the nineteenth century until the passage of the Eighteenth Amendment in 1919. Reformers and conservatives, wealthy and working class, Protestants and Catholics, political activists and moral suasionists, women and men, young and old were drawn to temperance activities. In Cleveland, as in the rest of the country, their ideologies, tactics, and organizations responded to those significant economic, social, and intellectual changes which also transformed the nation.

Cleveland's mid-nineteenth-century temperance organizations had their roots in the temperance agitation of the first decades of the century when improvements in distilling techniques, the unavailability of other beverages, and the need to relieve tensions created by the period's rapid social changes raised alcohol consumption to unprecedented heights. The first national temperance body was the American Temperance Society, formed in 1826 by New England clergymen and propertied gentlemen who objected to the wasteful, disorderly, and irreligious behavior of the inebriated citizens of the "alcoholic republic."[2]

51

Later opponents of alcohol would also stress both the physical and the moral, the individual and the social evils of liquor; eventually, they would successfully propose its banishment.

New Englanders who settled the Western Reserve brought with them the gospel of temperance as part of their intellectual and moral baggage. The first recorded temperance group in Cleveland, the Cuyahoga County Temperance Society, like its parent group, the American Temperance Society, and like the Cleveland City Temperance Society (formed in 1836), preached total abstinence from alcohol although temperance had originally meant only moderation in the use of alcohol. The shift is indicated by the change in the county group's name in 1841 to the Cuyahoga County Total Abstinence Society.[3]

The literature of the American Temperance Society blamed liquor consumption for "pauperism, crime, sickness, insanity, wretchedness and premature death," in keeping with the nineteenth-century belief that social evils have their origins in individual behavior. The remedy, however, moved beyond individualism to group action: the "diffusion of information, the exertion of kind moral influence, and the power of united and consistent example to effect such a change of sentiment." The Cleveland City Temperance Society also threw itself vigorously into information-gathering, as in its publication of a list of ninety-nine "breathing holes of hell" in the city where liquor was sold in 1837. Arguing that alcohol created both poverty and immorality, the Cleveland society urged that these places be closed through more restrictive liquor licensing laws,[4] suggesting that moral suasion be reinforced with pressure on local politicians.

These tactics were appropriate for men with political clout and social standing, who could believe that their upper middle-class examples would be beneficial and inspiring to others. The same tactics were employed by the leadership of the benevolent and missionary societies of the 1830s, which were, like these temperance societies, attempts to ameliorate the social ills created by a growing gap between the top and the bottom of the class ladder, particularly in urban societies.

A local example of this benevolent approach to temperance was the Marine Total Abstinence Society, which was formed in 1840 and survived almost two decades. Cleveland's thriving commerce in the 1830s and 1840s rested upon Lake Erie and the newly built canals. Lake sailors and canal men, therefore, became the objects of the city's first benevolent society, the Western Seamen's Friend Society, which maintained a chaplain and several missionaries. This society also founded the Marine Total Abstinence Society, whose lengthy roll of pledge signers included "names of every description, from men of note and high standing in society who occasionally look in upon the tars, give them a word of encouragement, and leave their names as an example worthy of imitation" by the seamen themselves.[5]

For the most part, however, the benevolent approach and leadership of the temperance movement in Cleveland, as elsewhere, were overshadowed in the 1840s by the Washingtonian movement. Washingtonian temperance was predicated on the evangelism and optimism of the period, often expressed in the religiously and secularly derived belief that the individual could save—perhaps even perfect—himself and his society. The goal of the Washingtonians was the spiritual reclamation of drunkards by their conversion to total abstinence. This salvation was to be achieved by temperance lectures, plays, and literature which relied on the techniques of revivalism. The Washingtonians' desire to save the less fortunate also linked them with contemporary democratic egalitarianism and humanitarian reforms, illustrated in Cleveland by the antislavery activities and the common school movement of the 1840s. Both the democratic and revivalistic tone are illustrated in a pamphlet whose author, Joseph Porketts, clearly an alcoholic, described a lifetime of hopeless binges until his own conversion to total abstinence: "When I came to Cleveland, I found twenty drunkards where there was not one in [my former city]. I continued drunk or crazy for nearly seven years. I often tried to quit drinking, but my dear brethren told me it would surely kill me and that I had better take a little for my stomach's sake." Finally, he "resolved to become and die a sober man." But the life of a teetotaler was not always a happy one, as he discovered in a Euclid tavern where "Two gentlemen from Cleveland took hold of me . . . and dragged me to the bar to drink whether I would or not." Fortunately, he wrote, "God . . . delivered me."[6]

Because the Washingtonians drew their leadership and their following from a broader constituency than the older societies, they stimulated a vigorous, if short-lived, flurry of temperance activity in Cleveland. Clevelanders heard famous speakers such as Theodore Weld and Lyman Beecher and his son-in-law Calvin Stowe from Lane Seminary in Cincinnati, and enjoyed temperance plays such as "The Reformed Drunkard." Established temperance groups benefited; the Cleveland City Temperance Society claimed fifteen hundred members in 1843. Several new groups were formed with direct ties to the Washingtonians, such as the Young Men's Washingtonian Total Abstinence Society and the Martha Washington and Dorcas Society, a women's benevolent and poor relief organization which also engaged in temperance activities. Despite this enthusiasm, however, attempts by the temperance forces to get a city "no-license" law were ineffectual.[7]

The Washingtonian movement lasted only through the 1840s since its emotionalism was difficult to sustain and organize. However, it had spread the gospel and broadened the base upon which Cleveland's next significant temperance groups, the Sons of Temperance and the Independent Order of Good Templars, would capitalize. Both were fraternal orders, with secret rituals and degrees and ranks of membership. These groups were also examples of the increasing number of voluntary associations which provided members with the sense of fellowship and community rapidly being eroded by midcentury industrialization and urbanization. The national Sons of Temperance was established in 1843 "to shield [members] from the evils of intemperance; afford mutual assistance in case of sickness and elevate [their] characters as men." As indicated, this was also a mutual aid society which furnished social security against the disasters of illness and death when there were few public social welfare institutions, and social respectability for the upwardly mobile in a time when outward signs of class membership were becoming indistinct.[8] Although not a mutual benefit society, the Independent Order of Good Templars, founded in 1851, was similar to the Sons in organization and purpose.

By 1848 the Sons had three divisions in Cleveland, and a decade later, the Good Templars had several lodges. Cleveland had lost its small-town quality; in 1850 its population of 17,034 was thirty times that of 1820, swelled by an influx of rural Americans and German and Irish immigrants. Its economic base had begun to shift from commerce to manufacturing and heavy industry, providing new opportunities but also necessitating new job skills and work situations. Membership in fraternal orders such as the Sons of Temperance, the Good Templars, the Masons, or the Odd Fellows, which also had flourishing lodges in Cleveland,[9] provided identity and a sense of solidarity and shared purpose. These were reinforced by the orders' discipline of members who broke the pledge or violated other group norms.

Both the Sons and the Good Templars also advocated political action to end the liquor menace. From 1852 to 1853, other Cleveland temperance groups also pushed for city and state prohibitory laws, forming a temperance alliance to strengthen efforts and inviting Neal Dow, father of the prohibitory "Maine Law," to speak. Since 1853 was a gubernatorial election year, and because the Democratic and Republican candidates would not commit themselves to prohibition, the Cleveland Temperance Alliance supported a Free-Soil Democrat.[10]

Temperance forces lost the election, but prohibition became an important goal from that time forward, and political action independent of the two major political parties was soon employed again.

Catholic temperance groups also flourished during the 1840s and 1850s in urban areas such as Cleveland. They were inspired partly by the preaching of Father Theobald Mathew in Ireland and in this country during his 1849 to 1851 visit, and more practically by a need for mutual aid and fraternity due to prevalent nativism. In August 1851, at the invitation of Bishop Amadeus Rappe, a proponent of total abstinence, Father Mathew preached to thousands of Clevelanders, many of them non-Catholic. Thousands took the pledge, including the mayor and the city council at one service. The Father Mathew Mutual Benevolent Total Abstinence Society grew out of this visit, the first of many Catholic temperance groups, reflecting the city's increasing Catholic population. These societies played an important role in offsetting local hostility and assimilating their members into American life.[11]

The Catholic church, unlike many American Protestant denominations, did not officially support temperance activities although many prominent clergymen, like Rappe, did. In 1870 the Catholic Total Abstinence Union of America was established. This group stressed the efficacy of prayer and the clergy—moral suasion—and the distribution of temperance literature. Local groups were encouraged to push for local liquor legislation, but the union did not support prohibition activity,[12] doubtless to avoid accusations of political meddling.

During the Civil War, Americans had turned their attention from temperance and the other antebellum causes, but at the war's end, the movement pushed forward with the political tactics with which it had experimented in the 1850s. This development was foreshadowed at a convention of the National Temperance Society in Cleveland in July 1868, attended by a variety of groups, most notably the Sons, the Good Templars, and the state temperance alliances. The Honorable Woodbury Davis told his audience that the "ignorance, vice, crime" caused by liquor could not be remedied by "love" or "moral suasion" or by licensing; the remedy could only be total prohibition of the liquor trade, as in the Maine Law. Most significantly, he concluded that this would be achieved only by the election of men dedicated to temperance, not by ordinary politicians susceptible to pressure from the liquor interests. A number of factors appeared to necessitate the formation of the third party which was implied in Davis's speech: a federal excise tax of 1862 which seemed to provide the protection of the federal government to the liquor business; the organization of the Beer Brewers' Congress in the same year; the lapse of many prewar state prohibition laws; and the corruption and moral bankruptcy of the national Democratic and Republican parties.[13] Also, the Republican party, originally formed around a single issue, provided an example of a successful third party.

But all temperance advocates were not immediately persuaded by Davis's arguments. When the Ohio State Temperance Alliance met early in 1869, the majority voted against independent political action. A minority, however, with its base in Cleveland's vigorous temperance movement, endorsed the formation of a third party, and in March 1869, they "nominated in the city of Cleveland, the first distinctively Prohibition ticket of which we have any record." Their nominee for mayor, Grove N. Abbey, got 1,049 votes. Encouraged by this, a small group then formed a state prohibition party in May of 1870 and in September helped form the national Prohibition party.[14]

At its first national convention in Columbus, Ohio, in 1872, the Prohibition party asked for federal and state prohibition but moved beyond this single issue to demand a sound national currency, honest and competent civil servants, regulation of postal and telegraph communications and of railroad and water transportation, expanded public education, and suffrage for all "citizens . . . who are of suitable age and mentally and morally qualified" without regard for "color, race, former social condition, sex, or nationality." In 1876 the party met in Cleveland, adding to the 1872 platform a plank calling for a federal constitutional amendment to validate national prohibition. However, in 1880, again in Cleveland, the party backed off from this broad approach. The only issue supported other than prohibition was woman suffrage, which, with the fulsome praises of the virtues of home and motherhood, was clearly intended to win women's support. Shortly thereafter the national Woman's Christian Temperance Union, formed in 1874 in Cleveland and led by Frances Willard, did endorse the Prohibition party, which became briefly the Prohibition Home Protection party. Initially identified with reformers and reform (the party called itself the Prohibition Reform party in 1876 and 1880), the Prohibitionists were the first national party to endorse woman suffrage, the direct election of senators, an income tax amendment to the Constitution, and national prohibition.[15]

The party often did better on the state than the national level, and its gubernatorial candidates ran well in Ohio through the 1880s, polling the party's largest vote in 1887. It is possible that the party sometimes held the balance of power on the state level during this period. In 1873 when a Democrat was elected governor of Ohio, the *Cleveland Leader* blamed it on the Prohibitionists: the Republican candidate, it declared, had been "kicked to death by the Prohibition Jackass." Until the end of the century, Prohibition party candidates ran for mayor and often for all city offices in Cleveland, including city council in most elections. The party, however, never ran as well as it had in 1869, trailing far behind not only both major parties but the various other third parties as well, such as the People's party in 1893 and a coalition People's party−Socialist Labor party candidate in 1895.[16]

Like other third parties, however, the Prohibitionists on the local and national level kept alive an issue which was too hot for the major parties to handle. In 1919 the Prohibition party would achieve the goal which it had been the first—and only—national political party to endorse, a national prohibition amendment.

The tactics and goals of the Woman's Christian Temperance Union were shaped significantly by the cultural ideals and the realities of nineteenth-century women's lives. The WCTU's perceptions of the evils of alcohol were simplistic and gender-based, as a Cleveland member explained in 1896:

> This Union began as organized warfare on behalf of the women of Cleveland and its homes against the saloon. This conflict has been carried on with earnest persistence because there is seen on every hand the devastation of homes and the wreck of woman's hopes . . . and it will be continued so long as mothers' hearts are broken, children's lives blighted, wives tortured and even killed outright by the fiends which the saloon produces.[17]

The WCTU's solutions to the problem, however, were broad-gauged and complex, combining moral suasion, political action, and the building of social welfare institutions.

The antecedents of the WCTU lay in women's participation in antebellum temperance activities, as in the Martha Washington and Dorcas Society. In 1850 the temperance activities of the society were taken up by the Ladies' Temperance Union, whose members also employed moral suasion to convert Cleveland men to temperance principles.[18] Although women's "sphere" narrowed to home and family by the mid-nineteenth century and made entrance into higher education or remunerative jobs difficult, the ideology of true womanhood described women as inherently more pious and moral than men; this allowed women to participate in movements, such as temperance, which were intended to improve male behavior, but at the same time limited them to moral suasion or other suitably pious tactics. The political approaches used by men were not forbidden—for example, women might sign petitions for local option—but such tactics were not as acceptable or as accessible. Women did join both the Sons of Temperance and the Good Templars, which probably provided them some political experience. Yet many women who became leaders and participants in the women's rights movement of the nineteenth century came to it from temperance where they had learned something also about political powerlessness.

Frustrated perhaps by these limitations in a movement which was increasingly turning to politics, women in the winter of 1873 to 1874 in small Ohio towns devised a dramatic variation on the moral suasion approach: the marches upon saloons by praying and exhorting women which became known as the "Crusades." Cleveland women read eagerly of the crusade elsewhere and soon followed suit. In March 1874 the president of the Women's Christian Association, a benevolent group which aided working women, called a meeting to formalize establishment of the Women's Temperance League of Cleveland, which had already begun its own crusading. A participant, Mary Ingham, described such a vigilante action of the league in a Public Square saloon: the assembled women read the Scriptures, sang the hymn, "There is a fountain filled with blood," offered a fervent prayer, and endeavored to persuade the "deathly-pale" bartender to give up selling liquor.[19]

The women called their work "gospel temperance," indicating its ties to the evangelical revivalism of the 1870s led by figures such as Dwight Moody. Their immediate goal was conversion to temperance; the ultimate goal, conversion to Christ. When the praying bands stopped visiting saloons, therefore, the Women's Temperance League established what were in effect city missions or institutional churches with daily religious services. The most successful and longest-lived was the Central Friendly Inn, established in 1874, where the pastor Janet F. Duty and her helpers created a parish of nearly two hundred persons by home visits and gospel preaching.[20] However, the women also provided for the material welfare of their charges. For example, Central Friendly Inn furnished men with cheap lodgings and meals and a reading room of temperance literature.

The Women's Temperance League eventually became active in politics. In 1874 members debated whether to canvass the city on behalf of a temperance issue, finally deciding that this would be inappropriate. The issue of political participation later created rival branches of the WCTU in the city. After the league's affiliation with the national WCTU, Cleveland women joined with the state WCTU in 1883 in gathering signatures for petitions asking that a prohibitory amendment to the state constitution be put on the ballot, and then campaigned actively for the amendment by distributing literature, sponsoring speakers, and raising funds. When the amendment did not pass, the leadership of the Ohio WCTU blamed it on the two major parties and in 1885 officially endorsed the Prohibition party at a state convention. In protest, a group within the Cleveland WCTU dissolved its affiliation with the state and national and called itself the Woman's Christian Temperance Union of Cleveland, Nonpartisan.[21] Cleveland women who remained loyal to the national group coalesced around the Cuyahoga County WCTU.

The stated issue was whether or not the WCTU, which described itself as nonpartisan, could endorse a political party; Frances Willard, then president of the national WCTU, claimed it could, especially since the Prohibition party endorsed woman suffrage and home protection. More logically, the dissident splinter group disagreed. In addition, most of the Nonpartisans were probably Republican supporters, reluctant to relinquish their party preference. Also possibly involved was the issue of woman suffrage, endorsed by the "loyals" but not by the Nonpartisans in Cleveland who did, however, support the temperance and school ballots for women.[22]

Cleveland became a center for the national and state Nonpartisan movement and organizations. Although historians of the WCTU maintain that this movement was insignificant because it involved only eleven states with one hundred local unions when the national or "loyal" majority had over ten thousand locals, in Cleveland the WCTU, Nonpartisan, appears to have been stronger than the Cuyahoga County WCTU. For instance, they commanded the support of John D. Rockefeller and other prominent Cleveland businessmen who served on their board of trustees and helped finance their institutions.[23] This support also suggests that class differences helped foster the schism.

The Cleveland Nonpartisan maintained the same "departments of work" as did the national: literature, social purity, kitchen gardens, prison and jail visitations, drinking fountains, juvenile work. What distinguished the Nonpartisan from the Cuyahoga County WCTU, however, was its flair—or financial assets—for institution-building. By 1913 the Nonpartisan had founded the Training Home for Friendless Girls, the Eleanor B. Rainey Institute, and the Mary Ingersoll Club for Working Girls, and had become a member of the Cleveland Federation for Charity and Philanthropy. In 1927 it became the Woman's Philanthropic Union, a small group which simply administered the investments and trust funds which partially sustained their institutions.[24] This group left as legacies to Cleveland, Central Friendly Inn, which had become a settlement, renamed Friendly Inn, while still under the Nonpartisan's management, and Rainey Institute, now part of the Cleveland Music School Settlement.

The Cuyahoga County WCTU's approach to temperance was political rather than philanthropic. In this respect, it more clearly reflected the expansion of women's sphere into the public arena, allowing historians to label the WCTU a feminist organization. The county WCTU's quarterly reports listed many loyal WCTU locals in Cleveland, and the departments of work carried on were similar to those of the nonpartisan union.[25]

The county WCTU stressed work with young people, the organization of loyal legions, and scientific temperance work, resolving in 1894 to use their recently acquired school ballot to pressure for enforcement of the state's law requiring temperance instruction in public schools. Underlying these activities was a persistent concern with political issues and power. The county WCTU in 1887 discussed the feasibility of petitioning the Ohio General Assembly, a "whiskey legislature," in regard to scientific temperance education, but concluded that petitions were useless in this instance, "especially petitions without a vote behind them." In 1894 the women resolved "that as we pray for the closing of the saloons we should work for the ballot as a means of power in answer to our prayers." Their support for woman suffrage and the Prohibition party reflected these concerns. In 1905 the county union worked to defeat Governor Myron Herrick for reelection because he had vetoed a state local option law; in 1912 members campaigned for a state no-license law and for woman suffrage, and in 1918 distributed at the polls literature supporting woman suffrage and a state prohibition amendment.[26] Unlike the WCTU, Nonpartisan, the loyal branches remained mostly temperance organizations.

Even more single-minded was the Anti-Saloon League. The league was born in 1893 in Oberlin where the "providential environment" of the Western Reserve was "full of the New England spirit of reform." The league was a more modern organization than the WCTU in that its strength lay in the evangelical Protestant churches, which provided funds and pulpits for league speakers and lists of registered voters. The league was also a national political pressure group staffed by paid professionals within a bureaucratic structure and utilizing the new techniques of mass communication. It was almost exclusively a single-issue group, its goal being ostensibly just an end to saloons. As such, the league represented the trend toward professionalization, specialization of interest, and bureaucratization which characterized other organizations of the period. Its political approach and its reliance upon devices such as constitutional amendment and the initiative and referendum also linked it closely with the Progressive movement.[27] So effective was the league that it became the model for later pressure groups, including those whose goal was the repeal of the Prohibition Amendment.

Initially there was some support for the league within the Prohibition party, especially from Prohibitionists who were disillusioned by the declining strength of their own political organization. However, the league's willingness to compromise temperance principles—to support a candidate who drank but voted "dry," to work for local option rather than prohibition, and most particularly, to support either or both of the two major parties—was distasteful to Prohibitionists. The resulting split between the party and the league also affected women who were temperance supporters. In Cleveland, although the WCTU loyalists backed the party, the Nonpartisan shared its headquarters in the arcade for many years with the Ohio league and sometimes aided their political efforts, which were technically nonpartisan. The Ohio league board included members of the Nonpartisan union from Cleveland. An Ohio Anti-Saloon League pamphlet illustrated both its ideological and tactical approaches: "A New State Temperance League, Inter-Denominational and Omni-Partisan, for Agitation, Legislation, Law Enforcement and Organization of the Boys. . . . The membership is made up of people of all political parties and religious creeds, and no creed whatever. It has no total abstinence pledge. Its sole aim and purpose is, as its name indicates, ANTI-SALOON."[28]

The league technique of publishing pro-temperance information dated back to the days of the American Temperance Society, but the volume and range of publications were new: its American Issue Publishing Company in Westerville, Ohio, produced an estimated 244,782,292 printed items between 1909 and 1923. The league also published yearbooks with information on the national consumption of alcohol, state and federal liquor laws, all the dry counties and cities in the country, and a list of all national temperance groups. The 1908 *Yearbook* listed Cleveland's 2,096 saloons and 12,535 arrests for drunkenness with the causal connection clearly made; in 1910 Cleveland was used as an example of a "wet" city with consequently rising taxes.[29]

Many of the publications were clearly designed to apply political pressure. In 1907, for example, the Ohio league published a bulletin endorsing several candidates for Cleveland City Council and Theodore Burton over Tom Johnson in the city mayoral race because Johnson allowed saloons to operate illegally and permitted "low dances" on the Sabbath. The league got the credit for defeating Governor Myron Herrick in 1905. It worked for state prohibition amendments in 1914, 1915, and 1917; the last cost the Ohio league $100,000 and the county leagues, $250,000.[30] All three amendments lost, but with decreasing margins. In 1918 Ohio did pass a state prohibition amendment, and in January 1919 ratified the Eighteenth Amendment to the Federal Constitution.

A combination of circumstances helped create this national victory for the temperance forces. Perhaps most important were the decades of education and agitation: scientific temperance education, mandatory in almost all states after 1902, which taught generations of children the virtues of abstinence and the evil of drink; ceaseless political activity beginning in the 1840s with the fraternal organizations and continued by both the Prohibitionists and the Anti-Saloon League; the conventions and meetings held; the newspapers, almanacs, and pamphlets which poured out of the temperance presses by the millions of pages; the temperance gospel preached in Protestant churches and the gospel temperance preached by the WCTU; and the caretaking institutions of the WCTU which provided an alternative and an antidote to the saloon.

Also crucial to the victory of prohibition was the entrance of the United States into World War I. War-time exigencies made prohibition an attractive means of saving manpower, money, and grains; the connection between German-Americans and the brewing industry added patriotic motives; the centralized authority in Washington made prohibition seem viable; and giving up alcoholic drinks was congenial to the spirit of war-time self-sacrifice.[31] Preliminary federal legislation eased the way for passage of the Prohibition Amendment: in August 1917 the Lever Food and Fuel Control Act banned the production of distilled spirits for the duration of the war; in November 1918 the War Prohibition Act forbade the manufacture and sale of all intoxicating beverages of more than 2.75 percent alcohol. By December 1917 both houses of Congress had passed the amendment, and slightly more than a year later, in January 1919, it had been ratified by thirty-six states and became effective a year later. Twenty-six states, including Ohio, already had state prohibition amendments.

Temperance forces hailed their victory and in the early 1920s claimed that it had brought all the benefits which they had promised.

In 1922 the Ohio Dry Federation, a league offshoot, claimed that "Ohio is prospering under Prohibition. . . . Drunkenness has decreased more than 50 percent. . . . AND THERE ARE MORE HAPPY AND COMFORTABLE HOMES," and fewer inmates in jails and city infirmaries. Recent historians, although less euphoric, also attribute to prohibition a measurable decrease in the amount of alcohol consumed by Americans at that time.[32]

Opponents of prohibition, however, were articulate and influential, particularly as the 1920s drew to a close, federal enforcement became less effective or determined, and the Depression created new economic conditions. Temperance groups had always faced the implacable hostility of the liquor industry—brewers, distillers, and saloon keepers—which had fought, with varying degrees of success and organization, the attempts to regulate or destroy them. Even before the passage of the amendment, however, several influential businessmen with no economic connections to the liquor industry formed the Association Against the Prohibition Amendment, which then played the leadership role in repeal politics; it was a single-issue, nonpartisan group modeled after the Anti-Saloon League. Like the league, it drew much of its political and financial support from Ohio and especially from Clevelanders. The AAPA argued that prohibition represented an unwarranted intrusion of government power into the lives of individuals and also that the inability or the unwillingness of the federal government to enforce prohibition eroded the legitimacy of authority, fostering disorder or anarchy.[33] Although the AAPA appeared to insist that prohibition worked both too well and not well enough, the arguments appealed to the politically conservative and business-oriented audience of the twenties.

In 1929 the Women's Organization for National Prohibition Reform was established by wealthy and socially prominent women such as Cleveland's Mrs. Amasa Stone Mather. In 1930 the organization held its first convention in Cleveland; it claimed a membership of one hundred thousand, of which twenty-five hundred were from Ohio. The WONPR maintained that prohibition created "wide-spread intemperance, hypocrisy, and corruption [which] threaten the structure of government." The significance of the WONPR was its attack on the idea, particularly as fostered by the WCTU, that women had a particular interest in prohibition. In 1931 the membership of the WONPR in fact exceeded that of the WCTU. Also active in repeal efforts were the Cleveland Crusaders, established in 1929 by a group of young businessmen led by Fred G. Clark. By 1930 the Crusaders sponsored radio debates and like-minded political candidates and claimed a national membership.[34]

These arguments of principle were made more compelling by the collapse of the economy in 1929. Supporters of repeal then maintained that it would bring back prosperity, creating jobs for workers and revenues for state and federal governments; enforcement of prohibition also cost taxpayers money which they could ill afford. In 1933 Ohio voted for repeal of both the state and the federal prohibition amendments, with Clevelanders endorsing repeal enthusiastically.[35]

The repeal of the Prohibition Amendment, like its passage, was facilitated by well-planned, well-financed political action combined with fortuitous circumstances. The temperance forces, however, had not abandoned the movement in 1919. The Prohibition party, whose principal assumption had been that no law could be enforced without sympathetic lawmakers in office—Prohibition party men—had the soundest rationale for continued activity. It ran presidential candidates throughout the 1920s, and its platforms demanded strong enforcement of the amendment. In 1932, as the repeal forces gathered strength, Prohibitionists once more re-stated their position on enforcement and also framed a program for economic recovery which was more specific about an active role for the federal government than that advocated by the two major parties.[36] The Prohibition party clung to its reformist origins longer than the other two temperance organizations.

The WCTU was always constrained by women's lack of political power even after the passage of the suffrage amendment in 1920. Its chief thrust, therefore, was education. In 1929 the WCTU still published millions of pages of printed material, including books, pamphlets, songs, pledge cards, and other scientific temperance publications which were distributed through its Young People's Branch, the Loyal Temperance Legions, Sunday School Department, Christian Citizenship Department, and Department of Fairs and Exhibits.[37]

The Cuyahoga County WCTU gained members, or at least organizations, during the mid-1920s, as the result of a million-dollar, million-member campaign begun by the national chapter in 1920, claiming two thousand members in December 1925. In 1924 the national WCTU celebrated its Golden Jubilee in Cleveland, reenacting the early crusades with the help of public officials who poured five-thousand-dollars-worth of whiskey into the gutter. The national held its convention in Cleveland again in 1934, making plans to raise another million dollars for temperance education on radio and in movies, and for temperance research. The membership of the local

WCTU, however, was dwindling by that time, and its focus narrowed to temperance education.[38]

Through the 1920s the Anti-Saloon League continued to argue forcibly against nullification of the Eighteenth Amendment. Its *Annual Yearbooks* continued to stress the benefits of prohibition, citing, for example, the decrease in arrests for intoxication (although Cleveland's arrests did not decrease). The league blamed repeal on "political manipulation" by the liquor interests supported by "Big Business," which employed political pressure and massive propaganda to achieve its goals.[39] The league was apparently unconscious of the irony of the opposition's use of its own tactics.

The Eighteenth Amendment seems to have become the law of the land precisely at the time when the values and institutional arrangements which made it possible became obsolete, for the Prohibition party, the WCTU, and the league had grown out of peculiarly nineteenth-century conditions. The party emerged in a politically volatile era of third-partyism when independent political action was a viable strategy for effecting social change; its constituency was upwardly mobile and imbued with middle-class beliefs about success resting upon self-discipline. The WCTU's appeal derived from a nineteenth-century definition of womanhood as possessing a nurturant and self-sacrificing morality which carried the obligation of playing private and public caretaking roles. Despite its modern bureaucratic structure, the league's strength was explicitly drawn from Protestant churches; its ideology and constituency were clearly sectarian and evangelical.[40]

In the years after World War I, however, the base of evangelical Protestantism shifted from urban areas such as Cleveland to the countryside, where the majority of Americans then lived, and identified temperance with a rural or small-town way of life which was fast disappearing. The virtue of self-discipline and self-restraint upon which abstinence from alcohol rested was eroded by a consumer economy and a lifestyle which rewarded gratification rather than control of individual desires and appetites. The hedonistic flapper replaced the philanthropist and the public-spirited activist as a desirable model for female behavior. Third-party activity was limited by the high costs of political campaigning through the mass media and by restrictive election laws.[41]

This estrangement of temperance advocates was not new. They had always been critics of their society: of crime, disorder, poverty, disrupted family life, sexual promiscuity, materialism, irreligion, and political corruption. Temperance principles had never had widespread support except perhaps at the time of the passage of the Prohibition Amendment. The tenuous hold these principles had on the American public was made apparent by the difficulties of enforcement and the speed of repeal.[42] The failure of "the noble experiment" then simply and finally discredited not only the goal but the tactics and belief systems associated with temperance.

History—and the American public—seldom side with a loser. In 1934 the *Cleveland City Directory* listed under "Temperance and Benevolent Groups" only the Ohio Anti-Saloon League and the Woman's Philanthropic Union with its several institutions.[43]

L O I S   S C H A R F

The Women's Movement in Cleveland from 1850

Progressive party float in the 1912 Cleveland woman suffrage parade

The organizational impulse by women to secure political and legal rights for themselves gained ground slowly in Cleveland. From the 1830s, however, association formation and institution building by women on behalf of other women and in support of social reform generally flourished. Female societies identified the needs of their less fortunate sisters and other needy and marginal members of a town—then city—finally metropolis—in constant flux. Through their societies they engaged in an evolving series of activities to salvage and uplift the souls of needy women, to nurture them in female-founded and administered institutions, and later to seek legislative redress for the unsavory aspects of female employment. As their associations emerged more prominently in the late nineteenth century and particularly during the Progressive Era, a strong woman suffrage campaign finally emerged within the broader framework of Cleveland's social feminism. After the passage of the Nineteenth Amendment both social and political feminism waxed and waned.[1]

The first outstanding benevolent reformer in the area was Rebecca Rouse who moved to Cleveland with her husband Benjamin in 1830. She found a town braced between its frontier roots and its commercial growth and development. Economic expansion and demographic change brought dislocations to which Rouse, along with the wives and sisters of the town's flourishing businessmen, brought benevolent charity and moral reform. They carefully balanced the domestic ideology of Victorian womanhood, which defined women as nurturing, moral guardians confined to home, with evangelical faith in perfecting their society outside domestic boundaries. Rouse became the leader in volunteer efforts to aid the destitute, visit the sick, reform prostitutes, and house orphans. She led the Martha Washington and Dorcas Society which provided poor relief, especially to women and children, and which engaged in temperance activities as well. The volunteer association counted 225 members before disbanding at mid-century. By 1853, fourteen hundred women belonged to the Cleveland Ladies' Temperance Union, just one of several female temperance organizations and auxiliaries. Fifty sewing women, with limited, short-lived support from more affluent Clevelanders like Rouse, organized and opened the Female Cooperative Union in 1851.[2]

Women's interest in issues concerning their political and legal disabilities was much more limited during the 1850s. Two hundred Ohio women who met in Salem in 1850 to discuss their grievances in response to a small notice placed in a Salem abolitionist newspaper concluded their session with a stinging resolution demanding redress. The women had met with no men in attendance (unlike the more famous Seneca Falls convention of 1848). In 1851 women's rights activists met in Akron where ex-slave Sojourner Truth delivered an eloquent speech which crossed the boundaries of race and gender while renewing the courage of the assembled women temporarily intimidated by the men in attendance. By 1852 the Ohio Women's Rights Association organized in Massillon and the following year Cleveland hosted the leading lights like Lucy Stone and Antoinette Brown of the growing national movement. But the city supported no local organization. Only one woman, Caroline Severance, who had moved from Boston when she married into a prominent Cleveland family, replicated the road a number of female evangelical reformers traveled from temperance to antislavery to women's rights. She attended a number of state and national conventions and on March 23, 1854, read her lengthy plea, "In Behalf of Women's Rights, in Respect to Prosperity and the Exercise of the Elective Franchise," to the state senate.[3]

After 1855, a series of laws were enacted that permitted Ohio women to retain and control their property and earnings. Child custody legislation was not passed during this period, but with the growing emphasis on women's special maternal capabilities, judges were less apt to revert to common-law principles and unquestioningly award children to fathers in cases of divorce. The first state-based suffrage association, formed before the Civil War, was established in Ohio, and in response, a committee of the Ohio legislature was the first in the nation to recommend that women be enfranchised. These gains and Severance's prominence notwithstanding, Cleveland women who chose public roles during the nineteenth century preferred benevolent charity and moral suasion to ameliorate the perceived disabilities of women.[4]

With the outbreak of the Civil War, pressure for legal change at the state level was temporarily suspended along with diffuse moral reform.

Feminists, who were fervent abolitionists even as they became concerned with their own disabilities, redirected their activities and affiliated with the National Women's Loyal League. The league, founded in May 1863 by national leaders Susan B. Anthony, Elizabeth Cady Stanton, and Angelina Grimké Weld, collected petitions in support of a proposed constitutional amendment prohibiting slavery.

Local women were among those who participated in the massive campaign, but larger numbers organized along less political and ideological lines during the war. One week after the fall of Fort Sumter, the Northern Ohio Soldiers' Aid Society enlisted the volunteer services of area women. Beginning as a neighborhood sewing circle with two gold dollars, it eventually encompassed 525 branches. Women organized in cities and in "localities where farm duties were engrossing, neighborhoods scattering and shipping facilities inconvenient." During the course of the war, the society, affiliated with the United States Sanitary Commission, raised almost one million dollars, including one hundred thousand dollars collected at a great fair held in Cleveland's Public Square in 1864. Funds were dispensed to hospitals and army units in the form of equipment, supplies, bedding, clothing, food, and books. A soldiers' home was established in Cleveland and staffed by volunteers to provide lodging and other amenities for army personnel between home and base.

When the war ended, a reduced staff conducted a special relief and employment bureau as well as a Free Claims Agency that expedited two thousand claims ranging from invalid and widow's pensions to requests for artificial limbs. For the thousands of women of the Cleveland area who transformed their missionary circles, church social groups, and benevolent associations into the branches of this vast network, the Soldiers' Aid Society provided both personal gratification and collective satisfaction through their organizational skills and contributions to the war effort.[5]

Cleveland temporarily regained the limelight of women's activism when the founding convention of the American Woman Suffrage Association (AWSA) convened in the city in November 1869. The founding of the organization stemmed from conflicts between male and female abolitionists in the aftermath of the Civil War. Before the war, the women's rights movement had been ideologically and institutionally tied to abolitionism. During Reconstruction, antislavery advocates placed their hopes for the promotion of freedmen's rights, including the vote, in the Republican party. The party, in turn, advocated guarantees for blacks at the expense of women through the Fourteenth and

Fifteenth amendments. Radical feminists like Susan B. Anthony and Elizabeth Cady Stanton refused to defer to black, male suffrage and formed the Equal Rights Association to demand franchise regardless of race or sex. In November 1868 a group of more moderate New England women formed the New England Woman Suffrage Association (NEWSA). Then Stanton and Anthony established the National Woman Suffrage Association (NWSA), the first nationwide feminist organization. In response, the New England association, with its Republican and abolitionist male supporters, issued a call to form a rival national organization. Caroline Severance, who had moved back to Boston, was active in the NEWSA and in the movement to go national. She may have been instrumental in selecting Cleveland for the site of the founding convention.

Many Clevelanders welcomed what seemed a sensible and moderate response to the Stanton-Anthony initiative. "We sincerely hope that the work of this Boston body may retrieve the mischief done to the cause and reputation of women by the discredible proceedings of the recent New York convention" chaired by the more radical Stanton and Anthony, said the *Cleveland Leader*. When the official call was issued for a rival organization to convene in Cleveland in November of 1869, the local YWCA invited all interested women to meet, appoint committees, and plan the hosting and entertainment of women who would attend the convention. But while Cleveland's women attended the public sessions, and four served as delegates, evidence indicates only a modicum of local support and organization after the departure of the founding mothers and fathers of AWSA. Hanna Tracy Cutler called a meeting to organize a Cuyahoga County suffrage committee. Caroline Severance stayed in Cleveland to help initiate the local group, but its future was an inauspicious one.[7]

The AWSA met in Cleveland again in November 1870 where the issue of union with the national association dominated proceedings and was rejected because Anthony and Stanton had alienated too many suffragists. After the assembly, AWSA attention focused on the state constitutional convention scheduled for 1873. Ohio women initiated a massive petition effort to influence delegates, with the major impetus coming from an active group of Toledo women. Even Painesville had a suffrage association with 150 members at a time when a comparable group in Cleveland numbered only thirty.[8]

Just as Caroline Severance emerged as the leading spokesperson for women's rights before the Civil War, Clevelander Louisa Southworth, widow of a wealthy businessman, filled that role in the last quarter of

71

the century. Yet while the local scene played host to the AWSA, Southworth identified with the Stanton-Anthony faction. She served as honorary vice-president of NWSA and chaired its Committee on National Enrollment. By 1888 she reported that forty thousand names had been collected and that she had borne the expenses of the drive. Southworth was committed to petitioning and when the tactic was abandoned, she continued to collect signatures in her capacity as chairman of the Franchise Committee of the Ohio Woman's Christian Temperance Union. Until the early 1890s she remained among a handful of women who traveled to Columbus in midwinter before each biennial legislative session to plead on behalf of votes for women. Still collecting signatures through the 1890s, her two daughters were active in the revitalized suffrage movement after the turn of the century.

In 1890 when the breach between the rival suffrage organizations was finally healed and the formation of the National American Women Suffrage Association (NAWSA) signaled the end of schism, Southworth continued to favor the national strategy that had been a hallmark of the Stanton-Anthony faction. In 1893 Lucy Stone, who had been an active feminist since her graduation from Oberlin and who was a founding force behind AWSA, proposed that the efforts of NAWSA focus on individual states. Anthony countered with a proposal to work for a federal constitutional amendment. Southworth supported her, but the Stone plan was approved at the convention. The state-by-state tactic would lead Cleveland women down an arduous, frustrating, and possibly unnecessary road given the intransigence of the Ohio electorate.[9]

While the movement for the vote floundered, Cleveland women responded to their changing social and economic environment through a number of organizations. In October 1868, six hundred women from area churches combined to form the Women's Christian Association of Cleveland. Like the voluntary societies of antebellum Cleveland, the initial motivation was benevolent and religious. A missionary committee visited families at home and men in saloons to distribute Bibles and religious pamphlets. But other committees soon formed to focus on the problem of growing numbers of women unable to cope with the rapidly changing conditions of urbanization. Recognizing increased mobility of rural migrants in search of gainful employment, the association clearly stated its desire to promote "the temporal, moral and spiritual welfare of women, especially the young, who are dependent upon their own exertions for support." Within a year of its founding, the organization created an employment committee to place women seeking work and founded a boarding home to meet the needs of many women, "strangers among us," for safe, low-cost housing. While the boarding house could shelter and protect those "whom destitution might lead to sin," another institution, the Retreat, was established to reform "the tempted and fallen who had already compromised their purity."[10]

By the turn of the century, the Women's Christian Association had founded additional homes for aged women, for chronically ill women, and for female transients. The organization also began a number of educational and social programs for working women and for mothers while launching projects that eventually developed into independent organizations: Woman's Christian Temperance Union in 1875, Day Nursery and Free Kindergarten Association in the 1880s, Federation of Business and Professional Women in 1920. In 1893 the association combined with the small, like-minded Educational and Industrial Union to form the Young Women's Christian Association, and affiliated with the national organization.[11]

For decades the activities of the YWCA made it the prototype for other women's associations; the homes for needy women of all ages were replicated by the WCTU of Cleveland, Nonpartisan, the Salvation Army, and later by black and immigrant women's clubs and associations. Programs that became the centerpieces of social settlement houses were modeled on classes and services first offered by the YWCA and were expanded for mothers and children. The association proudly proclaimed as its basic principle—"women helping one another to that 'more abundant life' for which they yearn"—a principle that occasionally permitted other salvagers of Christian souls to adopt conscious feminist sentiment. In 1893 the Salvation Army founded its Rescue Home for Fallen Girls, and appealed "to the heart of every woman who hears [the plea] . . . to stretch out her hand to a fallen sister. . . . Hitherto it has been quite in order to work for the rescue of fallen men and redeemed manhood has been welcomed into society again as though he had never been a drunkard or debauchee. But very little effort has been made to save fallen women, because of the prevailing idea that women seldom if ever can be reclaimed, and if she is lifted up she cannot be trusted, etc., etc."[12]

The feminist tone of the annual report of the Rescue Home was less common than a generalized female consciousness that seemed to affect Cleveland women in the 1880s and 1890s. Growing associations and clubs were only one measure of gender-based awareness and pride. As the city approached its centennial celebration, Mary (Mrs. W. A.) Ingham wrote and published a compendium and tribute to the educational and philanthropic work of Cleveland women. A former teacher, active church worker, and temperance leader, Ingham left little doubt about the origins and qualities of the women she praised—"noble woman, of true and best New England mould, with its educational and missionary spirit and active intellect." The contents provided no solace for exponents of a separate, private sphere for true Victorian or Protestant women of Yankee background. Ingham praised the domestic qualities of her subjects but reminded her readers that there would be no book if these women "would confine their influence simply to the home circle. They belong to the public. . . ."[13] Like antebellum reformers, these pushed against the constraints of prescribed domesticity to minister to the social needs of their community.

With the same pride in femaleness and women's capabilities, Gertrude Van Rensselaer Wickham engaged 216 volunteers in as many local communities to survey records for a centennial tribute to the pioneer women of the Western Reserve. Wickham noted the numerous biographies of male founders but the paucity of interest in and information on "their wives, who doubtless, had performed an equal though different part in laying the foundations of future civilization and prosperity." Five volumes eventually corrected the oversight.[14]

By the early 1890s, plans were underway for celebrating Cleveland's centennial. The debate over a proper format for exhibiting women's accomplishments—separate from or integrated with the men's—which had raged in Chicago prior to the World's Fair of 1893 was absent from the Cleveland scene. Surrender to separatism as symbolized by the Woman's Pavillion at the Chicago fair either convinced local women of the futility of full, integrated celebration with men or suited their gender-distinct perceptions. The latter seems likely.

The activities of the Women's Department of the Cleveland Centennial Commission culminated on July 18, 1896. The front page of the *Plain Dealer* was written by and about women. Women's Day of the week-long city celebration consisted of a reception and banquet where a casket with organizational records, newspapers, letters, and an address to the women of 1996 was sealed and deposited with the Western Reserve Historical Society. Ingham presided over all arrangements and events. Speakers were instructed to avoid controversial issues, but reference to suffrage by one woman brought more than a smattering of applause from the audience.

The topic of female enfranchisement was dormant but not dead as Cleveland's women celebrated their past with pride in their special qualities and contributions to their city. And for those women still concerned with the more specific political and legal rights of women, there were scattered successes to celebrate. By 1887 the last of the limitations on property rights were removed along with those on the ability of women to make contracts. And in 1894, Ohio granted women suffrage in school board elections.[15]

The twentieth century brought new distinction, achievements, and dislocations to Cleveland. The census enumeration revealed the city had passed Cincinnati in population, becoming the urban capital of Ohio. A reform mayor, three-cent streetcar fare, and plans for a new civic center placed Cleveland in the national limelight. But the problems associated with urban growth and rapid industrialization grew in tandem with positive developments. The voluntary, benevolent, philanthropic response of women to the economic hardship and social needs of other women and their families required new institutional and programmatic approaches. Women stood ready to cross the bridge between the charitable, moral-uplift thrust of nineteenth-century female associations and the professional social welfare and political activism of the Progressive Era.

Flora Stone Mather traveled a major portion of that distance. Daughter of one wealthy Clevelander and wife of another, Mather epitomized personal philanthropy on behalf of social and educational causes. The College for Women of Western Reserve University, the institutional creations of the YWCA, Lakeside Hospital, missionary societies—all benefited from her interest and financial support. In 1896 she helped establish and fund Goodrich House, one of several residential settlement houses gaining popularity in urban centers generally and in Cleveland as well. She became a trustee and eventually deeded the building and endowed a fund for the neighborhood social center. Activities at settlement houses were family- and especially child-oriented, and workers were usually well-educated college graduates who lived on the premises. But Goodrich House moved beyond kindergartens, clubs, and athletic activities for older boys and girls, vocational training for young men and women, classes for mothers. The center quickly launched a number of organizations that represented increased social concern and activism by women. The founding of the Consumers' League at the settlement in spring of 1900 indicated the role of the neighborhood settlement house as "spearheads for reform" as well as the new directions women were taking in response to an increasing female industrial labor force encountering exploitative wages, long hours, and hazardous working conditions. As one of the league's founders, Flora Stone Mather had traveled far from benevolent philanthropy.[16]

At the time of its organization, Consumers' League policy was modeled on that of similar leagues in eastern cities. Poor working conditions were studied, especially for women in retail establishments, and consumers were urged to boycott firms whose employment practices did not meet league-defined standards. At the time of Mather's death in 1909, however, league concerns had expanded and policies to engender reform had shifted. In cities like Cleveland, employment opportunities were growing, especially in light industry. Domestic servants, laundresses, seamstresses, and shop clerks still comprised the major share of Cleveland's working women, but new and growing woolen mills, garment factories, paper box manufacturing firms, and food processing plants offered additional employment opportunities for the increasing numbers of women flooding the city from neighboring farms and from the villages of southern and eastern Europe.

When the Cleveland league surveyed female-employing industries in 1908 and described deplorable working conditions and meager compensation, the local branch like those elsewhere agreed that their goals and tactics must change. The voluntary boycott of selected offenders was an inadequate means of pressuring employers to initiate "living" wages, shorter hours, and healthier work environments in a multitude of manufacturing establishments. The boycott gave way to insistence on protective legislation for women workers and legal limitations on child labor. And this new approach required that the Cleveland league engage staff members who were able to study issues, amass data, educate the public, and pressure legislators for action.[17]

As female reformers turned to legislative remedies to urban problems, their political disabilities and those of socially concerned women generally stood out in bold relief. The suffrage movement in the Greater Cleveland area finally rose from its long stupor under the able leadership of Elizabeth Hauser, a newspaper reporter from Girard, Ohio, who had collaborated with Tom Johnson on his memoir. Hauser worked for Harriet Taylor Upton, secretary-treasurer of NAWSA. When Upton moved back to her native Warren, Ohio, from Washington in 1903, she literally moved the headquarters of the national suffrage association with her. In spite of the association's proximity to Cleveland and Upton's domination of the movement in Ohio, it was not until 1911, when the Ohio legislature had called a constitutional convention to meet in January of the following year, that the time seemed propitious for Hauser to begin a Cleveland suffrage campaign.[18]

Along with a handful of committed suffragists, Hauser began an extensive membership drive especially among prominent Clevelanders. "[M]ore important Cleveland names were needed if the movement was to be recognized as socially respectable." While leaders of the drive remembered that "the homes along Euclid Avenue are, for the most part, strongholds of the Anti-Suffragists," the new organization began with the hope of appealing to Cleveland's elite.[19] However, the cross-class tensions that have been a continuous undercurrent in the history of women's movements quickly surfaced and highlighted the subtle distinction between women helping women on a benefactor-client basis and women helping women to help themselves.

In June of 1911, six thousand workers in the ladies' garment industry struck the city's cloak and suit manufacturers for improved conditions and union recognition. Josephine Casey and Pauline Newman were sent from the International Ladies' Garment Workers Union headquarters in New York to attend to the specific needs and issues of the fifteen hundred women who were among the strikers. Several days after the full-scale walkout began, violence broke out on picket lines and several young girls were arrested. During the early days of the walkout, newspapers reported that suffrage leaders would protect the interests of young women arrested while engaged in picket duty. When Casey, who was with the first group of pickets charged with disorderly conduct, posted bond she went directly to the newly established headquarters of the Cleveland Suffrage League. Casey asked that the league draft a resolution expressing sympathy for all women struggling to better their living conditions, supporting the principle of equal pay for equal work, and endorsing any movement that would improve conditions of female employment. A resolution was drafted and signed by several women, including Elizabeth Hauser, but with the note that signatures represented the support of individual women and not of their organization.

The position of the league was underscored at a mass rally of strikers and supporters held at the end of July. Casey again pleaded on behalf of "oppressed women," but a suffrage leader who presided at the rally reiterated the individual support of some suffragists, because the organization embraced a large membership of men and women whose sympathies and interests varied. Under these circumstances the league could not be expected to endorse any measure not pertaining specifically to woman suffrage. The handful of suffragists who did support the striking women promised an investigation of working conditions and a formal report on the issues. Rose Moriarty, student and social worker, undertook the preparation of the report on behalf of reform-minded women. But however honorable the intentions, the study failed to materialize; strikers felt disappointment and resentment as they drifted back to their jobs in October after four months of determined but futile protest.

Partial victories had been gained by female garment workers in New York and Chicago before the Cleveland strike, and in Boston and New York afterward. In these cases, the ability to forge concrete ties between immigrant workers and native-born reformers and suffragists had played important, if not decisive, roles in the outcome. The cross-class bonds were not without tensions, but middle-class women on picket lines and in courts helped legitimize the protests of strikers and their demands for union recognition. The absence of comparable cooperation in the failed strike in Cleveland revealed the important role joint effort could play.[20]

Timing was an important factor working against closer cooperation in Cleveland. Timidity characterized the early drive of the suffrage league. Full-scale participation in a labor confrontation, especially one marked by strife between frustrated strikers and intransigent employers, may have seemed like an invitation to self-destruction to suffragists. Within months, however, the group hesitantly adopted the "unladylike" procedure of soapbox oratory and even invited a militant New York suffragist who had been arrested in a Philadelphia strike to participate. Events in Columbus galvanized Ohio suffragists, and Cleveland proponents quickly realized the value of immigrant and working-class support.[21]

The Ohio constitutional convention assembled in January 1912 and heard forty-one proposed amendments. Number 23 adopted the suggestion of women's organizations that an amendment eliminate the words "white male" in the state's voting requirement and replace them with "every citizen." A special election was called for September 3 to vote on the constitutional amendments, and like their co-workers throughout the state, the Cleveland league began its campaign. Maud Wood Park and other national leaders helped local women. Six hundred women attended a public meeting in Cleveland and organizational matters were tackled at a series of teas. Cleveland and surrounding areas were divided into wards, and supervisors, ward leaders, and township leaders were appointed. Committees to arrange and oversee public meetings, membership, publicity, and finances were established and staffed. A number of officers and supervisors like Myrta Jones of the Consumers' League, Mrs. C. F. Thwing, wife of the president of Western Reserve University, and Elizabeth Baker, wife of Cleveland's mayor, were active women accustomed to public roles. But they were joined by others who had never participated in political affairs nor engaged in public speaking. The league organized a training class to furnish "lessons in voice culture and the art of speaking" as well as to practice arguments with which to present the case for suffrage.[22]

From May 31 when the proposed constitution was published until September 3 when the special election was scheduled, the women honed their skills as campaigners. In June, when Florence Allen, graduate of the College for Women of Western Reserve University and a law student in New York, returned to Cleveland, she immediately entered the suffrage ranks: she organized college women; attended rallies, luncheons, and women's clubs in Cleveland; traveled throughout the state standing in the back seat of automobiles and speaking on street corners, from courthouse steps, and at county fairs. Allen shared the native-born, middle-class social origins of her colleagues, but she shunned the "social motherhood and housekeeping" rhetoric on behalf of suffrage. These arguments focused on women's nurturing qualities, moral purity, and domestic skills which should be projected into the public sphere to promote protective legislation for women and children and to sweep away political corruption. This rationale was widely used for expedient reasons and because large numbers of suffragists truly believed it. But others like Allen eschewed this approach; she focused on suffrage as a natural right. By July 1912 the Cleveland league printed pro-suffrage posters in Hungarian, Italian, and Yiddish to take the message into the large immigrant neighborhoods. Perhaps appeals to ethnic, working-class women were self-serving as well, but they represented the willingness of the early Cleveland organization to come to terms with the realities of the city's demographics.[23]

The short but difficult drive resulted in failure. The amendment lost by a sizable majority. The Ohio Suffrage Association decided to collect the requisite number of petition signatures to initiate a suffrage amendment to the new constitution. Together with suffragists in other cities, Cleveland women shed what remained of timid, low-visibility tactics. Proponents took to the streets in impressive numbers. Women on horseback led the 1914 parade, ranks of middle-class women faced cheers and endured jeers, and a small group of male supporters composed a division. Marie Wing, daughter of a Cleveland judge and industrial secretary of the YWCA, led a group of young working women at the end of the marchers. The media response was positive, coverage was full, and editorial support was also positive. By the end of July 1914, over 131,000 names had been collected and filed with the secretary of state. Less visible educational activities continued on a smaller but unremitting scale. Still, in November the amendment again met resounding defeat.

After two failures, suffragists changed their strategy. Since the new constitution provided for home rule for cities whereby localities could adopt their own charters without going to the legislature, suffragists believed these charters could carry provisions enfranchising women in municipal elections. When East Cleveland, a middle-class suburb with a well-informed electorate, framed a charter in 1916, the Woman Suffrage League of Cleveland decided to make a test case. On June 6 a new charter containing a suffrage clause was submitted to East Cleveland voters and adopted. But the Board of Elections refused to permit the women to vote, and the suffrage organization initiated a taxpayers' suit. In October Florence Allen argued persuasively, the Supreme Court of Ohio concurred, but it did not announce its decision until the following April. After a vigorous campaign, Lakewood followed the example of East Cleveland in the fall of 1917.

Encouraged by these limited successes, suffragists sought additional gains through varied tactics. Several states had granted women the right to vote for presidential electors. Allen and her colleagues lobbied for similar legislation. Both houses of the Ohio legislature and Governor James A. Cox concurred, signing the bill February 21, 1917. Opponents immediately challenged the victory and circulated petitions calling for a referendum on the new law. Suspicion that numerous signatures on the opponents' petition were fraudulent was verified after an extensive statewide check. (In Cleveland alone seven thousand names were thrown out.) The challenges of suffragists were time-consuming and ultimately failed; the referendum proceeded. Legislation to extend the presidential franchise to Ohio women was recalled by 144,000 votes.

This bruising defeat on the heels of excited hopes undermined what faith remained for women obtaining the vote within the state. Ohio women turned their attention and efforts to Washington and Congress, lobbying their representatives and senators before passage of the Nineteenth Amendment, and then working for state ratification afterward. Yet even with ratification, the struggle continued. In 1918 the Home Rule Association (the most current cover for the liquor interests) ini-

80

tiated and obtained an amendment to the state constitution stipulating that federal constitutional amendments must be approved by voters before ratification by the legislature was valid. Designed originally to overturn prohibition, it was used in 1920 to try to nullify the woman suffrage amendment. Only after a decision by the Supreme Court that upheld the ratification power of state legislatures was the issue settled.

It can be reasonably argued that female enfranchisement should have been sought in Washington from the start, that Lucy Stone's state-by-state strategy had condemned countless Ohio workers to failure and frustration completely out of proportion to their efforts and skills. Still, the suffrage campaign mobilized numbers of Cleveland women under a single banner as no event or issue had ever done before. By 1920, eighty thousand women had enlisted in local suffrage leagues and parties, women who may not have identified with a campaign focused on Congress, 350 miles away. Goals no farther than Columbus and volunteer tactics that could be employed within reach of home combined with increased consciousness of inferior status to galvanize Cleveland women on behalf of an issue which for sixty years had been the radical, unappealing dream of a few. The numbers involved in this once dormant, unpopular movement also indicate that the women's movement had extended well beyond the confines of Cleveland's benevolent religious elite. Elizabeth Hauser represented one new kind of female activist—the educated, small-town migrant to the urban center. Marie Wing and Florence Allen were college-educated women for whom the suffrage movement was an apprenticeship for successful professional careers later. The faceless, working-class women who read the foreign language posters found only temporary common cause with the campaign's leaders, but they, too, were touched by the drive for suffrage. The women's movement would ebb and flow after 1920, but it would never again be the special preserve of Rebecca Rouse, Flora Stone Mather, or even Hauser herself.

The broadening base of female activism on behalf of the vote has often masked the outburst of female energy on behalf of social welfare that marked the first two decades of the twentieth century. American entry into World War I emphasized these diverse undertakings as war needs mobilized the efforts of women in industry, in service organizations, and in the home. In June 1917 the first issue of *Cleveland Women: Official Publication of the Womanhood of Cleveland* was published to publicize and encourage female organizational contributions to their families, city, and nation. The first issue featured articles on the Red Cross, Surgical Dressing Committees, and the War Relief

Society, as well as a recap of the fifteenth annual convention of the Cleveland Federation of Women's Clubs. Many of the seventy-four federated associations—ranging from study circles and mothers' clubs to the Consumers' League and the Suffrage Party of Greater Cleveland—and nonaffiliated groups like the Daughters of the American Revolution and the Women's Americanization Committee, responded to requests for informative articles and advertisements. *"Cleveland Women* is a publication for women," its editors wrote. "It differs from other papers in this, that it does not confine itself to the fireside. Every activity in which the woman of this day takes part is covered by this paper."[25]

The publication dramatized the wide-ranging organizational efforts of the area's women on behalf of social welfare, justice, and change. By 1917 a plethora of female-directed associations devoted time and energy "to win the war, to relieve French orphans, to rescue girls, to educate foreign citizens, to encourage civic betterment, to oust strong drink, to bear better babies."[26] Still, the publication was not all inclusive. Black and ethnic women also associated for purposes of institution building, neighborhood improvement, and same-sex sociability. But race and class provided distinct barriers to inclusion within this "mainstream" of the women's movement. The only exceptions were members of the Council of Jewish Women who were settled German-Jewish Clevelanders whose mid-nineteenth-century roots and economic status coincided with those of many of the city's elite. They were, in fact, inbred with many Anglo-Saxon values according to Mary Ingham, and even had an issue of *Cleveland Women* (February 23, 1918) devoted to their activities which paralleled those of their Protestant "sisters." The wave of female community building was even greater than publicists (and later historians) recognized.

War-related activities, especially the conditions of female employment, engaged the interest of several of the women's associations. One November 1917 issue of *Cleveland Women* featured the efforts of the Consumers' League both nationally and locally to encourage working women to avail themselves of nonconventional, well-paying employment opportunities caused by labor shortages. In addition, league members closely monitored working conditions to prevent the abrogation of hard-won legislative regulations of hours and safety standards. The league also provided personnel to proliferating public agencies: members sat on the Ohio Committee on Women and Children in Industry and Belle Sherwin chaired the Cleveland Women's Committee of the Council of National Defense of the Mayor's Advisory War Committee.[27]

Roles as watchdogs of working women were not always successful. One defeat achieved national attention. In late August 1918 the street-car company of Cleveland hired women as conductors. Male employees complained, and a Department of Labor investigation revealed that the scarcity of male labor was not large enough to justify the continued employment of the women. The women, in turn, protested their threatened discharge before the War Labor Board, represented by Florence Allen and supported by a number of women's organizations. But the men insisted that the employment of women streetcar conductors was a matter for the company and the union to settle, and on December 2, the union formally threatened to strike if the women were not fired immediately. The men struck the following day. The War Labor Board ruled that the women should be replaced within thirty days, but the strike ended when the union and company decided "that on and after this date there will be no more women employed as conductors; that the Cleveland Railway Co. will remove and displace the women that are now in its service as rapidly as possible."[28]

Protests from the women and their defenders resumed, and the War Labor Board reconvened to hear Allen plead once again. In March 1919 it finally ruled that the sixty-four women had been hired because of wartime labor conditions and were entitled to their employment. By this time they had been discharged and so were ordered rehired. The company decided to abide with its original agreement with the union, and the president wrote to the board placing responsibility for reinstating the women on board members.[29]

The War Labor Board could not enforce its decision. In spite of the cooperative efforts of female professionals, reformers, and workers, the cause was lost. Social feminists became firm in their conviction that the well-being of working-class women lay in protective legislation and not in voluntary unions. They could not be blamed for embracing this tactic, but that decision placed social reformers in solid opposition to the National Women's party and its proposed Equal Rights Amendment for almost one-half century after its introduction in 1923. Any perceived threat to protective legislation was anathema; any gains in female membership by unions through the efforts of male or female leadership (or rank and file in some cases) were made without the aid of the reformers.

But these divergent paths and their costs to the women's movement were not foreseen in the halcyon days of cooperation and suffrage victory. With great optimism, the Cuyahoga County Women's Suffrage party disbanded after Ohio ratified the suffrage amendment and turned over its membership lists to Belle Sherwin and the newly established League of Women Voters (LWV). The Consumers' League under the direction of Wilma Ball and Marie Wing concentrated on a minimum wage bill for women as well as tentative plans for unemployment insurance. And the YWCA, ever the program innovator and training center for Cleveland's social activists, initiated 1920 with a new publication, *The Cleveland Dial: A Magazine of Women's Interest*, "to serve all women, to compromise no ideals, to carry the message of the women's movement, to record permanently the achievements of Cleveland women—such is our 'excuse for being' "—at least for the six issues published.[30]

Just before publication of its short-lived periodical tribute to area women, the YWCA "mothered" a new organization. With the help of Lena Madisin Phillips of the national office and Marie Wing of the Cleveland branch, a number of women responded to the invitation to meet and form a chapter of the National Federation of Business and Professional Women. The response was gratifying—a tribute to the growing numbers of educated women who had achieved occupational success. Many of the founders like Wing, Florence Allen, Mary Grossman, and Clara and Lillian Westropp had earned their stripes in the suffrage campaign, as social reformers, and in professional fields. According to Grossman, the new organization was more than an institutional recognition of collective achievements of the past and setting for joint pursuits in the future. It was also founded to support Florence Allen's candidacy for common pleas judge in Cleveland.[31]

Allen's campaign succeeded, and with the continuing aid of a network of devoted and competent friends, she continued her climb up the judiciary ladder. Several steps behind, Grossman and Lillian Westropp followed. The latter and her sister founded the first female-financed and run savings and loan bank in the nation. Other federation members benefited from this supportive network also. Rosalind Goldberg became the first woman police prosecutor in Ohio. Marie Wing left her post at the YWCA, led the Consumers' League while attending law school, and ran successfully to become the first woman on Cleveland's city council. Dorothy Smith succeeded Wing at the YWCA before opening a successful insurance company. Eleanor Farnham founded her own public relations firm, handling the publicity for her friends in politics, social reform, and private business.[32]

These achievements mark a departure from the previous structures and directions of the women's movement. Trained within that framework in terms of leadership skills and collective action, these women gained success during the 1920s and after as individuals and within business and professional frameworks that could no longer be identified by sex. Bernice Pyke of Cleveland and Margaret Waite of Lakewood, for example, began long, devoted careers in the folds of male-dominated Democratic and Republican party politics respectively, not working together on behalf of women's suffrage or other gender-specific issues. The "sisterhood" endured, encouraging each other's goals, supporting each other's efforts, applauding each other's attainments. But achievements were now individual and personal.

The organizations persisted, but their directions after 1920 also underscored change. The League of Women Voters launched its local efforts to educate newly enfranchised women, to work for its legislative program, and to encourage women to enter the partisan political arena. Its first goal was admirably accomplished by instructing women on registration procedures and illustrating the voting process at model booths. When the local organization polled candidates on their stands on issues, published their responses, and sponsored debates among candidates, the Cleveland league initiated practices that became models throughout the nation.

On the legislative scene, the local group failed to pursue women-oriented issues as outlined by the national league's Committees on Legislation and on the Status of Women. At the national level, the league played prominent roles in lobbying (usually in tandem with other women's groups who formed the Women's Joint Congressional Committee) for equal citizenship laws for women, for the Child Labor Amendment, for repeal on bans inimical to the employment of married women, against the Equal Rights Amendment. At local and state levels, league branches promoted additional protective legislation for working women, especially minimum wage laws, and worked to extend political rights to all phases of participation. But the issues that held the attention of Cleveland members were increasingly civic and political rather than social and feminist. Civil service, city-manager government, school board reform, and reorganization of county welfare services were the issues studied by league members, occasionally to the extent that study, not advocacy, seemed the raison d'être of the group.[33]

In only one instance—early in the 1920s—did the Cleveland LWV initiate and lead a movement identified with women's interests. The second national convention was held in Cleveland in 1921, and at the general session Florence Allen introduced the "Cleveland Peace Plan" to amend international law to criminalize war. The language of the proposal was diluted, but the peace appeal struck a responsive chord. Belle Sherwin, president of the local group prior to assuming leadership of the national organization, formed the Women's Council for the Prevention of War and Promotion of Peace as a result. She feared that the popularity of the peace plan would identify the league too closely with one issue and subsume other league activities. But leadership of the two organizations was interlocking, and the movement gained force. In March 1924 Marie Wing led a peace march in downtown Cleveland, and the local council served as the model for the National Committee on the Cause and Cure of War. "The women of Cleveland . . . are spurring the women of other cities in this great task of womenkind," according to the LWV national chairman. Failure of the United States to join the world court in 1926 and international developments during the 1930s ignored and undermined the worldwide peace movement dominated by women, but not before it came as close to suffrage in unifying women's concern as any single issue for half a century.[34]

Growing emphasis on the study of political issues rather than action on a broad front of general reform mitigated the role of the LWV in turning its civic-minded investigators into active participants in the public arena. When one local league member did tread political waters, she was rebuked for running for public office before resigning her league post. The leadership reaffirmed its primary concern with issues rather than candidates and congratulated itself on having thwarted attempts by league members to use the organization as a political springboard. When former suffrage and league leader Lucia McBride resigned from the Cuyahoga County Republican Committee because of the treatment (or lack of treatment) accorded women, her action accented the difficult dilemma of politically oriented women. Although women were in need of a female support system to help sustain them within male-dominated political parties, the most politically oriented of women's organizations turned its back.[35]

Social feminists were more successful in retaining a clear vision of their goals, but they eventually suffered from their own successes and achievements. At first that seemed an unlikely outcome. The Consumers' League of Ohio spent most of the 1920s designing, lobbying, and experiencing painful setbacks in the movements for a minimum wage law for women and ratification of the Child Labor Amendment. Unemployment insurance continued to constitute an important plank in the group's program especially after Elizabeth Magee assumed the post of executive secretary in 1925 and the economy collapsed at the end of the decade.

Magee symbolized many of the changes that had characterized the social origins, status, and direction of female activists from the turn of the century. Like Elizabeth Hauser, she was not a Clevelander, but drawn to the city by the opportunity for work. A former YWCA worker from Denver and Detroit, her master's degree in economics from Columbia placed her in the company of the well-educated professionals who were concurrently carving out their individual careers. In effect, she immediately joined that group of Cleveland women who were still concerned with social welfare even as they left the actual task of transforming visions of reform into concrete public policy in the hands of capable, professional experts. Women like Magee completed the cycle from nineteenth-century benevolence to twentieth-century social and political activism, from Cleveland's elite ladies bountiful to geographically mobile professional experts.[36]

Within a brief period after assuming direction of the Consumers' League, Magee's ideological position and policy commitments were firmly stamped on the organization's policies. This was an implicit example of the individualizing of the women's movement and of women's personal rather than collective accomplishments. Unemployment compensation became the centerpiece of the league program and Magee's activities. Her statewide speeches, legislative testimony, and lobbying efforts attracted wide attention, and in 1931 she became director of the governor's newly created Ohio Commission on Unemployment Insurance. The 1933 report of the commission advocated legislation to create an insurance program, dubbed the "Ohio Plan," which became a model for other states. It floundered in the Ohio legislature, but its chief advocate was appointed to the National Committee on Economic Security when the Roosevelt administration became committed to a comprehensive, nationwide insurance program. Magee was closely involved in devising the unemployment compensation component of what became the Social Security Act of 1935. And after finally securing a minimum wage bill for women in Ohio, she returned to Washington to work with her widening circle of influential colleagues to help draft and lobby for the Fair Labor Standards Act of 1938, establishing hour and wage guidelines for men and women.[37] A century of social welfare and reform by women on behalf of their communities and the disadvantaged members of those communities was institutionalized in public policy at the federal level. The women of

Cleveland played a crucial role in this process which characterized the 1930s and marked the victory of female social reformers.

During World War II, Magee helped safeguard work standards for women and children, and like Belle Sherwin before her, became the national head of her organization. But more in the tradition of Harriet Taylor Upton, she made Cleveland the virtual headquarters of her national association, another sign of individual achievement at the expense of collective effort, a diminution of the women's movement.

After the war, Magee continued her feverish activities, tying the Consumers' League to other organizations committed to social welfare and reform in which she served in leadership capacities. As in the case of her minority report as a member of President Truman's Commission on the Health Needs of the Nation, her positions coincided with those committed to the unfinished agenda of New Deal liberals. In effect, her commitment to and articulation of social issues, her proposed legislative solutions, and her unquestioned identification with the Consumers' League provide a final assessment and a death knell for social feminism. The desire to smooth the ragged edges of industrial capitalism and urban dislocation—never exclusively but largely identified with women's social reform activities of the Progressive Era—was co-opted by the New Deal and American liberalism in the postwar era. Social reform suffered the fate of its success; it entered the mainstream of American political life and policy. But an important element was lost in the process. Social feminists were always concerned with a broad agenda of reform, but at the core lay the special problems of women. That thrust was dissipated as political and social policy advocated by the League of Women Voters and the Consumers' League was subsumed by male-dominated institutions. Individually and collectively, the women's movement lost its special female-defined composition and concern within broader structures. The tradition of reform endured but its feminist base was lost. Those women who continued their activist stance turned to the immediate postwar problems of displaced persons and the enduring issue of world peace.

When middle-class housewives read Betty Friedan's *Feminine Mystique* in the 1960s and young women moved from civil rights and antiwar protests to a reborn feminism, they revived the women's movement in a historical vacuum. Female organizations with roots extending to the turn of the century survived, but they held little appeal for a new generation, if that new generation knew of them at all. What time had done to the causes and commitments of earlier women's organizations was painfully revealed in a 1970 letter from Louise Stitt (another Cleveland YWCA alumna) to her friend Elizabeth Magee. Stitt had watched and admired young people protesting the American invasion of Cambodia, demonstrating their capacity to work for causes about which they felt strongly. And wistfully she wondered "whether those same young people could become sold on the Consumers' League program."[38] The answer would be a resounding no. Cleveland women of the late 1960s and 1970s created an entirely new institutional framework from NOW branches and rape crisis centers to a local chapter of the Coalition of Labor Union Women. They established a framework around Womanspace, a physical location to informally house the increasing memberships of diverse groups and organizations. The Consumers' League did not join the early coalition established to endorse the Equal Rights Amendment, although by the early 1970s it joined the League of Women Voters in reversing its position and advocating passage and ratification. The Women's Political Caucus was founded and filled the vacuum created by the issue-oriented, nonpartisan LWV.

The proliferation of new associations and attention to women's issues during the early 1970s was astounding. By October 1975, in conjunction with International Women's Year proclaimed by the United Nations, Cleveland women celebrated their accomplishments and discussed women's issues for three consecutive days. Over one hundred organizations participated; local and national figures discussed topics ranging from union organization of domestic workers to the current agenda of the Junior League. At a time when the social upheavals that had marked the 1960s and early 1970s began to wane, Cleveland women demonstrated incredible individual and collective intellectual vigor and social activism. And within that renewed women's movement, they retrieved the record of historical precedent and achievement as well.

Occasionally an individual embodies the continuity of a movement better than historical retrieval and narrative. In Cleveland, Josephine Saxton Irwin was such a woman. Born in Lakewood and educated at Western Reserve College, she rode the horse that led the great suffrage parade down Euclid Avenue in 1914. She marched in the Cleveland peace parade ten years later and remained active in antiwar activities through the 1930s and again in the post–World War II peace movement and Council on World Affairs. In 1976 she retraced an earlier route, leading a march down Euclid Avenue on behalf of the Equal Rights Amendment. And when the ERA failed, she spoke to "mourners" assembled at Shaker Square. If onlookers sometimes wondered if

BERTRAM WYATT-BROWN

Abolition and Antislavery in Hudson and Cleveland: Contrasts in Reform Styles

Rev. James A. Thome, minister (1848–71) at Cleveland's First Congregational Church and noted abolitionist

Abolition received no kind welcome in Cleveland. As village, town, and metropolis, the Lake Erie port was much too conservative to boast of preeminence in the sort of revolutionary undertaking that immediate emancipation entailed. Indeed, in the early Republic, no city except Boston had much of a record along radical lines. For northern businessmen, clerks, day workers, and artisans, the daily struggles of marketplace, factory, and building site were sufficient preoccupations. Besides, moral agitations were unsettling. For all classes, but especially the middle ranks, "respectability" was not merely a term denoting social place; it was a community value and personal aspiration not to be casually cast aside. In taking this view of the world and its ways, Clevelanders were scarcely different from other northerners.

Yet, the inhabitants did not react with alarm at the prospect of social and moral change, an absence of fear that set the community apart from many others during the controversy over slavery. Unlike Cincinnati, for instance, Cleveland was seldom the scene of proslavery mobs howling in the streets. To be sure, antebellum Cincinnati was a thriving, tumultuous city, whereas Cleveland was slow to become a major urban center. The pace of growth did not quicken until the late 1830s— after the ending of a serious depression. Size, however, never had much to do with popular antiabolitionism. For example, in 1836 Marius Robinson, a follower of the abolitionist William Lloyd Garrison, barely escaped several hundred rioters in little Granville, Ohio. Later he was brutally tarred and feathered at the tiny settlement of Berlin in Trumbull County.[1] Clevelanders were by no means so inhospitable as these crossroads rowdies. They viewed the antislavery crusaders as cranks, but not as monsters. To them abolitionism represented a religious more than a political cause (as later examined), and therefore the reaction was verbal rather than physical. The relative equanimity in the face of provocation from ideologues became a matter of local pride. The *Herald*, for instance, boasted in 1833 that the residents were "too discerning, too intelligent, to be made the willing instruments" of "fanaticism" whether on one side of the political spectrum or the other.[2]

Cleveland's mixture of fascination with social improvement, stability, and routine commerce reflected the spirit of the earliest settlers—the hard-working, pious folk of New England—and that tradition of practicality and restrictive but genuine idealism endured through the nineteenth century, if not longer. In regard to slavery, the two attributes were represented by abolitionism and antislavery. The terms require some differentiation. Antislavery connoted a hostility to the labor system, manner of life, and supposed moral deficiencies of the southern slaveholder. Under the pressure of sectional rivalry, opposition to slaveholders became a way for northerners, particularly those of religious and moralizing bent, to distinguish themselves from those who depended upon others to do their drudgeries and provide them with the gold for their allegedly luxurious way of life. While all abolitionists, however, were antislavery, not all antislavery folk were abolitionist. The latter term signified a conviction that slaveholding was not merely a curse upon southern whites, shackling them to sin and idleness, but a mockery of God, justice, and humanitarian ideal. Abolitionists, therefore, emphasized the importance of rearranging national priorities: making real the tenets of Jefferson's declaration by freeing the slaves on the soil, without masters' receipt of compensation, and with the rights of citizenship guaranteed. At first abolitionists anticipated that their goals would be achieved by acts of voluntary manumission when their exhortations, from pulpit and press, brought individual slaveholders to the proper point of contriteness. On the other hand, the antislavery proponent would be satisfied merely to prevent the spread of slavery from its existing borders and to propose gradual emancipation, perhaps with removal to another location on this continent or abroad.

Antislavery was by far the more powerful force on the Western Reserve. In this Whig-dominated section of the state, antislavery fed notions of moral superiority over the remainder of Ohio. The Democratic party was strong downstate and it was identified on the Reserve with the vices and hedonism of the South. Cleveland shared these simple prejudices along with a nobler distaste for the cruelties of slave subjection. Thus one could be a religious and social conservative and a sturdily self-conscious opponent of southern ways and institutions all at the same time. In fact, conservatism on the Reserve presupposed a commercially inspired devotion to Henry Clay's "American System" and a hardy puritan disapproval of southern sin.

Unlike antislavery, abolitionism could not be easily translated into such practical political programs as the exclusion of slaves from the western territories of an expanding America. Instead, it served as a dream of what might be, a theological humanitarianism laying down precedent and example for both present and future generations not on slavery alone, but on the purification of the world generally. Immediate emancipation was based on the divinity of man under God, as most abolitionists perceived the matter. Therefore it appealed almost exclusively to "New School" Presbyterians, Hicksite (evangelical) Quakers, Methodists, and Free Will and Missionary Baptists—all of whom held in common a belief in the perfectability or near-perfectability of mankind. Needless to say, sustaining so lofty a view required enormous emotional and spiritual efforts. Fear of sin and failure was all the more intensely felt, and surrenders to temptation harder still to admit. For this reason, abolitionism not only expressed hostility to a tyrannical political and racial institution but also a demand for faith over reason, individuality over institutional and social consensus, purity of heart over mere intellect (although intellectuals were scarcely excluded from its ranks). It was thus a demanding and often psychologically taxing philosophy and mode of action and therefore the number of adherents would always be small. On the Reserve, immediate emancipation was very closely tied to the revivalist "New Measures" of Charles G. Finney and his followers in the Presbyterian-Congregationalist "Plan of Union." But, whereas revivals were for everyone, abolitionism appealed chiefly to passionate intellectuals and other restless, self-examining spirits who found in the lonely cause a bond uniting them with a sacred band of likeminded friends.[3]

By itself, abolitionism would have died the moment New School revivals sputtered out in the mid-1830s. But when combined with antislavery, the more comprehensible, antisouthern movement, a dynamic fusion was created, one that made an impact in Cleveland and in the rest of the Western Reserve. The town presented no claims for originality or leadership in the emancipation cause, but just as the city merchants brought in material goods from the eastern states, the citizens imported reforms from the same source. The business leadership of the community transformed these potentially explosive ideas of black freedom and human perfection into serviceable materials for political aims and regional self-interest, at the expense of the South, and eventually of the old Union.

The local source for reform concepts that Cleveland later received was a small college town to the south and east. At first, Hudson, like its neighbors, supported the colonizationist movement.[4] Colonization enjoyed a rather impressive vogue among the "wise and good," the nation's squires and gentlefolk, including such Ohio luminaries as General and Governor Thomas Worthington of Painesville, and Elisha P. Whittlesey, Joshua R. Giddings's National Republican and Whig predecessor in the district's congressional seat. These and other gentlemen in the country approved colonization of freed slaves because first, the Liberian experiment, begun in 1817, was an imitation of Sierra Leone, Great Britain's antislavery depot for recaptured victims of the illegal African slave trade; second, it promised to remove the allegedly inferior black along with the evil institution. Colonizationists envisaged the Christianizing of Africa in that mission-minded era and, above all, sought neither to disturb the master's rights over human property nor to tempt the black to plan rebellions. The movement was, in a word, "respectable," so much so that its utter impracticality as a remedy dampened enthusiasm not a moment. For instance, David Hudson, shrewd old land speculator though he was, spoke with his heart not his head when in 1832 he wrote colonization headquarters in Washington in this vein: "Having through a long life considered that 'all men are born free and equal' . . . and convinced of the absurdity" of the "doctrine" of slaveholding, "I rejoiced at beholding the Colonization Society steping [*sic*] forward . . . like an Angel of mercy . . . to bless two continents. . . ."[5]

Hudson had taken his cue from local clerical authority. As early as 1830, on Independence Day, the Reverend Warren Isham, editor of the *Hudson Observer and Telegraph*, told the gathered residents of that village that Liberia's prospects might enable Americans to "avert these terrible judgments of Heaven which, we have . . . reason to fear, will ere long overtake us as a Nation." Already James S. Clark (or Clarke), an early industrialist, Samuel Cowles, and other town fathers had established the Cuyahoga County Colonization Society in Cleveland. In 1827 Cowles explained at a society meeting that blacks would be much improved to live in their homeland "under a salutary government, with the means of knowledge" and with "all the arts of civilized life."[6] Similar activity busied the wise and good of the wilderness settlements throughout the northeast corner of Ohio.

At the recently established Western Reserve College at Hudson, colonization was no less popular than in politically conservative Cleveland. The trustees and friends of the school were almost all active in the black repatriation effort. Moreover, President Charles Backus Storrs spoke for the cause and for other mildly antislavery endeavors such as the exclusion of slavery from the District of Columbia. The growing body of students formed a colonization society chapter, and the newly arrived professor of sacred literature, Beriah Green, an enthusiast for temperance, tract dissemination, and other measures, made colonization a part of his evangelical repertoire. (Nearly all future abolitionists began their interest in the cause as members of the colonization society.) Elizur Wright, Jr., the new professor of mathematics and science and son of a college trustee, however, failed to lavish praise on the Liberian cause. While an undergraduate at Yale, he had been exposed to the rowdyism and snobberies of wealthy slaveholders' sons, and he doubted from the start the efficacy of so circumspect a plan as colonization. He did not, though, immediately broadcast his opposition.[7]

Public harmony about colonization did not last long. In the winter and spring of 1831 to 1832, Isaac Israel Bigelow, an enterprising undergraduate at Western Reserve College, began his mission to convert the campus into a stronghold for immediate emancipation. His first target was his landlord, Elizur Wright, with whom he had already studied at Andover Academy, Wright's first teaching assignment. Bigelow left his copies of Garrison's *Liberator* where Wright and other faculty members were sure to find and read them. On one occasion, Bigelow later recalled, Wright dashed into the house, "his face all aglow with joy" to announce that Green and Storrs had been persuaded to renounce colonization and to adopt Garrison's "abolition doctrines" acknowledging the sin of slaveholding and the immediate need to free those in bonds.[8]

All three college leaders were dedicated evangelical or New School Christians who had studied for the ministry for varying periods at Andover Seminary in Massachusetts. Thus they represented a potentially dangerous element from the first, insofar as "Old School" or moderately Calvinist pietists were concerned. In fact, Wright later thought that the theological division was the hidden cause behind the battle over modes of antislavery action. From its founding in 1826 the college, he said, had been "the child of science including theology, of course, as the oldest of the sciences." In the opinion of "the clergy on the Reserve," Wright recalled, the college was to be "a nucleus of sectarian propagandism and in point of fact became its midwives." As soon as he arrived on campus, Wright made known his particular approach toward Christian faith. He denied the conventional historical proofs of revealed religion and instead relied on the subjective feelings of the heart and the notion of "judging the tree by its fruits." Harvey Coe, Caleb Pitkin, and John Seward (Wright's brother-in-law), all highly influential clergymen of the vicinity, were "scandalized" by his classroom lectures that sought "to reconcile science and religion by limiting the field of inspiration in the Bible." Everyone knew that the Portage Presbytery had turned down Wright's application for a license to preach prior to his college appointment. Nor were Storrs and Green spared similar complaints, "not so much for what they *did* preach as what they did *not*," Wright remembered.[9] There were too many hints of a political and moral agenda, too few exegeses on Calvinist themes. Even President Storrs's inaugural address had suggested the removal of "the oppressive load" which "the guilt of slaveholding had imposed." The more elderly divines and laymen on the Reserve could tolerate New School theology only within limits, even if it was the latest intellectual fashion out of Yale College at New Haven and other eastern locations.[10]

The growing tension had other, yet related, causes. The faculty and college president were very young to hold such high positions. Storrs was only thirty-six when appointed in 1830, and Wright, the youngest, was a mere twenty-five when he joined the faculty the following year. The trustees and town leaders were considerably older. Moreover, the scholars were fired with enthusiasm for such reform efforts as antitobacco, temperance, and antiprostitution. The clergy and laymen, though not altogether disapproving, worried that these moral crusades might become sources of community rancor. New England villagers put a high priority on consensus, and strenuous moral aims threatened that sense of public peace.

President Storrs and Professors Green and Wright did not allay such fears. In fact, the latter two faculty members displayed a righteousness and arrogance that seemed to accentuate the parochial and dullish conformity of their Calvinistic, antislavery neighbors and colleagues. As S. A. Whittlesey, one of Wright and Green's student allies, later commented, the inhabitants of the Reserve perceived their settlement to be "a second New England"—as remembered from earlier days. They were especially eager to reduplicate to the letter eastern styles of "education and Christianity." The moderates did not fully realize the changes that had taken place in the East, a region becoming increasingly commercial, urban, and secular in character. Still poor, underdeveloped, and dependent upon missionary charities from the eastern states, the college trustees felt acutely the need to be orthodox and unventuresome. Even the process of founding Western Reserve College, Whittlesey continued, had been "entered upon by many hesitatingly and tremblingly."[11] Hudsonians welcomed the prestige of supporting a nationally recognized college, but the corollary of lively intellectual activity had its unhappy side. The problem was one to be repeated in American educational history from then to the present era. In addition to these factors, another struggle still underway that would feed into the slavery controversy was the anti-Mason cause which grew into a temporary but northern-wide political party. Country folk on the Reserve accused townspeople of aristocratic, antirepublican behavior and denounced the "vanity" of the squires, lawyers, and grocers who were "loaded down, with [Masonic] offices and honors." The political agitation spilled over into the upcoming warfare between colonizationists (generally supporters of Masonry) and abolitionists (consistently hostile to the secret organization).[12]

Cautious at first, the antislavery moderates grumbled privately when Elizur Wright began on July 13, 1832, a series of essays in Warren Isham's *Hudson Observer and Telegraph.* The topic was familiar enough to the well-versed puritan churchgoer: the primacy of "conscience" over "expediency." But the illustration of evil was quite unsettling to the village subscribers. Wright used American pusillanimity over slavery as the example of deviance from God's command. Conscience, said he, required direct, unequivocal, and absolute confrontation with slavery and the immediate adoption of complete equality of the races. The moderates could not openly object to such sentiments, couched as they were in rather unspecific terms at the outset. For the antislavery moderates, God was "sovereign Lord" of conscience, in the words of the Westminster Covenant. Wright, though, made the inner voice answerable to his own chosen moral convictions, those which involved an iconoclastic dismissal of institutional form and orthodoxy in the adoption of abolitionism. Oliver Clark, a local critic, accused him, in effect, of heresy as well as political and social recklessness, but Clark was no match for the Yale-trained scholar.[13]

Not surprisingly, the trustees and their friends reacted with growing alarm to Wright's polemics. With each installment, he revealed his contempt for colonization with increasing clarity. It was an organization, he insisted, led by men who knew that they were playing falsely with the benevolent proclivities of the public by claiming to do for the slave and continent of Africa what was clearly impossible. Still worse for the trustees, the students, under faculty encouragement, had begun debating the relative merits of the two antislavery approaches at their Wednesday afternoon forensics class which Beriah Green supervised. As if to defy the concept of authority itself, ran the rumors, the professors entered the debating arena at these weekly meetings, placing themselves on a footing with their subordinates. Then starting in early December, to answer the mounting criticism, Green delivered a series of Sunday jeremiads at the college chapel on the pretensions and evils of colonization. Up went the cry of "politics in the pulpit," as if puritan divines had never assumed that function before. For the trustees, it seemed that rather than serving as a beacon of Christian enlightenment, Western Reserve College was becoming a seat of Jacobinism and godlessness.[14]

The intellectual vulnerability of the antislavery moderates only made matters more disagreeable. First, it meant that they watched helplessly as the radical professors gathered the brightest and most dynamic students around them, and second, it left the colonization camp demoralized and leaderless. Rufus Nutting, librarian and professor of ancient languages, did his best to advise the student colonizationists in their struggle. Nutting had come west with high recommendations from Andover Academy where he and Wright had served together, but he was not the kind to whom students rallied. Nor were the elderly trustees Harvey Coe and Caleb Pitkin in tune with collegiate life. Both were as contentious as Green and Wright but lacked their learning and genius.

As a result of these local deficiencies, the student moderates turned to national colonization headquarters for outside help. Horace Taylor and David O. Hudson, son of the founder of the town and college, complained to the secretary of the American Colonization Society in Washington: "A large portion of the students among whom are some of the most talented members of our association, have become 'all of a sudden' thorough-going *Abolitionists.*" Moreover, they added, Wright and Green had awed "into silence those [students] who would otherwise have opposed them." Colonizationists could not even hold regular meetings without an invasion from the abolitionist students, all members of the old society, who then outvoted their former associates. It was cold comfort to report, under these circumstances, that "in the country around us," at least, "abolition has very few friends." Realizing that the strategically located college carried much influence in the Northwest, the Washington leaders came to the rescue by dis-

when he resolved not to leave the country after all. For Green, as for Wright, abolitionism was a means to stave off the "hypo," as acute depression was sometimes then called. President Storrs also had similar visits from the "hypo." Though gifted with a strong, almost charismatic personality, Storrs was subject to episodes of despair—albeit expressed in theological terms peculiar to the puritan mentality. His striving for perfection left him so conscious of his worthlessness that a fellow minister declared that it should be said of him in his "despondence" as for all "the afflicted and penitent, 'Blessed are they that mourn.' " Storrs's emotional infirmity was compounded by recurrent seizures from consumption, the disease that was to carry him off before the close of 1833.[20] These emotional aspects of abolitionist makeup were to appear again in the later history of the reform in the region.

Finally, Theodore Weld, the "passionate liberator," as Robert Abzug, his most sensitive biographer, calls him, arrived on the campus during the rising furor over Wright's articles and student activities. For three weeks in the fall of 1832, Weld conferred with Storrs and company, attended the student debates, and conversed with the young men. He had come to lecture on temperance and the manual labor reform fad. Both of these causes were part of the college curriculum as well as being nostrums for the very agonies that Green and Weld himself (sometimes blinded from overstudy and overwork) had undergone as college students. Weld's conversion from colonization to abolitionism took place during those exciting weeks at Hudson. There can be little doubt that his own abolitionist activities as leader of student rebels and abolition disciples at Lane Seminary in Cincinnati and Oberlin Institute, near Elyria, from 1833 to 1836, were greatly influenced by the events that he had witnessed on campus.[21]

The denouement for the struggle over radicalism at Hudson was surprisingly swift after a school year of uninterrupted agitation. Storrs suffered a severe attack of tuberculosis in May after his speech in Cleveland. No doubt with relief, the trustees granted him permission to regain his health in the East during the fall semester, but he died there. His demise at once elevated him to the status of a much persecuted "martyr," according to Garrison and the evangelical Tappan brothers in New York, and John Greenleaf Whittier commemorated his passing with antislavery verses. Meanwhile Green left Hudson to assume the presidency of the Oneida Institute, a manual labor school based on the principle that learning to handle an axe instead of a whiskey bottle was the road to salvation and success. Then Elizur Wright "threw in" his resignation the day after commencement in August, as he gleefully wrote the dying Storrs. What a relief that gesture must have seemed to the recipients because Wright had embarrassed the authorities with abolitionist activities staged during the ceremony. Already Wright had obtained a job and new career from Arthur Tappan; he would be secretary of the newly formed American Anti-Slavery Society. But the young professor guessed—probably correctly—that he would eventually have been fired from his teaching position otherwise, despite his father's presence on the board of trustees.[22]

These events might give the impression that the college and the Western Reserve region in general were hidebound in their opposition to the antislavery cause. Such was not the case. Actually, the college admitted a number of black students in the next few years. Also, several of the leading colonizationists, including David Hudson, made the college town a stopping-place for fugitive slaves on their way to Cleveland and Canada. Whig Congressman Joshua R. Giddings could always count on the support of Hudsonians and neighboring town dwellers in his energetic antislavery campaigns for reelection from 1838 to 1860. Moreover, the college authorities sought to regain eastern reputation and prove that their institution was not averse to New School doctrine and benevolent works.

After George E. Pierce, Storrs's weighty successor (three hundred pounds of stately presidency), took the helm in 1834, he repressed student lecturing on abolition. At the same time, he urged the abolitionist Charles G. Finney, the noted revivalist, to take the theological chair that Arthur Tappan had established for Storrs. Notorious for failing to answer his mail, Finney did not reply; instead, he and a number of abolition students from Hudson and others from the similarly afflicted Lane Seminary in Cincinnati went to Oberlin. That school quickly became the rival of the struggling Western Reserve College and the center for abolitionism statewide. Nevertheless, the college, though not so radical as Oberlin, continued to serve the cause of antisouthern agitation. Some of those who fought the Garrisonians from 1832 to 1833 adopted sturdier reform positions against perceived southern encroachments in the years that followed.[23]

Many of the themes presented in the Hudson controversy were repeated in Cleveland: a conservative business mentality versus a more idealistic, religious, and intellectual angle. But Cleveland was already too diverse to permit the kind of one-on-one struggle that took place in Hudson. For instance, the various churches—not a college—were the focus of agitation between competing yet interconnected approaches to the slavery issue. In part, the difference was that Cleveland simply had more denominations than Hudson. In that village, the First Church and a Methodist congregation constituted the greater part of the resident populace. In Cleveland, Christendom was rather fragmented. Therefore antislavery took more variant paths and coordination was harder to achieve. It must be admitted, though, that with regard to chapters of the American Anti-Slavery Society, the membership usually consisted of volunteers seldom from more than one or two churches with a scattering of dissident stragglers from a handful of others. But at least they were involved, giving a certain ecumenicity to Cleveland efforts that would have been impossible in Hudson. As one would suspect, "Presbygationalists" dominated the Cleveland abolition affiliates, even though evangelicals from other faiths were also welcome. Such individuals as Solomon L. and John L. Severance, Samuel Cowles, a former colonizationist, John A. Foote, Edwin H. Nevin, and Benajah Barker—all of solid New England and Congregational background—were among the leading abolition organizers.

Experienced with arranging similar activity in behalf of Sunday schools, children's mite societies, tractarian work, and other benevolent, congregation-centered efforts, these young businessmen and professionals founded the Cleveland Anti-Slavery Society as early as the fall of 1833, just as the movement fell on hard times in Hudson. In the previous spring, Arthur Tappan had dispatched Charles W. Denison, first and rather tedious editor of the *Emancipator,* published in New York City, to help get the group started. In 1837 the same clique, with the support of scattered abolitionists in neighboring towns like Willoughby, Brooklyn (or Ohio City, after 1836), and Strongsville founded a county affiliate of the American Anti-Slavery Society. One may guess that most members of the Cuyahoga chapter were New School adherents, like Edward Wade of Willoughby, as were most other members of the Cleveland group. They were chiefly associated with the Stone Church where the Cuyahoga branch held its first meeting.[24]

It cannot be said that either the town or the county societies functioned with impressive vitality. If newspaper accounts accurately covered their doings, not much went on to enliven the cultural and moral scene. After Denison's brief appearance, two years passed before another major abolitionist figure visited the town under society sponsorship. Even when Theodore Weld, the movement's greatest orator at the time, gave six lectures at the Stone Church on Public Square, he could scarcely claim to have awakened the citizens to southern iniquity and the plight of the downtrodden. Though mobbed elsewhere on his famous Ohio tour in 1835, Weld gave no offense in Cleveland—and no apparent inspiration either. "We are happy to say, that in his lectures thus far, Mr. Weld has not found it necessary to use any exciting language, or come into contact with the friends of any other measures," the editor of the *Whig* remarked with relief. By abolitionist standards the newspaper review provided no compliments.[25]

Many years elapsed before another national abolitionist leader addressed a Cleveland crowd. In 1847 Frederick Douglass and William Lloyd Garrison, "celebrated expounders of the ultra abolition faith," said the *Whig*, graced the city but did not find a sponsoring organization to make preparations. Finally in 1860 Cassius Marcellus Clay, the redoubtable Kentucky squire and reformer, gave an abolitionist speech in 1860, but his appearance had more to do with the election of Abraham Lincoln than with root-and-branch emancipationism. Reformers had to be content to draw crowds with sporadic public meetings with local talent of uncertain quality. Such, for instance, was the nature of the protest gathering over the "martyrdom" of Elijah P. Lovejoy, shot in 1837 while defending his antislavery (and grossly anti-Catholic) press in Alton, Illinois.[26]

Antislavery enterprise, as distinct from radical measures, far outdistanced abolition in pre–Civil War Cleveland. The main activities took two forms, both of which were immediately rewarding in contrast to the utopianism implicit in abolition doctrine. The first was to help fugitive slaves in imminent danger of recapture; the second task was supporting officeseekers like Representative Joshua R. Giddings, Senator Thomas Morris, and Governor and Senator Salmon P. Chase, all three shrewd and, in their way, devoted enemies of slavery and the South. These moderate efforts were ones that abolitionists, to greater or lesser degree, could also support. Yet radicals seldom were allowed to lead the rescue of the fleeing slave or seek public office. Such activities belonged to the moderates, not to the racial egalitarians.

In regard to the fugitive slave issue, Cleveland was an especially significant location. After the Ohio Canal was completed in 1833, Cleveland dominated Ohio trade to Canada and therefore the blacks' access to safe territory. (In this respect, Hudsonians also were of some value. Such moderates as Western Reserve College President Pierce, the Reverend W. L. Woodruff, and David Hudson assisted in operations to transfer runaways from their hamlet to Cleveland.) While the "North Star" legend, especially in Ohio, was to claim thousands saved, the facts suggest scores. Some myths, however, had a kernel of truth. Legend once claimed that an elaborate tunnel under St. John's Episcopal Church provided fugitives secret access to the nearby waterfront, but it never existed. The church's belfry, however, did serve as a hideaway every so often. Lay people of the Stone Church also responded swiftly when called upon. Yet, as in other parts of the North, local blacks, not whites, spirited most fugitives to safety. In Cleveland their numbers were very small, but they did what they could for the refugees. The Fugitive Slave Society, as it was called, was active in the city throughout the 1850s.[27]

White participation was more vocal, probably, than helpful in individual cases that aroused human interest. Yet more significantly, the Cleveland papers, excluding the hotly Democratic *Plain Dealer*, found nothing radical at all in examples of disobedience to the much-resented Fugitive Slave Act of 1850. In 1855, for instance, an editor boasted that the city deserved high marks for its citizens' hostility to the law. Human property valued at nine thousand dollars, the *Leader* crowed, had passed through the community on the way to Canada in one week. Certainly the most famous incident of this kind was the famous "Oberlin-Wellington rescue" of 1859. A band of Oberlinites whisked a fugitive away from the jail in nearby Wellington and sent him on to Canada. The Oberlin participants and a Cleveland store clerk named Simon Bushnell were indicted and jailed by a federal grand jury for violating the much despised Fugitive Slave Law passed as part of the Compromise of 1850. Thousands gathered in Public Square to hear Giddings and other notables denounce the law and the alleged Great Slave Power of southern politicians who had fastened the measure on a free people.[28]

Much more important than fugitive-slave incidents was the development of partisan politics in the cause of antislavery. Organizing a political party required compromise and the uniting of self-interest with grander aims. To politicians, abstract differences mattered less than they did to doctrinaire abolitionists who prided themselves on their unpopularity. Reform-bent office seekers had to find some means to bring antislavery reformers of every description into harmony. As the abolitionist leader J. T. Sturtevant of Chagrin Falls satirically remarked in 1843, there were on the Reserve "old fashioned abolitionists, enthusiastic or hot-headed abolitionists, deliberate abolitionists," gradualists and ultraists, "subtle and Bondite abolitionists, and to cap the climax . . . a quite popular class of do-nothing abolitionists" who disapproved of slavery theoretically but criticized any reform measure that was proposed. Yet he exaggerated, as there were some genuine and active friends of the local black community who saw injustice at home as well as in the South. Franklin T. Backus, a Cleveland corporation lawyer and a Whig state senator in the late 1840s, opposed the proscriptive Ohio Black Laws which denied the race access to public schools. He was instrumental in the repeal of the hideous code, although the public school prohibition remained on the books. At a higher political level, Joshua R. Giddings represented the humanitarian feelings of Cleveland and the Reserve in the national Congress. Because of his strong antislavery position, the maverick Whig could not prevent Cuyahoga County from being severed from his district by state legislative gerrymandering in 1852. The hope was that Cleveland and environs would back a conservative replacement. Instead, though, Edward Wade, another antislavery stalwart, was chosen. With regard to presidential politics, however, the city and region took more cautious ground. Only a few Cuyahoga County citizens, largely churchmen, cast ballots in 1840 for the Liberty party's James G. Birney, the first abolitionist candidate ever to run for the office. What loyal Ohio Whig could turn his back on General William Henry Harrison, the state's favorite hero? These sentiments held Cleveland faithful to Whiggery of an antislavery nature throughout the 1840s. In the following decade, Giddings helped to swing the city and its hinterland into the Free-Soil camp and into the Whig–Free-Soil–Independent (antislavery) Democratic coalition that became known as the Republican party.[29]

If antislavery action took so cautious and benign an institutional form, so did proslaveryism. As the city grew, the Democrats capitalized on Cleveland's ethnic diversity. There were some politicians in the city like M. W. Holtslauder, leader of the Young (Democratic) Hickory Club, who thought that Yankee abolition "fanaticism" had no place in municipal or national life. Holtslauder was determined to defeat the New Englander Edward Wade, Giddings's fellow Free-Soil Congressman from the Reserve, a "notorious abolitionist" with "crazy notions," said Holtslauder, "about niggers and freedom." The young Democrat's party failed at the polls, but he was right about Wade's position. He had been a founder of the Cuyahoga County Anti-Slavery Society, but by the late 1840s and early 1850s, Wade's opinions were hardly thought eccentric any more, at least by the Reserve's standards. Even the Democrats were subject to antislavery influences. Jeffersonian Judge and Senator Benjamin Tappan, brother of the abolitionist Tappans in New York, Thomas Morris, and especially Salmon P. Chase were popular figures on the Reserve because of their antislavery principles. In the 1850s Holtslauder represented a proslavery minority locally, although his position conformed well with the national party's strong alliance with the South's Democratic majority.[30]

Although antislavery thrived in Cleveland, it did so quietly and perhaps at the expense of more radical possibilities. The reasons were partly intellectual. First of all, Cleveland had no major college where new ideas could flourish as they had in Hudson. Periodically, city leaders tried to rectify the deficiency. When Finney agreed to join the founding faculty at Oberlin in 1835, a group of Cleveland businessmen urged him to move the college's site to the mouth of the Cuyahoga, a more civilized and salubrious spot than the clay flatlands of Elyria, they insisted. As in the case of inquiries from President Pierce at Hudson, Finney did not reply.[31] Opportunity knocked once more in the 1850s when troubles at Oberlin led President Asa Mahan to resign and open "Cleveland University" with a few dissident faculty and students from Oberlin to fill the classrooms. On the Cuyahoga riverbank, just south of the city, John Jennings and other Cleveland leaders purchased several thousand acres for the campus. Such an institution, headed by so venerable—and irascible—an abolitionist as Mahan might have changed the moral climate of the town. But Mahan and the wealthy Thirza Pelton, Mahan's Oberlin ally, had a disagreement about the new venture. Abruptly Mahan resigned, and the college promptly dissolved.[32] Not until 1882 when Western Reserve College left Hudson did Cleveland obtain an institution of higher learning connected with the antislavery past.

Nor was the press in Cleveland a source of abolitionist excitement. Then as now, editors of Cleveland dailies nursed safe opinions, particularly in comparison with the lively Cincinnati or New York journalistic scene. There was no weekly reform journal to match the *Anti-Slavery Bugle* of Salem, Ohio, the *Oberlin Evangelist,* or the *Cincinnati Philanthropist.* Such a paper would have helped to counteract the virulently antiabolitionist *Plain Dealer.* Rumors started in 1847 that Frederick Douglass was planning to edit the *Anti-Slavery Bugle* and move it to Cleveland, but nothing materialized. (The distinguished former fugitive and abolition leader was, however, invited to address Western Reserve College at commencement in 1854 at which time he refuted the old canard that blacks belonged to a naturally inferior race.)[33] Without such an organ, abolitionism was bound to be restricted.

With the press limited to safe racial and sectional opinion, the only institutional forum for immediate emancipation efforts was the church. The Second Baptist Church, Plymouth Church, and First Presbyterian in Ohio City had the greater share of the city's abolitionists. On the whole, however, radicalism was held in check, although Cleveland was more antislavery than most others in the state. Clergy whom one might expect to have promoted immediatism failed to do so. For instance, Samuel Aiken of the Stone Church on Public Square was not the sort to lead crusades. Instead, like the city elite, many of whose members belonged to his congregation, Aiken placed himself somewhere between the Tappanite activists and the colonizationists, a disheartened group after 1833. Aiken spoke against slavery in the District of Columbia, a cause that Giddings helped to make respectable in Congress and on the Reserve. Also he tolerated abolition meetings in his church, an open-door policy that many other clergymen in Cleveland and elsewhere were too timid to adopt. He provided the same access to conservative antislavery groups, but he despised "ultraists" of any persuasion. "No good cause was ever more wretchedly managed than the cause of anti-slavery has been in the United States," he complained from the pulpit in 1851. As a result, he had to bid farewell to disgruntled worshippers, the largest group of whom left in 1852 to form the Plymouth Church under Edwin H. Nevin. Similar problems confronted Methodists and Disciples, whose official neutrality on the slave issue displeased minorities. Yet despite Aiken's rumored refusal to aid a fugitive seeking sanctuary in his church in 1850, he should not be altogether despised, as church historian David McMillan makes clear. Like many New School clergy (Aiken was once closely identified with Finney's 1830s revivalism), he tried to balance reform with order. In the 1850s he spoke eloquently against the Fugitive Slave Law, perhaps out of remorse for his earlier fall from grace. According to Cleveland black leader John Malvin, Aiken "proved" himself "a powerful friend to the colored people" in opposing, like Backus, the state black laws.[34]

Since Aiken was more antislavery than abolitionist, only one clergyman of long residence in the city could be said to have acted as a link to the more idealistic, doctrinally pure emancipationism of the Hudson period years before. James A. Thome, briefly professor of belles lettres at the ill-fated "Cleveland University," had been raised a slaveholder's son in Kentucky. In 1834 at Lane Seminary, Weld converted him to abolitionism during the famous debates there, those analogous to the Wednesday rhetoric sessions at Hudson only two years before. In

1848 Thome left his professorship at Oberlin, then in financial straits, and assumed leadership of the First Congregational Church in Ohio City at the corner of Detroit Avenue and State Street.

Like Green, Storrs, and Weld, Thome suffered periodically from depression. His first serious crisis of the spirit took place during the debates at Lane Seminary. The conversion process restored his faith in himself. Two years later, in 1836, he experienced another episode in which he found that the mere act of "praying so exhausts me," he had written Weld, that he could not attend regular services. Nevertheless, he pushed ahead, claiming that by active abolitionist work, he had come "to know nothing but Christ crucified," as he confessed to "Brother" Finney at Oberlin.[35]

From its founding in 1832, the First Church in Ohio City had always been in the front rank of abolitionism, although the membership was tiny. After Thome's arrival, however, the numbers, refreshed by revivals, increased with baptisms in Lake Erie (when the weather permitted). "Concerts of Prayer" for enslaved humanity were held every Saturday throughout Thome's ministry until the passage of the Thirteenth Amendment in 1865.[36] He often thundered from the pulpit the radical spirit of the early 1830s. For instance, he invited Weld to return in 1862 to deliver an antislavery address, one harkening back to those happy if contentious days. For complicated, emotional reasons, the great reformer had been silent for many years, but such was their long association that Weld agreed to speak for the cause at Thome's First Church.

Tragically, after this climax for Thome's discipleship in the aging movement, the congregation refused to continue its reformist position by supporting Radical Reconstruction. Just when the South was laid open for missions to both whites and blacks, war weariness and a resurgent materialism made reform seem threadbare and obsolete. Thome took the setback hard. "Broken in health and spirit," said a friend, he accepted a post in Chattanooga, Tennessee, in hopes of bringing to his native South something of the New School egalitarian spirit that he, like Weld, Green, Wright, and Storrs, had adopted some forty years earlier. His Southern white congregation did not understand him. Within two years he died.[37]

If, as some claimed, Storrs was really a martyr to his physical ailments rather than to immediate emancipation, the same cannot be said of James Thome. In fact, his efforts kept the lantern of idealism flickering in Cleveland. Yet, in a curious way, Thome and his predecessors, Wright and Green, had unwittingly helped to bring on that postwar materialism. Their perfectionism had been part of the movement away from a God-centered faith toward the cult of individuality and secular freedom. Impatient with the deficiencies of such institutions as the colonization society, they had sought the creation of a new man and a new America, freedom from sin as well as from slavery. That divorce of ethics from Old School dogma weakened religious defenses against modern hedonism, as exemplified in Cleveland's postwar business spirit led by John D. Rockefeller and Henry Flagler. In 1832 Hudson critics of Wright's theories on conscience had dimly sensed the problem. Perhaps Thome had helped to separate ethics from Old School dogma. Perhaps conscience about these matters sent Thome southward on his impossible quest, when he was weary of the struggle. But he, unlike Storrs, Weld, and Green—once so firm in evangelical, abolition conviction—had abandoned neither the cause of black freedom nor the Christian faith that inspired their participation. Thome was one of the few abolitionist leaders who did not turn away from any of his initial beliefs.

Aside from Thome's sad mission to reform his fellow southerners after he had spent too many years in New England's West, there were some other final ironies. In the interconnections of the rival approaches to slavery, Hudson's brief sojourn with radicalism helped to produce the most extreme exponent in the abolition ranks, the revolutionary John Brown. His father Owen, a trustee of Western Reserve College, had tried to defend the rebellious faculty against their trustee critics. For ten days in the spring of 1859 before the autumn assault on Harpers Ferry, John Brown stayed in Cleveland. There was a price on his head, owing to his bloody deeds in Kansas. No one turned him in. The city was in the throes of excitement and indignation over the Oberlin-Wellington fugitive slave case. The protest rally for the defendants at which Giddings spoke to ten thousand Clevelanders in Public Square helped to provide the cover and sympathy that Brown needed. He and his associates sauntered every day right by the federal marshall's office. His untouchability distressed the *Plain Dealer* and highly amused the *Leader*.[38]

In some respects, after his "martyrdom," John Brown brought together the threads that bound the twin policies regarding slavery. His Old School Calvinist principles seemed to be easier to understand than the more complicated evangelical bases for modern abolitionism. His use of violence—the reliance upon courage, manhood, and other familiar virtues—made more sense to the ordinary Western Reserve and Cleveland citizen than the headier, romantic notions of peace-minded, clerical abolitionists like Thome. Clevelanders might not have approved Brown's course, but at least his deeds were clear in intent and effect. At the same time, Brown's identification with the slave and with the abstract concept of liberty was very much in harmony with the ideological temper of the region.[39]

These mingled attributes of the new and old religious modes earned the Kansas fighter a respect, albeit a grudging one, among antislavery conservatives. Middle-class Clevelanders took him into their hearts. On December 2, 1859, the day of Brown's execution in Charlestown, Virginia, Thome preached a sermon, reprinted in full in the *Leader*, in which the old veteran of antiabolition mobs placed the Harpers Ferry hero in the company of Stephen, John the Baptist, and other martyrs for righteousness' sake. Flags in Cleveland flew at half-mast and bells tolled at the hour of Brown's hanging. Judge Daniel Tilden that evening told the fourteen hundred who gathered at Melodeon Hall that they should "baptise" themselves "in his spirit and stand upon a foundation of adamant and unalterable hostility to slavery." Some Clevelanders made pilgrimages to Hudson to express their feelings.[40]

When the young scholars at Hudson began their assaults on the elderly colonizationists, they had no way of knowing that an old man's violence and anger would be an immediate cause of secession and war. At the same time, it was the young who died for the sake of the Union and emancipation. The tensions as well as the reciprocity between abolitionism and antislavery, intellectual and businessman, Old School and New School, trustee and faculty, student and elder that had been played out on the stage of Cleveland and Hudson helped to bring about that inspiring—and tragic—conclusion. Yet even if Cleveland and the Western Reserve fell short of abolitionist hopes, the inhabitants had accomplished great things. Although no monument attests to the work of Elizur Wright, Joshua Giddings, or James Thome, they and their supporters should be remembered for helping to advance the cause of human freedom.

C H R I S T O P H E R   W Y E

At the Leading Edge:
The Movement for
Black Civil Rights
in Cleveland, 1830–1969

Part of the group attending the tenth anniversary conference of the NAACP in Cleveland in June
1919

T he history of the quest for black civil rights in Cleveland is
the history of a movement deeply affected by the unique-
ness of the community in which it took place. Among cities of equiva-
lent, and sometimes different, size and time, the Forest City almost
always offered black citizens an urban context that was in the vanguard
of prevailing liberal sentiment. Though this liberalism has been rede-
fined many times in response to changing circumstances and issues, its
long-term direction normally has been on an ascending path, and frequently has been at or near the best that a given period of the American
national experience had to offer.[1]

Partly, this liberalism was an outgrowth of historical geography,
and its implications. As a northern, urban industrial city, Cleveland
was far removed from the economic, political, social, ideological, and
even psychological currents that underlay the southern plantation system with its dependence first on the enslavement of blacks and, subsequent to the Civil War, their subordination through custom and law.
But Cleveland's liberal views on race were also a reflection of the city's
early settlement pattern, for the Western Reserve attracted a large infusion of settlers from northern New England who brought with them a
strong evangelical religious commitment and an inclination toward
reformist movements.

In the early years of the nineteenth century Clevelanders were barely
and perhaps even indifferently aware of their black neighbors. With
only a handful—probably less than a hundred—black residents in a
total population of several thousand, the city's black community was
not sharply defined in the minds of local whites.[2] The views of the
latter on race issues were indistinguishable from those of many others
who lived in similarly situated midwestern urban centers. There was a
pervasive sense of distance from the national debate, then just beginning, over the issues of slavery and race. Many had only a vague sense of

the human rights side of the issue, and felt that preservation of the Union was the only issue of real merit. To the extent that local citizens were inclined to a more activist position on race issues, many were sympathetic to the colonization movement, a movement which had as its goal the gradual abolition of slavery and the colonization of blacks in Africa. Clevelanders roundly condemned the more militant position being articulated by New England abolitionists as a dangerous threat to the peace, prosperity, and even survival of the Union.[3]

The views of Cleveland's black citizens in the early years of the nineteenth century, especially before 1830, are unknown since no written record has survived to provide a direct account or reflection. We know that George Peake, his wife, and their two sons crossed the Ohio River into the Western Reserve on a journey from Pennsylvania, purchased one hundred acres of land, and became Cleveland's first permanent black settlers in 1806.[4] We also know that Peake and his family were followed by a very small number of other black families, which if they came in equal numbers up to the year 1850, numbered no more than six individuals a year.

Beginning with the 1830s, the attitudes and activities of both whites and blacks toward race issues changed significantly, and Cleveland became more liberal on the question of civil rights. The immediate impetus for the change in white attitudes was the infusion of new settlers from northern New England. These new settlers, born and raised in a section of the country that spawned a rich variety of evangelical religions and reformist causes, brought with them a dynamic, activist, liberal inclination toward a broader and higher definition of the quality of life. Many of them supported the abolitionist movement and the Underground Railroad. Beyond the abolition of slavery, opinions were remarkably diverse, with some people feeling that blacks were innately inferior, and some believing that blacks should stand equal with whites before the law.[5]

If the 1830s marked the beginning of Cleveland's reformist tradition on the issue of race, it also marked the beginning of recorded black activity and expression on civil rights. As the country became increasingly divided over the issue of slavery in the years before the Civil War, leading black Clevelanders publicly supported the abolitionist movement, and some actively helped escaped slaves reach Canada and, ultimately, freedom. John Brown, a successful barber, and John Malvin, a well-known canal and lake boat captain, were two who personally helped fugitive slaves. A few, especially farmers like Alfred Greenbrier whose land and buildings provided a measure of both distance and security, allowed their homes to become regular stations on the Underground Railroad. Later, as the city became a major terminus on the road to freedom, local black citizens formed a vigilance committee to coordinate activities in support of fugitive slaves, including the provision of food, clothing, shelter, and assistance in securing passage across the Great Lakes.[6]

By their active support of runaway slaves, Cleveland blacks showed the strength of their opposition to the institution of slavery. In terms equally clear, they demonstrated their rejection of any future which included a separate status for blacks. In the 1840s and 1850s a number of movements developed around the idea of colonizing blacks in separate communities in Africa, South America, or in isolated areas of the United States. Cleveland blacks denounced all colonization schemes in terms that were unequivocal, one going so far as to call it "nefarious and diabolical." Far removed from the worst of the slave regime and located in a city that offered them an enticing glimpse of a better future, local blacks wanted nothing to do with a movement whose goal was the removal of black citizens from the mainstream of American life.[7]

In every way, black Clevelanders of this period confirmed their commitment to the ultimate achievement of full citizenship rights. They labored to improve their skills, supported and contributed to community activities, participated eagerly where they could, and waited impatiently where they could not. They encouraged their children to hope for a better future than theirs, and worked hard to help them achieve it. When the outbreak of the Civil War threatened the dissolution of the Union, they were among the first to volunteer for active combat. And when they were initially rejected on the grounds that the Ohio Constitution forbade their enlistment, many served in an all black regiment established in Massachusetts, until in 1865 the state of Ohio authorized the recruitment of black troops.[8]

Very little is known about the personal lives of leading blacks in this period. For the most part, the record contains only chance glimpses of their attitudes and activities on race issues. One early black leader about whom some information has survived is John Malvin. As a young man Malvin worked at a variety of positions ranging from cook to carpenter to sawmill operator before signing on as a working hand on a local canal boat. Once there he demonstrated a natural ability at mastering navigational skills as well as at working with the interracial crew, and he was eventually appointed the boat's captain. Later, having expanded his skills to include open water navigation, he bought a boat and developed a business carrying limestone on Lake Erie for Cleveland industries.[9]

Malvin's views on race issues and the eventual (if not immediate) status to which blacks should aspire symbolized the consensus among contemporary black leaders. He abhorred the insitution of slavery, spoke out against it on public occasions, supported the national abolitionist movement, and actively worked with the Cleveland Anti-Slavery Society. In support of the activities of the local Underground Railroad he personally assisted escaped slaves on their way to Canada. He opposed any movement which had as its goal a separate status for blacks, including the colonization movement in all of its variations. And he fought tirelessly against the restrictions of the black laws, setting a personal example by his refusal to ignore segregated or discriminatory accommodations or treatment in public or semipublic facilities. In 1836, for example, Malvin was the successful leader of an eighteen-month campaign to eliminate a segregated "colored gallery" at the predominantly white First Baptist Church of Cleveland.[10]

Beginning around the 1870s and gaining considerable momentum in the years just before and after the turn of the century, new strands of thought increasingly influenced the civil rights strategies of black leaders. The Civil War, with its catharsis over the issues of sectionalism and slavery, left the country weary of intense debate, especially on issues related to blacks. In a different but related development new schools of thought emerged, some in the highest academic circles, around the notion that blacks were biologically inferior to whites and hence lacked the natural aptitude required to exercise full citizenship rights.[11]

In roughly the same period but especially during World War I a related demographic trend had an important impact on race relations. Seeking to escape the increasingly hostile environment of the South and, especially during the war years, hoping for better jobs in northern war industry, black migrants streamed into the Forest City. In the fifty years following the Civil War the Cleveland black population grew from just under one thousand to about eighty-five hundred, reflecting a very modest annual increase of about one hundred persons a year. But between 1910 and 1920 it grew to almost thirty-five thousand—a nearly 400 percent increase in ten years. Virtually overnight these migrants transformed the black presence in Cleveland from that of a relatively unobtrusive racial cluster to that of a full-blown ghetto.[12]

This influx of southern blacks substantially increased the pressure on race relations at every point along the margins of interracial contact, generating greater friction and discrimination in contexts ranging from employment to education to recreation. While still more liberal than many midwestern cities, Cleveland now joined other northern urban centers in redefining and circumscribing the status of black citizens.

Although the Ohio legislature had passed a civil rights law in 1883, by the beginning of World War I almost every type of public and semipublic facility which it covered—including restaurants, theaters, amusements parks, and swimming pools—had manifested some form of antiblack prejudice. In this period, discrimination became more evident in hotels, playgrounds, drugstores, hospitals, and train cars. One of the clearest examples of the mounting tide of prejudice was the situation blacks faced in the public school system. Until the great migration the local public schools had appeared to be relatively free of discrimination, but after the influx there were increasing complaints of segregated classes. And throughout World War I blacks reported growing difficulty in obtaining both warrants and convictions under the civil rights law.

At the same time, while the growth in the black population led to increased friction in race relations, it also gave rise to increased race consciousness and community development. Almost all of Cleveland's black lived on the city's East Side, in the Central Avenue section bordered on the north by Euclid Avenue, on the east by East 55th Street, on the south by the New York Central Railroad tracks, and on the west by the downtown business district. As the black community grew in size and complexity, it developed a more distinct identity, including its own tradesmen and professionals, newspapers and journals, churches and lodges, banks and insurance companies, drugstores and groceries. By the early twentieth century black Clevelanders lived in an area that had come to resemble a city within a city.[13]

Members of the new entrepreneurial group of black businessmen moved up the economic, political, and social ladder within the black community, and came to occupy key leadership positions in civic and political organizations. By the turn of the century these young leaders were challenging the established leadership, setting the scene for a division of thought between an older generation whose careers were, in substantial part, rooted in the white community, and a younger generation whose careers and ambitions were rooted in their own black community.[14]

Against this backdrop of changing circumstances and more uncertain times, black leaders all over the country were divided in their thinking. In the mid-1890s Booker T. Washington, then headmaster of Tuskegee Institute, emerged as the spokesman for those who favored a strategy of accommodation. While affirming a commitment to the ultimate achievement of full citizenship rights, Washington advocated a public posture that deemphasized civil and political protest in favor of self-help, thrift, hard work, and racial solidarity. He believed that blacks should develop an independent economic and institutional base to provide the jobs, services, and products not available through the white community. In the same period, W. E. B. Du Bois, a noted black sociologist and author, espoused a more integrationist position. Du Bois felt closer to the racial leadership of the early nineteenth century, to men like Frederick Douglass who worked actively to overcome the limitations faced by blacks. Like them, he believed that blacks should exercise full civil and political rights and that they should reject the establishment or use of separate facilities or services.[15]

Cleveland's new black leaders naturally reflected the national pattern of black thought, with some emphasizing an accommodationist approach and others an integrationist approach, although in more muted tones. Among those leaders committed to an integrationist approach, John P. Green exemplified the position often espoused by upper-status moderates. Green was born in North Carolina in 1845 and came to Cleveland when he was 12. Thereafter, he graduated first from Central High School and later from Union College of Law before before establishing a career as a lawyer and politician. As an active Republican, Green had a long and distinguished career. In the 1870s he was repeatedly elected justice of the peace, in the 1880s he was twice elected to the lower house of the state legislature, and in 1891 he became the first northern black elected to the state senate. In 1897 President William McKinley recognized Green's work in support of his campaign by creating a special position for him, that of postage stamp agent in Washington. Throughout his career Green maintained extensive social and political contacts within the white community—including the influential politician Marcus A. Hanna—and most of his electoral victories were based predominantly on white votes.[16]

With his heavy dependence on the white electorate and easy access to white leadership circles, Green developed a very cautious approach to the public discussion of race issues. In private life, he would occasionally appear in court in behalf of a black client facing obvious discrimination. In public, however, he was much more circumspect, meting out his political capital only on issues which were not likely to elicit strong sentiments from whites. He believed that the path to success for blacks lay in achievement, and that achievement had to take place within the context of the times. He believed that the problems faced by blacks were largely economic and that "with better fortunes . . . [they] shall attain power and . . . [their] status will be elevated." Yet, notably, he never espoused the accommodationist position being enunciated by Booker T. Washington. While recognizing the virtues of hard work, self-help, and discipline, Green rejected the implicit assumption underlying the Washington philosophy—that the only immediate opportunities available to blacks were in the black community itself. His whole career testified to a strong belief that a successful and aggressive career could be won in the white community.[17]

If John P. Green represented the moderate wing of the integrationist group, Harry C. Smith represented its more militant wing. Smith was born in West Virginia in 1863 and came to Cleveland as a young child. After attending Central High School where he graduated in 1882, Smith established the *Gazette*, a small black weekly which he published for the next fifty years. An active Republican like Green, Smith was appointed deputy inspector of oils in 1885, and he was elected three times to the Ohio General Assembly for the terms 1894 to 1896, 1896 to 1898, and 1900 to 1902. While a member of the assembly he helped enact the Anti-Mob Violence Act and the Civil Rights Act, both in 1896.[18]

A biting critic of what he referred to as Washington's "fool" accommodationist racial philosophy, Smith stridently condemned the "Uncle Tom" tactics of "white folks Negroes" who favored the establishment of separate organizations and espoused a compromising approach to the white community. Although he advocated black support of black business, he saw this as a temporary expedient that should in no way postpone a vigorous campaign for full equality. From the beginning of his career in the 1880s through to his death in 1941, the militant editor argued for the right to complete and immediate participation in every aspect of American life.[19]

Green and Smith, as well as others who shared their integrationist outlook, tended to share organizational affiliations such as the Cleveland branch of the National Association for the Advancement of Colored People. This branch, founded in 1914, evidenced a muted version of the legalistic protest strategy set forth by the national office. Reflecting both its roots in the relatively more comfortable racial atmosphere of earlier years as well as a tendency to underestimate the increasing erosion of the city's liberal heritage, the Cleveland NAACP pursued a cautious and unobtrusive program of local community activity. Its meetings were little more than polite discussions in the homes of comfortable and well-off blacks, and its program of activity, while paying dutiful lip service to principle and protest, was more in the nature of community relations than of legal action. Among the more prominent of its early members were three black lawyers, Harry E. Davis, Clayborne George, and Charles W. White, as well as one white social worker, Russell E. Jelliffe.[20]

But the integrationism that Smith so ardently supported increasingly lost ground to the new strain of accommodationism. This new emphasis was evident in the thinking of J. Walter Wills, a prominent businessman and civic leader of the period. Wills was born in southern Ohio and educated at Antioch College. Following college he came to Cleveland to learn the insurance business, holding a number of positions until 1904 when he became co-director of the Central Avenue Funeral Home. Several years later Wills established his own funeral home, and within a very short period of time he dominated the business in Cleveland, functioning as one of its leading representatives for the next thirty years.[21]

Wills also participated in community affairs, developing a reputation as a leading advocate of the economic self-help theory. In 1905 he founded the Cleveland affiliate of Booker T. Washington's National Negro Business League. The primary function of the league was to mobilize community support for black business. Wills tended to see such support almost as a racial obligation, sometimes arguing that white people would be incredulous if black people did not support their own businesses. Still, while he was a strong advocate of racial self-development and Washington's accommodationist approach to civil rights issues, Wills also actively supported the local NAACP and sometimes lent his support to lawsuits against discrimination in public and semipublic accommodations.[22]

As much a businessman as Wills and even more of an ideologue—in fact the Cleveland ideologue—on the self-help issue was Nahum D. Brascher. Born in rural Indiana and educated in southern Ohio, Brascher came to Cleveland in the 1890s in search of a career. He worked at selling real estate and advertising before joining Thomas W. Fleming and Welcome T. Blue in establishing the *Cleveland Journal*, an all-black newspaper, in 1903. With Brascher as its managing editor, the paper was published on a weekly basis until 1912.[23]

Brascher and the *Journal* were the accommodationist counterpart to Smith and the *Gazette*. If Smith referred to Washington as a "fool"

121

accommodationist, Brascher termed him "the Wizard of Tuskegee," and if Smith condemned the "Uncle Tom" tactics of the accommodationists, Brascher ridiculed the "slap back," "indignation spirit" of Smith and the integrationists. Through the pages of the *Journal* Brascher became the most articulate spokesman for the conservative ethic. The only way "to become recognized as a factor in this great land," he wrote, was to "become thoroughly established in the commercial field" as a businessman. Week in and week out he preached the virtues of self-help, hard work, thrift, and accommodation. His editorials appealed to race consciousness, pride, and group solidarity.[24]

Brascher, Wills, and others who supported Washington's self-help philosophy, gave their support to a variety of community organizations with a wide range of purposes. Prominent among these were the Phillis Wheatley Association, a social welfare institution similar in function to a Young Women's Christian Association, and the National Negro Business League. But most, if not all, felt especially close to the work of the Cleveland Urban League, the local affiliate of the National Urban League. Founded in 1917 under the leadership of William R. Connors, a bright young black social worker with a doctorate from the University of Pennsylvania, the league evidenced a strong commitment to Washington's emphasis on racial elevation by means of self-improvement and a tactful approach to the white community. The league held health education meetings at churches, clubs, and social settlements; developed home and neighborhood improvement associations; and conducted classes in home management, sewing, civics, English, and history. The hallmark of the league's approach was a scrupulous avoidance of confrontation and controversy in favor of cooperation and persuasion.[25]

By the early thirties a rising tide of discrimination against blacks as well as the economic collapse engendered by the onset of the Depression contributed to a worsening of the racial climate. The times were not hospitable to the civil rights issue. Northern white liberals were content to let the South deal with the black population in its own way. And scientific thought seemed to confirm the belief that blacks were biologically inferior and hence less entitled to full citizenship rights. At the same time, as Cleveland entered the first years of the Depression, its black labor force suffered severe dislocation. Within the black community, which by now included over seventy thousand persons, unemployment among wage earners averaged 50 percent, and in some neighborhoods was as high as 90 percent.

This worsening racial climate combined with the severe economic collapse to place new pressures on Cleveland's black leadership. Although the basic ideological division among black leaders continued to be between those who emphasized accommodation, self-help, and gradualism on the one hand, and those who stressed protest, activism, and institutional change on the other, during these years new leadership groups and positions began to appear across the full spectrum of black thought, especially within its more activist segments. Both wings of the established leadership were challenged by the new clusters, one associated with the Communist party, another advocating an alliance with the labor movement, and another espousing the use of economic boycotts and pickets. These emerging groups had the effect of broadening the variety of strategies, tactics, and objectives, and, at the same time, of shifting the entire range of black thought in a more aggressive direction. As the newer groups attracted support and influence, the older ones were compelled to listen to their views, or risk a possible loss of influence and leverage in community affairs.[26]

The Communist party was especially active among blacks in this period, although its blatant effort to exploit the hopelessness and despair among unemployed workers for political reasons as well as its ideological extremism and commitment to the ultimate destruction of American capitalism "root and branch" severely limited its appeal to blacks. For example, in 1931 the Cleveland Unemployed Council, a Communist-sponsored organization, staged a hunger march in the downtown area to dramatize the plight of the poor, and in the same year it staged several demonstrations at East Side branches of the Cuyahoga County Relief Administration to protest inadequate relief allowances.[27]

Although the evidence is scanty concerning the nature and extent of the interest in the Communist party expressed by blacks, scattered contemporary references in the press together with information obtained from interviews suggest that it was limited in size, confined largely to the lower class, and nonideological. At several of the demonstrations staged by the local Communists, it was reported that only a few blacks were present and most of them were "of the working class and not of the bourgeoisie." Summing up the attraction which the Communists held for some lower-class blacks, one observer commented that "they may never have heard of Karl Marx and know little of Russia, but they do know when they are hungry and cold, when they are pushed out of even low wage employment, and finally evicted from dwellings which their white neighbors spurned long ago."[28]

Another of the new groups to emerge in this period called for greater attention to the economic problems of the black masses and advocated an alliance with the labor movement, especially the industrial union movement which was just beginning to gather steam under the leadership of the Congress of Industrial Organizations. Consisting largely of a small number of well-educated upper middle-class individuals, this group criticized the community's established leadership for its "highbrow attitude toward the black masses." In their view neither the Urban League nor the NAACP could effect programs that would "feed the Negro babies in Cleveland" because the former was controlled by "white philanthropy" and the latter was dominated by an "excessive number of attornies steeped in the 17th Century legalism." They felt that the economic problems faced by black workers could be solved only if mass pressure was brought to bear on the white power structure and that the best avenue for the expression of that pressure was the labor movement.[29]

In 1935 those who held this view became active in establishing a Cleveland affiliate of the National Negro Congress, an organization then being established nationally to revitalize and redirect the overall thrust of the black community's advancement effort. Its purpose was to bring together all of the existing black labor, religious, fraternal, social welfare, and civic organizations into a "great federation" in which the "masses will be united to throw off political and economic oppression." Although the congress supported legal action and public demonstrations on many community issues, its primary mission was to mobilize support for the unionization of black workers. Charles W. White, Cleveland's most influential black exponent of this view, remarked that it will be "the tragedy of the twentieth century . . . for the American Negro to permit a proletarian movement to develop without his being an integral part of it."[30]

The NNC never really got off the ground in Cleveland, however, largely because the Communist party tried to push it in a more radical direction, but also because the success of the CIO in organizing black workers in the middle and late 1930s seemed to obviate the need for its existence. Toward the end of the Depression, the group came under the influence of Maude White, a well-known and self-avowed black Communist, with the result that earlier and less radical leaders, like Charles White, steadily dropped away.[31]

The final new leadership cluster which made its appearance in these years espoused the use of economic pressure tactics to obtain jobs for blacks. Apparently influenced by a similar movement launched in Chicago in 1929, a campaign involving boycotts and picket lines was started by several Cleveland organizations to employ blacks in white-owned stores located in the ghetto. The most prominent of these local groups was the Future Outlook League. Funded in 1935 by John O. Holly, a thirty-two-year-old shipping clerk, the league consisted largely of a small group of ambitious younger representatives of the lower middle class who served as its leadership core, together with a larger number of recent high school graduates who manned its picket lines. The league was an outgrowth of the frustration felt by young, hard-working, upwardly mobile blacks whose ambitions were thwarted by the Depression and whose frustration was aroused by white merchants who, while located in the black community and serving a predominantly black clientele, refused to hire blacks. Much of the league's program as well as its frustration was summed up in its catchy slogan, "Don't Spend Your Money Where You Can't Work."[32]

In the middle thirties the FOL employed pickets and boycotts against dozens of white-owned businesses, ranging from small groceries and pharmacies to large food and theater chains, eventually securing hundreds of clerical and sales positions for young blacks. Among the white businesses which came to employ blacks as a result of the league's activities were the Jules Dress Shop and Hoicowitz Dry Goods Store, the East Side A&P Company and Fisher Brothers, and the Quincy and Haltnorth theaters.

As the league became more successful, it expanded its activities to include a wider range of targets, and in the process substantially broadened its spectrum of mass pressure techniques. The organization ventured outside the ghetto for the first time in 1941 when it simultaneously conducted a picket line and a telephone campaign in an effort to get the Ohio Bell Telephone Company to hire blacks at its downtown office. When the country entered the Second World War, the FOL tried to obtain jobs for blacks in local defense industries. In 1942, for example, the league successfully picketed the Standard Tool Company, a large supplier of war material operating under contract from the federal government. A year later the organization sponsored a court case against the Warner and Swasey and Thompson Products companies, both of which refused to employ blacks in war production. And when the wartime demand for housing led landlords to charge exorbitant rents, the league laid the groundwork for a rent strike, although quick action by city officials made the actual implementation of the strike unnecessary.[33]

By the late thirties and early forties it was clear that the Future Outlook League, the National Negro Congress, and, despite its almost total rejection by blacks, even the Communist party had achieved a considerable impact on Cleveland's established black leadership. Race leaders associated with both ends of the traditional ideological spectrum—from the gradualist Urban League to the activist NAACP—were beginning to take into account the newer strands of thought. Both showed greater concern for the economic problems of black workers, and understood the increasing importance of the labor movement. Both evidenced more interest in the work of the FOL, and recognized the effectiveness of its boycott technique. And both realized the need to broaden their base of support within the black community. Thus, while the accommodationist-protest cleavage continued to characterize much of black thinking on race issues, the entire compass of black thought had shifted toward a more aggressive stance as well as toward a focus on the economic problems of black workers.[34]

These two emerging characteristics—greater assertiveness and sharper focus on economic matters—were a direct outgrowth of the black experience in the dark years of the Depression. The economic collapse created a sense of urgency, fear, and impatience. Among the burgeoning number of black citizens who were unemployed or otherwise adversely affected by the hard times, there was a rising feeling of desperation, a sense that something had to be done. These tensions were exacerbated by the failure of the existing leadership groups to adapt their strategies to the times. With the local NAACP continuing a low-key program of political activism and legal protest and the Urban League maintaining an even lower-key program of social welfare and self-help, the pressing economic problems of the day went unaddressed. As black unemployment and business failure rose to unprecedented and devastating levels, the established leaders appeared aloof and insensitive to the problems facing the masses of black workers. In this climate of rising discontent and unaddressed issues, it was almost inevitable that new leadership groups would challenge existing groups, and that the NAACP and Urban League would have to broaden their strategies or face dwindling community support.

Underlying the evolution of black thought in this period, and in part responsible for it, was a series of interwoven generational, career, and class imperatives. In general, at the outset of the Depression, the age, career status, and class position of black leaders followed an ascending path from the newer groups like the FOL and NNC through to the Urban League and NAACP. The key leaders of the NAACP were older individuals, like John P. Green and Harry C. Smith, who were at or beyond the middle of their careers and who had achieved recognition in the early years of the twentieth century. Many of these elders had close economic or social ties to the white community. The Urban League's central group was somewhat younger, closer to early than to mid-career development, and slightly lower in social status. Most were businessmen and professionals who rose to prominence by building careers in the expanding institutional and economic structure of the black community. William R. Connors, the league's executive secretary, exemplified these emerging leaders. Young, in his middle thirties, clearly establishing a career in black affairs with few social contacts in the white community, Connors symbolized the parvenu elite.

The composition of the newer groups, like the FOL and NNC, was quite different. Though both tended to attract younger individuals who were just beginning their careers, the similarity between the two groups ended here. The FOL was made up of lower middle-class individuals, the sons and daughters of the working poor. Most had a high school education, some had been to college for a few years, and a small number had a college degree. Their aspirations were toward entrepreneurial or mid-management positions, as well as to solid middle-class respectability. The NNC, by contrast, was comprised of middle- and upper middle-class people, the progeny of those who were aggressive aspirants to upper-class status. They were frequently college students or graduates, and they were intellectually aware of the new and challenging ideas of the times, prominent among them the industrial union movement. As the Depression decade drew to a close, some of the individuals in both the FOL and NNC began to move up the social and leadership hierarchy, and a few became associated with the NAACP and Urban League, bringing with them a wider range of ideas and strategies.

However, while social and demographic trends help to illuminate the evolution of black thought, they do not fully explain it. The recently emerging groups were successful in gaining adherents because they raised the right issues, and because they raised them in a void. With the effects of the economic collapse everywhere apparent, and with the established leadership nowhere in evidence, the stage was clearly set for the emergence of new ideas and leaders. There was a time in the mid-1930s when the FOL and NNC seemed to have come center stage, and when it seemed they could achieve a position of preeminence. This moment was very brief, but that it existed at all symbolized the extent to which the established leaders were initially insensitive to the issues raised by the Depression and unprepared to devise new strategies to deal with them.

As the NAACP and Urban League selectively took into account some of the emerging strands of thought, groups like the FOL and NNC began to decline in importance. This is not to say that the established leaders officially endorsed the new thinking. The street tactics of the FOL and the ideological radicalism of the NNC were far beyond the social and intellectual limits of the upper-status individuals who constituted the inner leadership core of the NAACP and Urban League. Nor did many of the leaders of the newer groups—especially those of the FOL—make the transition to the upper stratum; the social gulf was too large. But if the central message of the newer groups was that the established leaders needed to be more aggressive and more focused on economic issues, then the NAACP and Urban League, each in its own way and within the limits of its overall strategic emphasis, clearly got the point.

Ultimately, however, the extremism evident in the thought of newer groups like the FOL and NNC was deflated by the return of economic prosperity. When the country entered the Second World War, American industry was strained to capacity to meet the needs of defense production. Although the first jobs in war industry went to whites and though blacks had to wait on the sidelines until local labor shortages made their employment inevitable, by the early and mid-forties black workers were streaming into Cleveland's steel and ironworks, many moving into skilled positions frequently never before open to them. Those who did not find jobs in industrial production found employment in positions newly opened to blacks as clerks, bus drivers, motormen, and supermarket checkers, while whites moved into higher paying jobs in war industry. With the entire community—white and black—returning to full employment, and many holding better positions at higher wages than ever before, the radical ideologies of the discouraging thirties lost their relevance.[35]

Also, the war was fought on the basis of an antifascist, prodemocratic ideology. The racist theories and fascist doctrines expounded by Nazi Germany elicited a strong American counteroffensive. Though the American war effort was not free from racial tension—indeed hostility between black and white workers, urban riots and threats of violence, and discrimination in the armed forces were widely reported—still the country was forced by the logic of its own wartime ideology to face the race issue directly. In Cleveland this was symbolized by a renewed commitment on the part of the municipal government to consider the needs of its black constituents. In 1943 the Cleveland Welfare Federation announced the beginning of a two-year study of the black community. The Central Area Social Study, as it came to be called, was designed to provide a total look at racial and economic conditions in the city's black community, including population and housing characteristics, employment patterns, educational and recreational opportunities, health conditions, and family life. Its purpose was to "determine the factors that underlie the mass of racial problems . . . [and to] support measures for coping with the conditions."[36]

Although the study never really fulfilled its action-oriented promise to identify the "real potentially organizable forces" which might be used as a "channel for implementing programs of community welfare," it did provide the informational base for a new concept of the predominantly black area. The study depicted the area as a distinct community with its own institutions, organizations, businesses, social hierarchy, and ideological perspective. In so doing it moved away from the traditional view of the area as a "ghetto" or "slum" toward a more sophisticated view of the black population as a functioning subcommunity distinguished from the broader Cleveland community on the basis of color. The study concluded that an "artificial community has grown up in the Central Area—artificial in that its main criteria are color and color's implied difference."[37]

In the same year that the Central Area Social Study began, the city's incumbent mayor, Frank Lausche, established the Committee on Democratic Practice. Composed of the city's leading black and white civil activists—including such well-known blacks as Charles W. White, assistant city law director, Clarence W. Sharpe, president of the Cleveland NAACP, and William O. Walker, editor of the *Call and Post,* and whites such as Charles McCrea, president of National Malleable Iron and Steel, Frederick C. Crawford, president of Thompson Products, and W. J. Holliday, president of the Cleveland Chamber of Commerce—the committee was assigned the task of developing a broad educational program against racial intolerance and of working toward the eradication of specific problems, such as discrimination in employment, housing, and public accommodations. Although the committee's early work was limited largely to public statements issued through the press, it symbolized the city's growing awareness of its black citizens.[38]

Many issues contributed to the broadening of black protest movement during the Depression and the Second World War. The judicious receptiveness of the established black leaders to newly emerging protest groups with different ideas, the return of economic prosperity with the beginning of war production, the essential commitment to the

American way of life which the wartime emergency elicited among blacks, the democratic and antiracist ideology of the war against fascism, the Central Area Social Study with its effort to view the black population as a distinct community, and the Committee on Democratic Practice with its attempt to focus public attention on race issues, all contributed to a new atmosphere in which a debilitating sense of pessimism was replaced by optimism, and despair gave way to hope. As Cleveland entered the postwar years and the work of the Committee on Democratic Practice seemed to suggest the possibility of a better future, the Forest City once again affirmed its position at the leading edge of the best that the country had to offer, in that day and time, for its black citizens.

But in later years, especially in the fifties and sixties, and despite a continuing reputation as one of the country's most liberal urban environments for black Americans, the future of race relations in Cleveland became increasingly unclear. On the one hand, the city's black citizens made steady, though incremental, progress in municipal civil rights and local politics. On the other hand, they faced deteriorating conditions in housing and public schools. Both of these trends, though reflecting divergent outcomes, were closely related to a single impelling force—a large increase in the city's black population caused by the continued immigration of southern blacks.

Following the large increase in Cleveland's black population which occurred during World War I, the city's black community continued to grow in size each decade, although at a reduced rate. Whereas the black population increased 400 percent to 35,000 between 1910 and 1920, it increased by a much smaller (100) percent to 72,000 by 1930, and by only 18 percent to 85,000 by 1940. But again, as had been the case during the First World War, during the Second World War, the black migration to Cleveland accelerated dramatically as poor, rural, southern blacks streamed into the Forest City hoping for jobs in the burgeoning war production effort. Between 1940 and 1950 Cleveland's black population almost doubled to 148,000; in the fifties as the city's industrial production continued at high levels and southern blacks continued to come north in search of jobs, the black population again almost doubled to 251,000.

While these population increments do not reflect percentage increases as great as those in earlier years, they had a similar, and possibly even greater impact on race relations in the city. Whereas the effect of the four-fold increase in the city's black population during World War I was cushioned somewhat by a 50 percent increase in the white population, the effect of the nearly 100 percent increase in the black population during World War II was accentuated by a net decrease in the white population, as white families moved to the city's surrounding suburbs. The same pattern was repeated in the fifties as the city's black population grew while the white population shrank, leaving a black presence in the city that was becoming more and more sharply defined.[39]

One effect of this growth in the black community was an increased role for blacks in local politics, for as the black population increased, so too did black voting strength and political representation. In 1947 Harry E. Davis was elected to the state senate, the first black to hold such a position in over fifty years. Jean Murrell Capers became the first black woman to serve on the city council in 1949, and Hazel Mountain Walker became the first black member of the Ohio Board of Education in 1961. The first black elected to the United States House of Representatives from the newly created twenty-first congressional district was Louis Stokes in 1968. And over the twenty years following World War II the number of blacks elected to positions on the city council increased from three to ten.

Also related to the growth of the city's black population was the enactment of new municipal civil rights legislation. In these years the increasing importance of the black electorate, together with the continuing influence of the city's liberal heritage, gave rise to broadened legal recognition for black civil rights. In 1945 a new city ordinance transformed the city's Committee on Democratic Practice into the Cleveland Community Relations Board with a broader mandate to foster improved race relations through a program of public and legal action. The board developed a national reputation and became a model for the promotion of community-wide racial improvement. A year later, the city council passed a municipal civil rights law which provided for the revocation of the license to do business for any firm legally convicted of discriminating against blacks. And in 1950 the council enacted the first Fair Employment Practices Law in the country. The law gave the Community Relations Board the responsibility to receive complaints, conduct investigations, and make recommendations relative to discrimination in employment.[40]

But, if the World War II influx of blacks had the positive effect of increasing black political strength and broadening black civil rights, it also had the negative effect of heightening tension in many areas of race relations. This was especially the case in regard to the adequacy of housing. Beginning around the turn of the century a small slum area

131

had emerged in the southwest corner of the East Side ghetto, close to the downtown commercial area. During the thirties and forties this area was rebuilt with new public housing facilities but the rents of the new units were beyond the reach of the poorest black families, with the result that low-income families in search of housing were forced into adjacent neighborhoods where conditions soon became as intolerable as those they left behind. In the 1950s slum conditions were intensified by the urban renewal program which, though intended to rebuild some of the worst areas, actually accelerated the spread of urban blight, as whole neighborhoods were demolished in preparation for the construction of new units and facilities, many of which were never completed.[41]

The most notorious of these areas was the Hough neighborhood in the northeastern section of the city's East Side black community. As recent migrants streamed into the neighborhood, housing conditions that were already strained to their limits went from bad to worse, with building code and sanitary violations becoming an accepted standard. Garbage pickup was irregular, leaving the streets and alleys littered with refuse and the air full of the stench of decaying food. Policy operators sold numbers and announced winners with little fear of police interruption. Prostitutes, encouraged by a police department that publicly supported the idea of a segregated vice district, plied their trade without restraint. Police activity was minimal, prejudiced, and sometimes brutal, with beatings of blacks for apparently minimal offenses frequently the subject of passionate complaint from black leaders.

While the incoming migrant families put increased pressure on the ghetto housing market, their children strained the capacity of public education facilities. One problem was that many migrant children had begun their education in segregated, rural southern schools which did not adequately prepare them for the Cleveland system, and were in need of special remedial education courses. Another problem was the sheer number of new students. The school program serving the black community was taxed far beyond its limit by the incoming migrant families. In order to accommodate them, each school day was divided into a morning and afternoon session, with each student attending for only one-half day sessions. By the early sixties the inadequacy of the public education available to black students was a sensitive and potentially explosive issue within Cleveland's black community, as well as a source of frequent hostility between white and black community leaders. One knowledgeable contemporary has described the situation as

132

"chaotic." In 1961 black protestors staged a demonstration at the Board of Education building. A year later Harry E. Davis Junior High School, a new school named for Ohio's first black state senator, opened its doors.[42]

But in 1964 the issue came to a head once more in an escalating spiral of protest by blacks and counterprotest by whites. Angered by continuing discrimination and segregation in the city's schools, blacks picketed the Board of Education; in response, whites staged a countermarch into black neighborhoods, overturning cars, breaking store windows, and beating black citizens; blacks then staged spontaneous sit-ins in school headquarters and buildings; whites countered by proposing three new schools although all were in locations that blacks previously had opposed; blacks and sympathetic whites led a demonstration to stop construction during which a white minister was run over by a bulldozer; local courts issued a permanent injunction against interference with school construction; blacks boycotted the white school system and opposed a school levy. In the end, however, all three schools were built and all in locations unacceptable to blacks.[43]

As blacks became more and more frustrated with their inability to influence important areas of community life such as housing and public education in spite of their growing political importance within the city, black protest thought again moved in a more aggressive direction. Within the established leadership, both the Urban League and the NAACP began again to reflect some of the newer strands of thought. Although both retained their traditional core values and strategies—the league emphasizing social issues and an accommodationist approach and the NAACP emphasizing civil rights and a legalistic approach—each in its own way became increasingly more assertive. The league began to devote considerable attention to the issue of housing, eventually appointing a second executive to its staff with specific responsibility for housing issues. The NAACP acquired its first full-time executive director in 1945 when L. Pearl Mitchell accepted the post. Charles P. Lucas then served as executive director from 1945 to 1954. Under their direction, the NAACP broadened its activities to include legal and political action in support of a wider range of issues, prominent among them, housing and public education. It also broadened its tactics to include judicious support of mass demonstrations and ghetto-based boycotts.

In turn, the more aggressive positions being taken by the established leadership organizations like the Urban League and the NAACP were, at least in part, a response to even more militant positions being enunciated by a rapidly growing array of newly established protest organizations. The Congress of Racial Equality sought to unite all black action groups in support of community self-determination. The Southern Christian Leadership Conference, founded by Martin Luther King, worked with churches in support of black youth, as well as on consumer- and family-related issues. At the extreme end of the ideological continuum and representing the most militant elements of the black community were a number of organizations which shared an orientation toward black separatism or black nationalism. These included such groups as the Black Panthers, United Black Alliance, United Black Student Alliance, Republic of New Africa, and Afro Set.[44]

By the early sixties the divergent forces set in motion by the rapid increase in the size of the black community—the one tending toward increasing black political power and the other toward growing black frustration over ghetto conditions—came to a head at virtually the same historical moment, as the city almost simultaneously elected the first black mayor of a major urban center and experienced the demonstration of a major race riot. In 1966, following a barroom argument between a white bartender and a black customer, the Hough section of Cleveland erupted in four days and nights of interracial violence. At its conclusion forty-six people were reported injured, seventeen hundred National Guardsmen were stationed in the city, and losses from looting and arson were estimated in the millions. Two years later violence again erupted in the Glenville area as a gun battle took place between black nationalists and local police in what became known as "The Glenville Shootout."[45]

In between those two events, in 1967, Carl Stokes was elected as the first black mayor in Cleveland. With a straightforward and moderate image among both blacks and whites, Stokes capitalized on the growing frustration of the black community and the tattered, but resilient liberalism of the white community to defeat the incumbent mayor Ralph Locher in the Democratic primary and the Republican candidate Seth Taft in the general election. Two years later he was again successful, defeating Robert J. Kelly in the Democratic primary and Republican Ralph J. Perk in the general election.[46]

More than any other, these two consummate events—the eruption of the Hough riot and the election of Carl Stokes—symbolized the emergence of a new element in Cleveland's race relations: uncertainty. True, the city's election of the first black mayor of a large city was an event of tremendous significance. But so, too, was the Hough riot, for it showed that, at least in some respects, race relations in Cleveland were not much different from race relations in other cities. By the middle sixties it was apparent that Cleveland's liberalism, at least that part of it related to black issues, clearly stood at a crossroad. What direction it would take in the years ahead and whether it would remain at the leading edge of liberalism on the race issue remained an unanswered question.

EDWARD M. MIGGINS

The Search for the One Best System: Cleveland Public Schools and Educational Reform, 1836–1920

Woodland Hill School library, Cleveland, ca. 1910

The heritage of New England greatly influenced Cleveland during its development from a pioneer village of Connecticut's Western Reserve to a major commercial city of the Civil War era. Believing in education as the bulwark of both church and state, transplanted New Englanders led the establishment and reform of public education in both Cleveland and Ohio during the nineteenth century.

The early settlers of Cleveland had already opened a school in the front room of Lorenzo Carter's cabin shortly before Ohio's admission as a state in 1803. In addition to teaching "the three R's," children were taught "how to shoot"—a clear indication of the social realities of a pioneer settlement in which only fifty-seven persons lived by 1810.[1] In 1817 the village's trustees reimbursed public-spirited citizens who had constructed a little wooden schoolhouse on St. Clair Street. In 1821 Carter and a group of citizens built a secondary school—the Cleveland Academy—a two-story brick building near Public Square. Harvey Rice, a graduate of Williams College, was appointed its principal in 1824.

Despite the advocacy of public education in Ohio's constitution, most townships did not tax themselves for the support of public education. Formal schooling was seen as both a private responsibility and educationally less influential than the home, the church, or the workplace. Parents employed teachers at their own expense or paid tuition to allow their children to attend schools like the Cleveland Academy. Like advocates of common schools elsewhere, Cleveland's pre–Civil War reformers wanted to establish a state-supported, compulsory system of public education as a right available to all people.

In 1825 Ephram Cutler, an Ohio judge and son of a New Englander who had influenced the provision for public education in the federal land ordinances of 1785 and 1787, secured the passage of a law which required the establishment of public school districts to teach "the three

R's." The state charter under which Cleveland became incorporated in 1836 also allowed the city council to select a board of school managers to operate the public schools. John W. Willey, a descendant of one of Boston's most prominent merchant families and the first mayor of Cleveland, strongly advocated a common school system in his inaugural address to the city council: "Our character, our manners, our habits and our means require an entire change, the introduction of a liberal and well adjusted system of education in our city." The city immediately took over the only free school, known as the "ragged school," located in the basement of the Protestant Bethel Chapel.[2] In 1837 the city built separate schools for girls and boys in each of the city's wards and purchased the Cleveland Academy to accommodate approximately eight hundred students. The city's wards jealously guarded their neighborhood schools by resisting centralization, even though it would bring greater economy. The school system employed male teachers at forty dollars per month to teach the boys, and women at twenty dollars per month to teach the girls. No attempt was made at classifying or grading beyond the creation of senior and primary divisions. The lowly condition of the schools was apparent by the fact that children brought their own textbooks and the average daily absence amounted to nearly 25 percent in the 1840s. The salary of teachers was reduced and the school year occasionally shortened because of the dire financial condition of public education. Public education had a difficult time overcoming the image of being a charity school for the poor.

The city council appointed Charles Bradburn, a retailer and wholesaler and son of a New England cotton manufacturer, and George Willey, a lawyer and the brother of the mayor, to the board of school managers in 1841. The former served as a member and business manager of the board for thirteen years and was called "the father of the Cleveland Schools."[3] Willey served fifteen years and concentrated on improving the quality of the educational program. By 1842 the city's schools enrolled twelve hundred pupils in fifteen buildings. Although the board prescribed a uniform system of textbooks, teachers divided their schools into as many classes as expedient and determined the amount of time spent on each subject. Teachers were required to pass tests on spelling, mathematics, and reading, and to furnish evidence of a good moral character for employment.

Bradburn and the board of managers campaigned in 1844 for a high school to teach the "higher branches of knowledge." Mayor George Hoadly endorsed the idea before city council: "This would present a powerful stimulus to study and good conduct. The poorest child, if possessed of talents and application might aspire to the highest station in the Republic. From such schools we might hope to issue the future Franklins of our land."[4] Despite opposition from wealthy taxpayers who contested the legality and expense of public schooling beyond the elementary level, Cleveland opened Central High School for boys in the basement of a Universalist Church on Prospect Street on July 13, 1846—the first public secondary school west of the Alleghenies. The board appointed Andrew Freese, who had studied New England's public schools, as the first principal. A girls' department was organized the following year.

In 1847 the Cleveland school system received support from the state's approval of Akron, Ohio's school law authorizing the election of a board of directors for the entire management and control of all schools in a single district. The law also allowed the board to establish a high school supported by general taxation and free to all who passed an entrance exam. The state applied the Akron law to all school districts the following year. In 1853 Ohio authorized a school levy to eliminate all student fees for public education, to reestablish a state board of education under the sponsorship of Harvey Rice, and to empower local school boards to organize graded elementary schools and high schools—a major step toward the autonomy and standardization of public education. The Cleveland City Council created a board of education with the power to appoint a manager and a superintendent of schools. The board chose Freese as the first superintendent and built a new facility for Central High School on Euclid Avenue at the cost of twenty thousand dollars in 1856. In 1859 the state allowed each of the city's eleven wards to select members of the school board for a term of one year. The new board appointed a Board of Examiners to issue a certificate of qualification as a prerequisite for employment as a teacher.[5]

Freese returned to teaching in 1861 and was replaced as superintendent by Luther Oviatt, a graduate of Western Reserve College and a teacher and principal in the public schools since 1848. Freese had previously attempted to grade and classify the schools by dividing the elementary system into three divisions and by introducing a course of study for each grade. His successor initiated "object lessons"—an outgrowth of the work of Friedrich Froebel, a German educator who believed in the educational value of playing games and manipulating objects. A professional gymnast was also employed to help the teaching staff introduce physical exercise in the schools. These small changes were the beginnings of a larger transformation of the city's public schools which would occur after the Civil War as services were enlarged to cope with the problems of the industrial city and to compel the attendance of school-age children.

Educational reformers and other civic-minded people and groups struggled to find solutions to the problems that arose from the rapid growth of American towns into industrial cities after the Civil War. These reformers shared Horace Mann's vision of the public school as the chief instrument for educating and disciplining the citizens of modern America. Public education would restore social harmony and the habits of honesty, hard work, and thrift—virtues often idyllically associated with the village and farming people of preindustrial America. The schools were also expected to assimilate foreign immigrants into America's Anglo-Saxon culture, to promote the mobility of virtuous, hard-working students, and to adjust the children to modern society. To achieve these purposes, educational reformers in the post–Civil War era transformed the simple common school into a highly diversified, bureaucratic system of modern education. The expectations of what the public school system could accomplish were increased enormously during this period, but, concurrently, so were the conflicts and debate over its failures and what constituted the best means to achieve what one historian has described as "the one best system."[6]

In 1866 Anson Smythe, then superintendent of Cleveland's public schools and former state superintendent, claimed that the public schools could compensate for the lack of moral culture and religious instruction not only by "a thorough instruction in those things contained in the textbooks," but also by the inculcation of "good social and moral principles and habits."[7] Reformers believed that better school facilities would attract a greater number of school-age children. The schools enrolled 9,270 students but the superintendent estimated that the number would reach twelve thousand if there were sufficient accommodations.

Andrew Rickoff, the former head of Cincinnati's public schools and a highly respected educator, was selected as the next superintendent. He and the school board exercised a freer hand in operating the public schools after the passage of the 1868 state law which eliminated the city council's control except for approval of new sites and buildings. In 1873 this last restraint was removed. The board of education now derived all its power from the state. Eighteen to twenty-six members were bienially elected from the city's wards.

Rickoff reclassified students into twelve grades because of the lack of uniformity in the work of different school departments. Some second-ary schools were doing the work of primary schools and vice versa. He devised a uniform system of student classification by grade and divi-sion level—primary, upper primary or grammar, and high school—and the separate division of boys and girls was eliminated. The super-intendent claimed that the prescribed course of study allowed teachers to fit their students between the work of the class above or below their grade level. In addition, teachers could now be held accountable for the educational progress of their students. Reformers maintained that the graded system which grouped students in classes according to age or ability replicated the modern industrialist's division of labor and was more efficient than the heterogeneous grouping of students of different ages in the one-room schoolhouse or ungraded classroom of the "common school." A new course of study was also introduced to econ-omize the time of teachers and to provide greater opportunity to illus-trate subject matter through object lessons. "It is an attempt on the part of the primary schools," explained Superintendent Rickoff, "to make its instruction more like the home."[8]

Rickoff reduced the number of grammar schools because of poor attendance in the upper grades and their former principals were made assistant superintendents of the school system. In 1868 the superin-tendent established the office of supervising principal to control meth-ods of instruction, discipline and classification of pupils, and informa-tion to the public. Women teachers were appointed to these positions at the end of the school year and relieved of all instructional responsi-bilities. Women were also given the posts of teachers and principals of the grammar schools. Since women were not able to vote, Rickoff be-lieved that they were less involved in partisan politics and would gov-ern the schools more efficiently and humanely than men.[9]

The quality of the teaching staff was also upgraded. During the fall of 1868 a normal school for the training of teachers was conducted for one week. The success of this program led to a permanent program at Eagle Elementary School in 1874. A committee of teachers from the normal school and Rickoff were given the authority to approve the appointment of graduates of the year-long prescribed course of studies. School leaders expected to gain greater control over the selection of teachers who were often hired in the past as a political favor to ward leaders. The superintendent also proposed a merit system to award sal-ary increases on the basis of ability as well as length of tenure.[10]

Rickoff introduced semiannual promotion of students to increase the efficiency of the school system and the teaching of subjects in German in 1870. He believed that the bilingual program would draw the approximately two thousand children of German immigrants who attended German-speaking private schools into the public schools. The superintendent argued that it would "not tend so much to Germanize America as it does to Americanize the Germans."[11] Both native and German youth would also benefit from a mutual sharing of cultural traditions. Almost a decade after the inception of the program, the number of German students not attending the public schools was reduced to approximately two hundred students.

During the latter half of the nineteenth century, educational reformers like Rickoff constantly defended the existence of the high school which enrolled only a small number of students at the financial expense of the general public. The superintendent argued that the reason only a small number of students enrolled in the high school was due to the overemphasis on academic studies and college preparatory courses. As part of the effort to expand nonacademic programs, music education was introduced throughout the system. The English course was shortened to three years and German substituted for Latin to induce parents to keep their children in school longer.

Superintendent Rickoff urged the board to furnish a secondary education more suitable to "industrial pursuits" outside the learned professions. In addition, a more practical education directly related to successful entry into the machine shop and factory would encourage working-class families to send their children to high school. The school board revised the secondary course of study by adding courses in analytical geometry and mechanical and commercial pursuits. The superintendent also hoped that more students would pursue "the mechanical arts rather than the overcrowded professions."[12]

In 1876 the Cleveland schools moved students from the old Central High School, located in the downtown business district, to a new location at East 55th Street. Rickoff assisted architect Levi Scofield in designing the new school, a Gothic building with the classrooms arranged around a central well extending from the large main hall to the roof.[13]

Rickoff and other public school reformers realized that it was not enough to provide new facilities and programs to attract children to the schools. New methods would have to be found to discipline troublesome or recalcitrant youth, of whom the majority were at the bottom of the economic system or the children of recently arrived immigrants. In March 1877 the school board established a "school for incorrigibles" for disruptive students. Rickoff believed that the school provided a better and more economical remedy than turning such children out into the streets. Ohio also strengthened its compulsory school laws to enforce attendance by children between the ages of eight and fourteen for at least twelve weeks a year. In 1880 the Newsboy and Bootblacks' Home and the public schools jointly offered an evening program for employed youth who had left school early.[14]

Rickoff received national recognition and acclaim for a school system which grew from 9,643 to 26,990 pupils, from 123 to 473 teachers, and which constructed award-winning school buildings during his tenure. But local controversy influenced the school board to replace Rickoff with Burke A. Hinsdale, the president of Hiram College, in 1882. The latter had previously criticized Rickoff before the Ohio Teachers' Association in 1876. Son of an old New England family and friend of President James Garfield, Hinsdale contended that the public schools were more interested in buildings, equipment, and numbers than in the educational development of each child. He described the graded school as "a system of platoons" in which the personal authority of the teacher was diminished. Rickoff defended the new system as superior to the ungraded schoolhouses of the past which had spent too much time on group lessons, rules, and definitions, and not enough on individual students. Local newspapers widely reported the conflict between the two educators and it appeared that Hinsdale won the debate. In addition, the newspapers also carried stories of unsanitary conditions which led to the spread of diseases in some of the most overcrowded schools. A group of school board members boycotted the proceedings of the board after they thought a supporter of Rickoff had illegally manipulated his election as president of the board. After the critics of the superintendent won a majority of seats on the board and refused to renew his contract, Rickoff became superintendent of the public schools in Yonkers, New York.[15]

Hinsdale believed in a more conservative philosophy than Rickoff: the schools should develop "moral character" through "lessons in punctuality, regularity, obedience, industry, cleanliness and decency of appearances." He visited and advised teachers during the first months of his tenure and declared that what the schools needed was not a revolution in "external organization" but a more flexible and thorough education of children in "the essentials."[16]

J. H. Schneider, the president of the school board, advocated the elimination of the last two years of high school and the organization of a ten-year grammar school. Hinsdale argued that such a grammar school would make parents think that they did not have to educate their children any further. He defended the high school as part of a democratic common school system which enrolled students from many walks of life and different nationalities. He cited the fact that enrollment had grown 348 percent between 1870 and 1884 as proof of the public's confidence.[17]

Hinsdale attempted to ease the transition from grammar to high school by assigning ninth grade students to a single teacher for the preparation and recitation of most of their lessons. Corporal punishment was eliminated and quarterly exams and teacher evaluations were substituted for the annual test for promotion. The superintendent also argued that physical exercise should not be left to chance and introduced a program to promote the "harmonious physical development" of children. In opposition to critics of German instruction, Hinsdale claimed that the program had broken "the class distinction between American and foreign emigrants" and that its participants performed better academically than the rest of the student body.[18]

In 1886 immigrant ward leaders successfully campaigned against Hinsdale and his Republican friends on the school board. The new board did not renew his contract. Hinsdale later advocated, in his subsequent position as a professor of history and pedagogy at the University of Michigan, the total removal of politics from schools through the replacement of popular selection of school boards with an appointive system.[19]

The board selected Lewis Day, a veteran teacher and administrator of sixteen years, as the new superintendent. He responded to the growing pressures from the business community and educational leaders for a more practical program in the secondary schools. In 1884 Newton M. Anderson, a teacher from Central High, rented an empty barn near 40th Street and started an after-school program in manual training. It offered classes in carpentry, woodturning, mechanical drawing, machine shop, and work at a forge for high school students. Three years later a course in cooking was opened in the Manual Training School— one of the first of its kind in the country. The public schools paid the tuition of students in manual training through funds from a levy that was authorized by the state in 1887. The school board opened the West Manual Training School in the upper floor of West High School in 1890 and added a two-year business course to the secondary curriculum.[20]

The public schools also expanded the evening program to admit girls and added courses in psychology and physics. The evening program which enrolled close to two thousand students in 1887 increasingly focused on teaching foreigners the basics of English and civics to pass naturalization exams. The school board also hired its first truant officer to enforce the compulsory attendance law of 1889. This law required children to attend school twenty weeks a year and children between the ages of fourteen and sixteen, who could not read or write English, to attend school either one-half day or in the evening.[21]

Despite his cooperation with leading businessmen, Day was criticized by the *Cleveland Leader* for his partisan award of textbook contracts, illegal use of building materials, and slow response to the misuse of funds for private loans by the school board treasurer. Businessmen, municipal reformers, the *Cleveland Leader,* and the Republican party saw the problems of the schools as part of the larger deficiencies of municipal governance which needed greater centralization and control by professional administrators. In 1891 a reform coalition successfully sponsored the passage of the Federal Plan to revive both Cleveland's municipal and school charters. All legislative power was placed in a school council of seven members of whom five were elected at-large and two from special districts. All executive authority was vested in a school director, elected directly by the people, who could then appoint the school superintendent. Overcoming the opposition of the Democratic party, *The Plain Dealer,* and the *Catholic Universe Bulletin,* all of which charged it with advancing the interests of the Republican party, the coalition successfully elected the majority of the new school board and H. Q. Sargent, a businessman, to the post of the school director. Sargent appointed Andrew Draper, the state superintendent of New York, as the superintendent of the Cleveland Public Schools.[22]

A former lawyer from an old New England family, Draper believed in the power of the schools to ensure "good citizenship, the protection of property and the preservation of the state." He appointed new supervisors and principals and attempted to upgrade the teaching staff through university extension courses, training programs at the normal school, and by dismissing over one hundred teachers for incompetence. The school system developed a new science course and a program for dropouts. In 1893 the school board purchased the Manual Training School and opened a manual training room in Central High. Assisted by the passage of a state law to educate disabled people, the board simultaneously opened the Cleveland Day School for deaf children. In May of 1894 Draper resigned his position to become the president of the University of Illinois.[23]

Sargent selected as Draper's replacement Lewis H. Jones, the superintendent of the Indianapolis schools, who continued to expand the educational and social-welfare programs of the public schools. He abolished annual exams in favor of teacher evaluations for promotion of students.[24] Believing like many leaders in the infant field of child and educational psychology that the ages between four and six were the most formative, the new superintendent established six kindergartens during the 1896–97 school year.

Jones also published a comprehensive and detailed course of study to allow teachers to know the work required of students. In 1900 the supervisor of physical education and school hygiene prepared materials for the teachers to detect defective vision in their students despite the objections of some parents who resented the program's intrusion in private affairs. The supervisor also personally administered technical exams and supplied free glasses to indigent children. And a program of physical education to improve physical well-being, scholarship, and self-discipline was introduced.[25]

The evening program to Americanize the city's "rapidly increasing number of foreigners" was expanded under Jones.[26] In 1901 he successfully advocated the provision of free textbooks as another means to encourage greater attendance by poor children. "Steamer classes" were also instituted in Harmon School as a special language program for non-English speaking children who had just arrived in Cleveland.

Both Sargent and Jones believed that the Federal Plan was responsible for the educational progress of the schools and the reduction of political interference by the "uneducated and unthinking classes." The plan did not prevent, however, the demise of the schools as a result of Jones's refusal to reconsider his dismissal of several young women from the normal school. The women won a court suit which reinstated them and one later joined the Democratic party's successful campaign for a replacement of Sargent in the election of 1900. During the fall of 1901 local newspapers also criticized what were described as the "frills and feathers" of the school adminstration. Faced with growing criticism and opposition, Jones accepted the presidency of the Michigan State University's Normal School in 1902.[27]

Educational reformers and their allies in Cleveland discovered that their victory over the wards did not ensure domination over the community. They would continue to search for more effective means to achieve what they thought was best for the public schools. Reformers wanted to enroll a greater percentage of school-age children, especially those from poor immigrant families, and isolate them from what they perceived as the evil influences of the street and home life. But only 54.6

percent of the children of school age were registered in the Cleveland Public Schools and only 40 percent attended school the entire year in 1900.[28]

The careers of the superintendents of the Cleveland schools reveal the strengths and weaknesses of educational reform between the Civil War and the turn of the century. The public schools developed a number of educational and social-welfare services as a bridge between the child and America's industrial-commercial life, but the motives of reformers were often based on a self-serving, ethnocentric view of immigrants and poor people. The schools were the custodian of the community's children, but immigrant parents and the lay public were seen as obstacles or political threats to their smooth operation.

Faced with the growing size and heterogeneity of the student population, standardization of the educational program and the classification of students was an improvement over large ungraded classes. On the other hand, the triumph of this system became an affliction for some educational reformers. Superintendent Hinsdale saw the school system as playing a beneficial role as "an averaging machine" to develop cultural homogeneity.[29] But the schools had still not adapted, in his opinion, to the individual needs of students. What became a means to an end often evolved into an end in itself as the public schools were consumed with the problems of expansion and conflicts over educational and political issues.

Cleveland's school superintendents embodied the characteristics of a new middle class of professional administrators who sought personal advancement through the expansion of modern, bureaucratic systems under their control.[30] But their idealist vision of stability and control over the city and its people was often contradicted by the realities of urban life. When reformers were able to coax recalcitrant youth into the school system, they often had to isolate them in such programs as the steamer classes or schools for incorrigibles. Despite the advocacy of the high school as a poor man's college, the poor did not attend in any significant number. Although reformers organized the public schools as a vehicle to assimilate different nationalities, the children of Cleveland's immigrant groups attended parochial schools which taught the languages and culture of the Old World.

Equality of educational opportunity meant universal attendance in the common schoolroom for antebellum school reformers. The definition changed during the last quarter of the nineteenth century as equality came to mean separate programs for children with different backgrounds and abilities. Many of the contradictions were glossed over as reformers inflated the role of the administrator and the school system to deal with the problems of urban America.[31] The response to failure was a call for greater centralization and expansion of the system. Educators of the Progressive Era would look to scientific management and new educational programs to train and assimilate children into American society. Faced with the choice of either seeking broad social change or utilizing the school as a surrogate for other institutions, late nineteenth- and early twentieth-century school reformers chose the latter.

Educational reform in Cleveland during the Progressive Era from 1900 to World War I was rooted in the theories and practices of post–Civil War leaders who developed more humane and realistic programs that expanded the role of the public schools. Progressive educators were also confident in the ability of the schools to cure the social and economic problems of twentieth-century America and to compensate for the deficiencies of children living in an urban-industrial environment. They would search for what Superintendent Jones had referred to as "a science in education" in the fields of child psychology, pedagogy, and professional administration.[32]

American educators and the public became more concerned with the social efficiency of education in promoting the general welfare of society.[33] Influenced by sociologist Edward A. Ross who spoke openly of education as an economical system of police, one group of reformers interested in efficiency believed that education should shape the entire personality of the student to conform to the usages and life values of the group to which he belonged. A different group, inspired by the writings of John Dewey and the work of social settlements like Jane Addams's Hull House in Chicago or George Bellamy's Hiram House in Cleveland, stressed the role of the school as an agency to provide a wide variety of services for the youth and adult members of a community.

Twentieth-century school reformers were convinced that informal educative systems were unable to provide the literacy and skills needed for a person to function successfully in society. This belief was strengthened by the influx of new immigrants from rural, non-English speaking cultures of southern and eastern Europe, who often lived in ethnic ghettos like Cleveland's Warszawa, an enclave of the Polish-American community. Between 1900 and 1910, the city's population from northern Europe declined by 2,346 to 69,852, while the number of new immigrants increased from 43,281 to 115,870 out of a total population of 573,872.[34]

In 1901 despite the opposition of the city's businessmen, the people

of Cleveland elected as mayor Tom L. Johnson, a maverick businessman who had become a disciple of Henry George and the hope of the
local Democratic party.[35] As a result the business community enjoyed
greater success with controlling the public schools. In 1904 the state
legislature abolished the Federal Plan by allowing five board members
to be elected at-large and two by wards. The board was empowered to
select a superintendent who would appoint all employees, supervise
the schools and teachers, and promote pupils. The board could also
appoint a director to manage the finances and facilities of the school
system. In January 1905 Samuel P. Orth, the head of the school board,
recommended the creation of an education commission of the city's
leading citizens to investigate the public schools. Orth stressed the need
to know why the school system lost the great majority of its students
after the sixth grade and whether a manual training high school was
needed. The commission selected as its chairman J. G. W. Cowles, a
real estate businessman and former president of the chamber of commerce. The commission's report criticized the schools for concentrat-
ing too much on what were considered nonessentials, such as athletics,
public exhibitions, and field day exercises, with not enough emphasis
on basic fundamentals. The commission found a high degree of waste
and inefficiency in the school system and called for greater differentiation in the functions of the high school and the establishment of separate manual and commercial high schools.[36]

The school board hired William H. Elson, the head of the public
schools in Grand Rapids, Michigan, as superintendent in 1906. Elson
believed that since "radical changes" had taken place in industrial and
social life, "the school shall fit for efficiency in a life that is predominantly industrial." A revised course of study gave greater attention to
manual and constructive activities, drawing, and "the three R's."
Foremost among his efforts was the opening of the Technical High
School in September 1908. The school was an impressive, English-
Gothic building on East 55th Street and included mechanical arts for
boys and domestic and applied arts for girls. The superintendent
claimed that the 90 percent of Cleveland's high school boys who did
not go to college made industrial occupations their lifework and that
girls needed, not a background in literature, but training to become
"ideal" homemakers.[37]

Reformers believed that a more practical curriculum would both encourage a greater number of students to pursue secondary education
and best suit students with immigrant and working-class backgrounds. Former Superintendent Draper argued, for example, that the

149

lack of industrial education had led an "undue proportion of youth to literature and scientific study which too often ends in idleness or insipidity, or in professional or managing occupations for which they are not well prepared and which are already crowded." In response to businessmen who wanted better training of students who pursued jobs in offices and stores, and to the high failure rate of students in commercial courses in the academic high school, the school board established one of the first commercial high schools in the country in 1909. The curriculum emphasized the application of traditional subjects to commercial life as well as specific courses in commercial training. Industrial education transformed the older conception of the high school as a program of general education for all social classes. It was part of the increasing differentiation of public education along social class lines —the very opposite of the democratic ideology of the common school. "Democracy implies equality of opportunity," declared Elson, "but equal opportunity does not necessarily mean the same opportunity."[38]

Elson believed, like many progressive school reformers, that specialized programs would accommodate the needs of children with different social and economic backgrounds. The schools, therefore, developed a system of course differentiation and classification of students into "slow and fast" grades in the elementary program. In 1909 the Elementary Industrial School was opened in Brownell School to solve the problem of "the premature breadwinner," the average or nonacademically talented boy or girl who would ordinarily drop out in the seventh or eighth grade.[39]

The school system enlarged its social welfare programs to exert greater custodial care over students. In 1903 the public schools had opened eleven vacation schools and playgrounds "to keep the kids off the streets" and "to reduce crime and vandalism."[40] Elson introduced play equipment and expanded the program to counteract the restriction of muscular activity in "the day of the city and of the machine." A gardening program for school children, first opened in 1903, was placed under the supervision of a curator of gardens. In the fall of 1908 the board appointed a physician in charge of medical inspection and opened a medical dispensary—the first of its kind—in a school in the Murray Hill district of Italian residents. The school system also opened fresh-air schools for the care of tubercular children, a free dental clinic, luncheon rooms in the high school, and classes for the blind. In order to better educate the city's adults, Elson organized the Lectures and Social Center Development Committee in 1906.[41]

Elson believed that the administrators and teachers must accept the fact that "the school is but a machine . . . to do a specific type of work" and subject to "definite tests of efficiency." The efficiency of the schools could only be measured by "the facts," and the superintendent believed that his reports on enrollment and course selection were the beginning of the collection of data to measure the work of the schools. To improve the performance of teachers, the program and facilities of the normal school were upgraded. In 1904 a system of competitive exams for admission to the school was instituted. After the school was legalized in 1908, a building for it was constructed at University Circle the following year. The program included courses for teachers of special or backward children and extension courses to improve the quality of teachers already employed in the system.[42]

A new coalition elected to the school board did not renew Elson's contract in 1911, in response to critics who denounced him as an insensitive elitist and for his alliance with Francis Haserot, the head of the school board who had been accused of fraudulently awarding construction contracts after the disastrous Collinwood school fire had killed 173 students in 1908. But the new group was soon accused of malfeasance for appointing one of their former members to the post of assistant superintendent and for changing the system's textbooks during the summer of 1912, only a short time after a different set had been purchased. Progressive reformers and social workers criticized the board for charging fees, for using the evening schools as social centers, and for the negative attitude of Superintendent James Frederick who claimed that the public schools could not provide enough facilities and trained teachers for the burgeoning student enrollment that had increased from 63,409 in 1912, to 71,394 in 1913. The board aroused more public anger by dismissing teachers who had attempted to form a union to fight for higher wages and better working conditions, and for its refusal to adopt the "double-shift" schools of the Gary Plan to relieve overcrowding. The schools were ripe for another investigation.[43] The public schools thus became one of the early investigations of the Cleveland Foundation, a local charitable institution established in 1914 by Frederick Goff, president of Cleveland Trust Company, as the first community foundation.

After surveying the city's welfare system, Allan T. Burns, a former social worker and the director of the Cleveland Foundation's survey program, announced the appointment of Leonard Ayres, the director of the Russell Sage Foundation's educational division, as the head of an investigation of the public schools in March 1914.[44] Ayres advocated scientific management and the creation of specialized programs for immigrant children. He supervised the work of twenty-five locally and nationally prominent researchers, and released the reports of the school survey between April 1915 and June 1916. The survey criticized the inefficiency of the Cleveland school system in a series of highly publicized public meetings, newspaper reports, and publications. Its reports constantly revealed the disparity between the glowing reports of the school administration and the actual performance of the educational system. Ayres estimated, for example, that two-thirds of the student population left school before the legally required age of sixteen for girls and fifteen for boys. The survey claimed that a more centralized and progressive administration would improve the efficiency and quality of the schools.[45]

Edward Bushnell, the president of the school board, dismissed the survey as a self-serving attack by a group of outside consultants. To overcome such opposition, the Cleveland Foundation organized a powerful campaign to implement its recommendations. In 1916 Ayres helped the school board select Frank E. Spaulding, the head of the Minneapolis public schools, as the next superintendent. Spaulding's educational philosophy and background as a social efficiency expert perfectly matched that of Ayres and the school surveyors. In 1917 a nonpartisan committee of fifteen residents chosen by the Citizens' League campaigned successfully for the election of school board candidates who had promised to support the school survey.[46] Spaulding reduced the power of the school board as he centrally reorganized the school system around his office. Supported by a new Department of Reference and Research, the school administration often allowed the board little time to deliberate its requests. In response to the survey's criticism of the "dual system" of administration, the separation of the business and educational departments, the new superintendent exerted greater control over school expenditures.

Spaulding and the majority of the school board supported the removal and prosecution under the Espionage Act of a socialist board member who publicly opposed America's entrance into World War I. The school board also terminated the teaching of German and required a loyalty oath from teachers as part of the wartime campaign for "100 percent Americanism." In addition, it hired Raymond Moley, a professor of political science at Western Reserve University, to improve and expand its citizenship programs as part of a citywide effort to Americanize foreign-born immigrants.

Spaulding developed new junior high and vocational training programs and instituted a department of mental testing to place students within educational tracks. Vocational guidance and mental testing did not escape the distinctions of race, ethnicity, and class it had been designed to overcome. "The school pigeonholed immigrants," according to a recent analysis, "as it prepared them for the world of work while educators confidently proclaimed that aptitude tests enabled children to rise to the level of their ability." A double-shift plan was expanded to relieve overcrowding. The superintendent claimed to have also improved the efficiency of the school system by increasing the promotion rate of students before he left to become a professor of education at Yale University in 1920. However, the gain was due more to the acceleration or continuous promotion of the most qualified students than to the improvement of the schools' total population. The dropout rate actually increased in schools with the greatest number of immigrants from southern and eastern Europe. The Cleveland Foundation declared that an educational revival had occurred but its efforts did not solve the problems of nonattendance, congestion, and nonpromotion of children with the greatest needs for assistance.[47] The public school's policy of continuous promotion, mental testing, and differentiation of students served better those it had always served best.

Progressive school reformers and professional educators believed that the public schools would transform both immigrants and cities. Faced with obstacles to their plans, educators demanded further expansion of the schools' role and attempted to further isolate the city's youth from what they perceived as the negative influences of their environment—the immigrant home and the street. Often educators overstated what they could accomplish and defended themselves by blaming the deficiencies in the backgrounds of children from the impoverished families of immigrants.[48] Although social efficiency experts wanted the school to operate like a factory, they feared the dislocations of industrialized society. Technological and industrial progress accelerated the social changes which destroyed the progressive reformer's vision of social stability and order.

The beginning of specialized programs which social efficiency experts believed were commensurate with the backgrounds and abilities of children created a very different educational system than that envisioned by Samuel Lewis, an Ohioan and antebellum school reformer. He had advocated the mixture of different students in the same classroom "until their different life circumstances fix their business for life." Progressive educators like Elson and Spaulding believed that the older philosophy of the common school was anachronistic in the face of the social and economic realities of a modern city like Cleveland.

They believed that the "circumstances" of both the child and the prevailing social-economic order must be taken immediately and continuously into account by the school. To the extent that services were made available to children with specialized needs and groups allowed to achieve desired social or educational ends, the philosophy and reforms of Cleveland's progressive educators and their nineteenth-century predecessors benefited the city and its people.[49]

Political conflict always accompanied educational reform. Reformers and their allies in late nineteenth- and early twentieth-century Cleveland attempted to remove the schools from the control of ward politicians and their immigrant working-class supporters. Advocates of the Federal Plan and the school survey believed that citywide elections and centralized management would create a better school system under their control. Draper believed that since "unrestricted suffrage" had made it more difficult to have strong and experienced men to manage great cities, it was imperative that "the intellectual elite" evolve a plan and educate "the masses" to support it.[50] However, the triumph of the corporate model of elitist reformers did not eliminate political conflict, as indicated by the fate of Superintendents Jones and Elson. Different political coalitions and Republican or Democrat machines continued to battle over the schools as well as other areas of political patronage and control.

Centralization provided greater authority to school administrators and accelerated the growth of a complex school bureaucracy. Education leaders enjoyed far greater freedom than when the schools were the handmaiden of Cleveland's city council before the Civil War. Even this triumph did not prevent an endless debate over what constituted "the one best system." Hinsdale warned, for example, that the schools should never replace the civilizing force of the home or the church and cautioned the public against undue expansion of the public schools. He also rejected vocational education as too specialized and limited to a too-small segment of the population for the common school. In 1914 William C. Bagley, a professor from the University of Illinois, told the National Education Association that separate vocational schools would create an undemocratic system of social stratification—too high a price to pay for "social efficiency." His colleagues did not heed his advice. By 1918 the Cleveland public schools enrolled 106,862 students in a wide variety of specialized schools and programs. Of the 9,619 high school students, 4,715 were in commercial-technical high schools. The school system had more than honored the previous request of Superintendent Rickoff for "a judicious modification"—the provision of an education for what educators thought was best suited to a student's capacity or ability.[51]

Despite the debate and conflicts over many of the changes in the Cleveland public schools between 1836 and 1920, educational reformers consistently upheld the common school as an equalizer of social condition. The faith in the school's ability to reduce social and economic divisions and to secure the greatest happiness of the greatest number became a major ideology of modern democratic life. It affirmed America's cherished belief in its commitment to individual freedom and equal opportunity within an open society.

A number of recent critics of public education have attacked this ideology as "a smoke screen" to hide either the need for structural reform or the role of the school as a perpetuator of the inequities of social class and race in America. Social scientists have also challenged the belief in the power of schooling to secure economic success or mobility. On the other hand, Cleveland's NAACP successfully filed a desegration suit in federal court in 1973 to achieve greater racial equality in the public schools. Since the 1960s community activists and advocates of alternative schooling have rejected the domination of schools by professional educators—no matter how enlightened. Even more radical are the proponents of "deschooling," the creation of learning opportunities outside the formal educational system.[52] This healthy and necessary debate continues "the search for the one best system."

JAMES F. RICHARDSON

Political Reform
in Cleveland

Peter Witt, Tom L. Johnson, and Newton D. Baker, Cleveland's foremost Progressive politicians

There may be a more ambiguous and potentially misleading term in the vocabulary of American historians than
reform; if there is it does not come readily to mind. For most historians,
reform conjures up positive associations of greater social justice, or a
better fit between political institutions and democratic principles, or at
least a more efficient and less haphazard method of conducting public
business. Marxist scholars reject such a set of associations; in their view
reform is a Band-Aid on the social cancer generated by capitalism, or
the illusion rather than the reality of positive change, or the manipulation of public policy by private groups to achieve goals of economic
order and stability not attainable through the private marketplace
alone.[1] Even non-Marxist historians, when they come to look on a case
by case basis at the causes and consequences, both intended and unin-
tended, of actions touted as reforms realize that many of them are
drenched in ambiguity. Different groups espouse the same cause for
quite different reasons, and the results of some actions cause many of
their original supporters heartburn. Still we use the word *reform* and
more often than not with positive connotations even when we know
better, just as students of *suburbs* think of low-density, single-family
residential areas when they hear the word even though they know that
suburbs come in many land use patterns.

For purposes of this essay, then, political reform should not be considered automatically a "good thing," but rather as proposals and actions of varying degrees of merit to change the structure and operations
of Cleveland's government. Much of what follows will concentrate on
structure because governmental structure—such as mayor-council
compared to council-manager, or ward versus at-large representation,
and partisan vs. nonpartisan elections—is important in deciding the
political issues of who gets what and who pays for it. A concentration
on structure also provides a convenient principle of selection in deal-

ing with such a potentially vast subject as political reform in a major city over a century within the confines of an essay.

As a municipal corporation, Cleveland, like every other American city, had to operate within the organizational and financial limits set by the state legislature. Until the adoption of the home rule amendment in 1912, the Ohio General Assembly could intervene in, transform, and restructure the city's governing arrangements virtually at will. The state's constitution of 1851 required that all laws relating to cities be general, that is, apply to all cities equally. But this provision proved unworkable, and until 1902 the courts permitted the legislature to adopt laws for different classes of cities and to establish classifications consisting sometimes of one city only.[2]

Under this dispensation, Cleveland received in 1891 a charter well-adapted to its needs and one quite different from that of Cincinnati. Cleveland's "federal charter" provided for a strong mayor in contrast to the independent boards and commissions of Cincinnati's form of government. This arrangement in Cleveland, a generally satisfactory one to public officials and private organizations with an interest in public affairs such as the Municipal Association, lasted until 1902 when the Ohio Supreme Court voided cities' charters as special legislation and insisted upon the adoption of a uniform municipal code. The Republican-dominated legislature, hostile to Cleveland's Democratic Mayor Tom L. Johnson, imposed the Cincinnati model upon all of the state's cities. Johnson confounded his enemies by winning election victories large enough to allow him to control these supposedly independent boards.[3]

In 1912 Cincinnati's Herbert Bigelow and other urban leaders succeeded in pushing through a home rule amendment to the state constitution which ended some of the egregious "ripper bills" that had come out of Columbus. Cleveland took advantage of the opportunity the following year to write its own charter under the leadership of Mayor Newton D. Baker. This instrument, which incorporated many of the popular innovations of the period, contained the initiative and the referendum and provided for nonpartisan elections. The commission thought seriously about at-large elections, a mode calculated to centralize decision making and raise the class level of council members, but decided to retain ward elections because of the city's ethnic and social diversity. (The census of 1910 showed that three-fourths of Cleveland's population was either born outside the United States or had at least one foreign-born parent.) Terms for mayor and council remained at two years under the new charter; Baker thought that frequent elections were useful because of the educational value of campaigns.[4] The level of campaigning then was much higher with more substantive discussion of the issues involved than is the case in our era of the television spot commercial.[5]

Although the state granted cities power to determine their own form of government, it kept them under tight financial control. Until 1910 Ohio reappraised property only every ten years, so that in the years between 1900 and 1909 the city received only limited benefit from the rapid rise in property values during that period. When reappraisal raised the city's tax duplicate, the total value of taxable property, from under $300,000,000 to more than $750,000,000, the state severely limited the amount of taxes the city could collect by the notorious Smith Act, which limited the total amount of taxation for all state, city, county, and school purposes to ten mills or 1 percent of appraised value. The voters by referendum could approve an additional five mills. The Smith Act was the product of a coalition of rural interests that could not understand cities' need for revenue, and of large urban taxpayers whose understanding was more than counterbalanced by their desire not to pay.[6]

The Smith Act crippled Cleveland's operating revenues, especially with the inflation accompanying World War I. By 1919 the city had accumulated seven million dollars in operating deficits, financed first by short-term notes and then by "Revenue Deficiency Bonds." Leaders in Cleveland, Cincinnati, and other Ohio cities banded together to secure financial relief. In this instance relief did not refer to intergovernmental transfer payments but rather to removing some of the state's shackles and allowing the cities to tax themselves adequately. The state did permit referenda on measures to increase the city's tax rates. In Cleveland a broad-based coalition secured the necessary positive votes in the fall of 1920 to alleviate the most serious of the city's financial woes.[7]

On other issues there was no such agreement. Cleveland politics in the early years of the century revolved around the struggles between Mayor Tom L. Johnson on one side and large taxpayers and the public service corporations, the so-called natural monopolies, on the other. Johnson, a self-made, and by 1900, wealthy businessman, proclaimed his mission as mayor to be ensuring that businesses and the wealthy paid their fair share of taxes and bringing utilities under municipal control. Unfortunately for the mayor, Ohio's constitution forbade municipal ownership, and state boards of equalization and the courts protected large taxpayers from increases in their assessments and rates.[8]

159

After a long and bitter struggle, in 1908 Johnson forced the street railway company to lease its property to a new company organized by the mayor and his associates. Although, under Ohio law, this new company had to be a corporation organized for profit, its intent, according to Johnson, was to secure the benefits of public ownership without the legal form. Its directors pledged to operate the traction system in the public interest and at lower fares. Johnson's dream came to naught the following year when his new company was forced into receivership. Under the compromise solution then reached in the Tayler Grant, Cleveland did have the benefits of a substantial amount of public control over the operation of the private company and the city did enjoy lower fares than other American cities.[9]

Even the editors of *Electric Railway Journal*, hostile to anything that smacked of public ownership, admitted that Clevelanders were satisfied with their streetcar service under the Tayler Grant. A more concrete form of evidence of satisfaction was the failure of the jitney movement to take root in Cleveland. Jitneys were automobiles operated by individual owners over fixed routes for a five-cent fare. They were widespread in American cities and provided severe competition for street railway companies. These companies and their political allies banded together to outlaw jitneys in other cities.[10]

Johnson and his associates conducted a tax school to demonstrate the reality and the effects of capricious assessments. His opponents were able to win a court judgment that the school was an unwarranted expenditure of public funds and brought the school to an end. Johnson also raised the assessments of public service corporations, especially of their personal property. The companies successfully appealed to the state board of equalization and had these increases rescinded. The courts held that the state board's action was not reviewable and that the board did not have to supply any rationale for its actions.[11]

Johnson's opponents dominated the chamber of commerce, an organization of business and professional men which exercised great influence over public policy. The chamber could command the time and attention of the most important people in the city. It also had the resources to produce well-researched and written reports and recommendations about important policy issues. The chamber was not always at odds with the mayor. It supported the group plan, Cleveland's version of a civic center, and it promoted improvements in public education, health, and the development of a modern housing code. Chamber leaders wished an orderly and efficient city, one that would be attractive to live and work in. So long as public policy proposals did not unduly threaten their private interests, they were willing to take a progressive view of the city's responsibilities. To this end they cooperated with urban professionals such as City Engineer Robert Hoffman and Health Director Robert Rockwood to increase the level of professional competence in these areas and to expand the scope of activities carried on by these departments. The chamber also supported such structural innovations as a more rational budget procedure. Yet, overall, the organization was more concerned with what was done rather than how. The chamber focused more on the substance of policy than on the form of municipal government and the niceties of procedural purity.[12]

The Municipal Association, subsequently known as the Civic League and still later, the Citizens League, was a more self-consciously good government group. It evaluated candidates for elective office on the basis of their formal educations and their presumed fitness for office, kept a close watch on payrolls to assure that the civil service laws were not being violated, and generally used its influence to weaken the power of the party organizations.[13]

After World War I, the Citizens League had a severe credibility problem with city officials since so many of its active members lived in the suburbs. Why, asked Cleveland politicians, should we pay attention to people who live in Shaker Heights and presume to tell Clevelanders how to manage their affairs? Some suburbanites objected that their fortunes were tied up with those of the city and that they should therefore have the right to vote on the city's form of government. Mayo Fesler, secretary of the organization both before World War I and after 1923, was a man with a strong belief in his righteousness and rightness. This characteristic did not always increase his or his organization's political effectiveness.[14]

Other private groups with an active interest in public policy included the League of Women Voters, a very active group from the 1920s on, the Association of Building Owners and Managers, whose prime concern was keeping the tax rate down, and the Board of Real Estate Dealers. The last group initiated the movement for a city manager charter for Cleveland in 1916.[15]

The city manager form was the prime panacea of structural reformers from 1913 on when Dayton, Ohio, adopted the innovation in the aftermath of a disastrous flood. In 1916 the National Municipal League, a nationwide organization interested in promoting the cause of honesty and efficiency in government, adopted the city manager form as part of its model municipal program. It was not enough to throw the rascals out and elect good men; rather a structure had to be created which would allow good people to function most effectively. The city manager would be the appointed expert whose task it would be to administer city services in the most efficient manner possible. The appointing body would be a small council elected on an at-large basis to minimize the parochial thinking common in a ward-based electoral system. At-large elections would also raise the class level of decision makers by assuring that successful candidates would have citywide reputations and, therefore, come from the ranks of executives of large organizations and major professionals rather than the skilled workers and small businessmen chosen from working-class and ethnic wards. The model was obviously the business corporation where a small and carefully selected board of directors chose the chief executive officer who would in turn appoint, promote, and transfer subordinates.[16]

The result, in Professor Frank Goodnow's famous phrase, would separate policymaking from administration. The council would make policy and the manager would carry it out without the constant intervention of ward council representatives seeking special favors for constituents and political followers. In this ideal world, administration would rest upon impersonal and universalistic criteria rather than on which council member could exercise the most pressure to get the streets in his ward cleaned first or whose protégé would receive the next promotion to captain in the police department.[17]

When Cleveland adopted a city manager form of government, it did not follow this model exactly, nor did the structural innovation yield the results expected. The discussions begun by the Board of Real Estate Dealers in 1916 for a city manager charter continued until 1917 when they were suspended because of the nation's entrance into World War I. When the war ended, the movement for a city manager resumed under the leadership of Peter Witt, a long-time gadfly of Cleveland politics and follower of Tom L. Johnson, and Professor A. R. Hatton of Western Reserve University. To the surprise of many local political leaders, the city manager charter was adopted in a referendum in the fall of 1921, to go into effect in January 1924.[18]

This charter did not provide for a small council elected at large. Instead, council would have twenty-five members elected via proportional representation from four districts with five to seven members each, depending upon population. This arrangement would escape the parochialism of wards while still giving some scope for the city's social diversity. It also preserved one historic cleavage, that between the East Side and the West Side, a division with deep roots in Cleveland's past and some of whose effects lingered well into the twentieth century and probably will still be found in the twenty-first. The smaller of the two, the West Side, formed one district, while the much larger East Side was divided into three districts, roughly near east, far east, and south. These districts were too large to be homogeneous; at the same time, they represented a rough ethnic and class division with the East End, the area around University Circle, as the most exclusive and expensive in the city although it was then in the process of losing its more affluent residents to the suburbs.[19]

The charter's proponents never achieved their goal of separating policymaking from administration. The leaders of the Cuyahoga County party organizations, Republican Maurice Maschke and Democrat Burr Gongwer, got together and arranged a satisfactory patronage split and agreed upon a single choice for manager, Republican W. R. Hopkins. As the majority party in Cleveland, the Republicans also received most of the city hall jobs.[20]

Through the rest of the 1920s the Citizens League praised Hopkins and attacked the organization leaders in council, especially Herman Finkle, the Republican floor leader and heir to the throne of "Czar" Harry Bernstein of old Ward Sixteen, a classic tribal chieftain of the late nineteenth and early twentieth century. Council members who were attorneys represented policemen under charges before the Civil Service Commission and in other less formal ways constantly intervened into the operations of the city's administrative departments. Hopkins, a promoter by nature and experience, devoted his time to big projects like the airport which now bears his name and the lakefront stadium rather than to the details of municipal housekeeping. In so doing, like many another manager, he became an advocate and not simply an executor of municipal policy.[21]

By 1930 the differences between Hopkins and Maschke had become irreconcilable, and the organization Republicans in council voted to remove the manager from office. Hopkins claimed that his offense had been to stand up for the city's rights in negotiations with East Ohio Gas and with the Van Sweringen Brothers, the promoters of the Terminal Tower office and hotel complex being built on the air rights over the new railroad station. Hopkins took advantage of the charter provision that a manager under fire was entitled to a written statement of charges and an opportunity to respond to those charges. The only one that had substantial merit was that Hopkins was insufficiently attuned to the wishes of council and unduly involved himself in the making of policy. Hopkins was more advocate than administrator as

163

even his supporters admitted, but this conception of his role probably indicated more the unworkability of Goodnow's separation of policy from administration than any malfeasance on his part. Columnist Jack Raper of the *Cleveland Press* thought Hopkins's regime notably corrupt. There were fraudulent land deals during his time in office but probably more attributable to crooked councilmen than to the manager. Others thought Hopkins's defense a more than adequate accounting of his stewardship. Hopkins may have had the arguments, but his opponents had the votes, and he was removed from office in January 1930. Council chose Daniel Morgan, a respected attorney and one time Republican member of council, as his replacement.[22]

Hopkins's removal and the fact that he went out with guns blazing provided considerable ammunition to those who wanted to return to an elected mayor. A key figure in this drive was Harry L. Davis, former mayor of Cleveland and governor of Ohio. Davis, whose political stock-in-trade was a warm smile and a friendly handshake, had earlier led unsuccessful referendum drives to end the city manager charter. He finally succeeded when a broad-based coalition of organization Democrats and anti-Maschke Republicans gained enough votes in 1931 to return to an elected mayor and a council of thirty-three members chosen by wards. Ironically, the first mayor elected under this new charter was Democrat Ray T. Miller, who had made a name for himself as county prosecutor by indicting and convicting Republican officeholders involved in the fraudulent land deals. Davis's turn came when he defeated Miller's bid for reelection in 1933.[23]

Many of the proponents of the city manager plan also supported some sort of metropolitan government. Before World War I this took the form of proposals to annex the suburbs to the central city. Annexation was responsible for much of Cleveland's growth in population in the late nineteenth and early twentieth centuries, but by 1910 the larger suburbs such as Lakewood and East Cleveland had developed to the point where they could provide their own services and had little interest in becoming part of Cleveland. Proponents within the city such as the chamber of commerce and the Citizens League stressed the importance of a larger population in making the nation conscious of Cleveland's greatness as well as the gains in efficiency that supposedly came from eliminating small political units and combining them into a greater city.[24]

After 1915, a massive migration of the affluent to the suburbs on the high ground south and east of Cleveland took place and changed the way many of Cleveland's leaders looked at the problem. The Chamber of Commerce Committee on Annexation, formed in 1916, changed its name to the Committee on Cooperative Metropolitan Government in 1924. By the mid-1920s its members talked about a dual form of metropolitan government that would reap some of the benefits of consolidation and at the same time preserve the independence of the suburbs and prevent their complete absorption into the city. They seemed most interested in preserving the quality of suburban schools and local control over land use to prevent the incursion of business and industry into their residential districts. Other services, less local and perhaps less sensitive, would be turned over to the consolidated government. The chamber of commerce and the *Plain Dealer* expressed interest in New York City's borough plan which consolidated some governmental functions and left others to local units. Another and more useful model was the London County Council, responsible for some functions over much of Greater London. Long-established cities and boroughs within the boundaries of the London County Council area continued to exist and provide specific services.[25]

By the mid-1920s there were active discussions between city officials and suburban and civic organizations about the possibility of a metropolitan government form that would not simply obliterate the suburbs. The major support for these proposals came from businessmen with their traditional interest in efficiency and economy rather than officeholders who feared change. The strongest objections came from suburban officials who did not want their positions eliminated or downgraded in a metropolitan reorganization.[26]

The gantlet that proponents had to negotiate was a particularly severe one. The first task was to secure an amendment to the Ohio Constitution that would make metropolitan government possible. Beginning in 1917 proponents led by Cleveland's Citizens League proposed such amendments every two years, only to see them defeated either in committee or on the floor in the legislature. Legislators from rural areas and small towns as well as those with ties to suburban politicians combined to defeat such efforts on the grounds that central city imperialism constituted an unacceptable threat. In the 1920s Ohio was an urban state whose legislature was still dominated by rural and small-town representatives organized into the Cornstalk Club. Robert A. Taft of suburban Cincinnati was the leader of the urban forces within the Ohio House of Representatives. He and other urban legislators also had to contend with Governor A. V. ("Veto Vic") Donahey of New Philadelphia. To overcome the resistance of rural interests, supporters of metropolitan government then sought alliances with the

Ohio State Grange and the Ohio Chamber of Commerce to neutralize their opposition.[27]

The amendment succeeded only when its backers forced a statewide referendum in 1933. Central cities and elite suburbs provided a disproportionate share of the affirmative votes, an indication of the association of structural innovation and central city business interests. However, the amendment was only the first step. Before metropolitan government could become a reality, voters within Cuyahoga County and its various subdivisions would have to agree to form a charter commission, choose a fifteen-member commission, and then approve the document the commission drafted.[28]

Each step in the process was more difficult than the one before it, especially since the courts decided that the final document had to be approved by a majority of the voters in a majority of the governmental units within the county as well as a majority of the voters of the county and the city of Cleveland. Opponents, organized into the Self-Government League of Cuyahoga County by Mayor Frank Cain of Cleveland Heights, took advantage of these structural rigidities to gain time and increase the level of resistance to possible domination of the suburbs by the city of Cleveland. These debates and campaigns took place during the most serious depression in American history, one in which the Cleveland area with its specialization in capital goods such as steel, automobiles, and machine tools suffered particularly harshly. The Depression both gave increased urgency to arguments on economy in government and increased fears about possible negative effects of change.[29]

The voters did approve the formation of a charter commission in 1934. Three slates of candidates came forth: one from Mayor Cain's group opposed to any substantial change; the second from the Citizens League committed to a thoroughgoing metropolitan reorganization; and the third led by Saul Danaceau and other members of the "Soviet Table" of the City Club. This last group was primarily concerned with protecting the interests of city residents in any reorganization scheme. Its members distrusted the Citizens League and other proponents of metropolitan government such as former mayor of Cleveland and Secretary of War Newton D. Baker. Danaceau and his friends had been leaders of the movement to abolish the city manager charter in Cleveland. They were afraid that the same elitist, antidemocratic groups behind the city manager plan were now supporting metropolitan government for much the same reason: to reduce the power of the majority of Cleveland's voters who were of ethnic social origin and blue-collar economic position.[30]

The election results showed that the commission would consist of thirteen people from the Citizens League group and two from the Danaceau slate. The commission's deliberations led the majority to back off from its original commitment to thoroughgoing reorganization of governmental functions within the metropolitan area and to settle instead for a restructuring of county government. The proposal abolished the existing county commissioners in favor of a legislative board and an elected county executive. Elected officials such as the sheriff and the coroner were to be replaced by administrators appointed by the county executive. At this stage, the Ohio Supreme Court ruled that this proposal constituted a change in the powers of local government and therefore required approval by each of the following: a majority in the county, a majority in the largest city, a majority in the county outside the city, and a majority of the existing units of local government. The proposal did secure a majority in the county as a whole, but it could not win the approval of most of the existing units of local government. On the whole the more affluent suburbs were most in favor of the innovation. Their residents responded most enthusiastically to the possibilities of greater economy and efficiency. Blue-collar areas and the least urbanized rejected it. Within the city itself there were also breakdowns along income and class lines with the higher income areas supporting change.[31]

After this failure to establish metropolitan government, proponents succeeded in again bringing the issue before the voters in 1949 and 1958. By the late 1950s, the professional and popular literature about the negative impacts of suburbanization and political fragmentation of metropolitan areas was reaching flood tide. The central theme of much of this writing was the gap between needs and resources within the central city which bore disproportionate burdens of cultural resources and poverty support for the metropolitan area as a whole. The central city had more than its share of the poor and had more of its land off the tax rolls for nonprofit organizations of various kinds.[32]

In the face of these fiscal trends, one would think that metropolitan government would have greater support within Cleveland than in any of the suburbs, and that the percentage of urban yes votes should rise over time. Such was not to be the case. Black voters especially rejected consolidation because of their fears that any chance they had for political power within the city would be eliminated by the white suburban majority. Proposals for metropolitan government in southern cities received much white support for precisely this reason. Some white ethnic political leaders such as Ralph Locher and Frank Lausche also opposed metro government. In contrast, some of the same affluent suburban areas which had supported the notion in the 1930s continued to do so in the 1950s, but not enough to see it adopted.[33]

In recent decades the ideal of dual level metropolitan government modeled on the London County Council or comprehensive integration has given way to a number of single service districts which encompass the entire metropolitan area. Unfortunately, the Regional Transit Authority and other such bodies are not really responsible to anyone except themselves. Moreover, while such agencies may provide coordination within the limits of their service mandate, this does not mean that they will cooperate in any effective way with other single service agencies. Single service metropolitan districts may rearrange but they do not eliminate the problem of governmental fragmentation. In effect they substitute functional fragmentation for a geographical fragmentation.[34]

If metropolitan government proved unattainable, there was still the possibility of making Cleveland's municipal government more efficient. A perennial issue among structural reformers was the size and mode of election of city councils. In unreformed cities, councils were large and elected by wards. As previously noted, the city manager system almost invariably involved a small council elected at-large on a nonpartisan ballot. Cleveland had not followed this model during its city manager years, and in 1931 when the city reverted to an elected mayor, its revised charter called for a council of thirty-three members elected by wards. Cleveland's council subsequently acquired an unenviable reputation as one which was not only large but also highly contentious and where the operative principle was "what have you done for me lately?"[35]

It was not until 1981 that reformers led by the League of Women Voters succeeded in reducing the size of council from thirty-three to twenty-one members. This last attempt came only after at least ten previous tries. Those who pressed for reduction made the same case about parochialism and limited capacity as had their predecessors three-quarters of a century before. Members of council elected from small wards were likely to be small-minded with limited knowledge and understanding of how city government worked. Most lacked the capacity and the desire to initiate and lead and were, therefore, passive followers and reactors rather than leaders.[36]

POLITICAL REFORM

After 1950 two new arguments or considerations came to the fore. The first was population decline. Between 1950 and 1980 Cleveland suffered a net loss of more than three hundred thousand people, from more than nine hundred thousand counted in the census of 1950 to less than six hundred thousand in that of 1980. In 1950 each member of council represented more than twenty-seven thousand people; in 1980 the comparable figure was only about seventeen thousand. This drop in the number of constituents per representative coincided with a serious financial situation for the city. In 1978 Cleveland was in the unenviable position of being in default. Inflation drove the city's costs up relentlessly whereas its revenues remained virtually stationary. Under the circumstances a case could easily be made for reducing the size and, therefore, the cost of council.[37]

But cost was a less important consideration than race. Like other central cities, Cleveland had a rapid rise in the proportion of its total population classified as black. Early in the twentieth century, Cleveland was thought to be a relatively enlightened community on racial matters although it was by no means a paradise for blacks even then. After World War I racial animosity and segregation intensified, ironically enough under New Deal-supported public housing projects, as well as the private real estate market. Since the 1950s, race has been the most serious source of division within the city's political life, and any proposal for change was sure to be scrutinized closely for its racial implications. This was especially the case when Carl Stokes was mayor and later when George Forbes became president of city council. Both Stokes and Forbes are black attorneys. In Cleveland as in other American cities, the power of the party organizations has diminished in recent decades. Strategically placed officeholders, whether elected or appointed, have moved into the power vacuum. In the 1920s it seems as though Herman Finkle's power derived from his position in the Republican party organization; in the 1970s James Stanton's or George Forbes's importance stemmed from the office of council president, not from close ties to the Democratic party leadership.[38]

In the opinion of those who wanted a reduction in council size, most council members followed George Forbes's lead rather than that of the mayor, whoever he might be. Yet the theory of mayor-council government presumed that it would be the mayor, the only city official elected by and answerable to a citywide constituency, who would set the agenda for public policy and submit proposals for council action. Yet mayors such as Carl Stokes found that getting a majority of thirty-three council members to approve any initiative was an excruciatingly difficult task, especially if the president of city council refused to go along.[39]

The case for reduction was thus a strong one. Its success, however, was not a foregone conclusion. Racial arguments were common at every campaign for reduction from fears of a black majority if council were smaller to concerns that a particular ethnic group might lose its representative with larger ward boundaries. It took a concerted effort by the League of Women Voters, the daily newspapers, and the Democratic party organization to overcome the resistance of Forbes and other blacks who feared that a smaller council would reduce rather than increase black political power. And, as in every change in the numbers of representatives, the question of new district boundaries was vital to incumbents, aspirants, and groups interested in whether or not they could elect one of their own to council.[40]

Although Forbes did not succeed in blocking reduction, he did draw the new ward boundaries in such a way as to reward his friends and punish his enemies, especially Councilman John Lynch, one of the leaders of the reduction drive. These new boundaries were especially significant in that the council elected in 1981 would serve for four years in contrast to the two-year terms that had long been the norm in Cleveland. In 1913 Newton D. Baker could defend frequent elections for their educational value in that campaigns kept voters abreast of issues, policies, and alternatives. In more recent decades, the costs of short terms and frequent elections seemed clearly to overshadow the benefits. However, it was not until 1980 that groups favoring change could overcome the forces of inertia and the status quo.[41]

This discussion has concentrated on structure of government because it is not only important in itself but also because of the clues that it gives to some of the persistent cleavages in the city's political life. Centralizers have usually stressed the interdependent nature of the city's economy and have seen all parts as constituent elements of a whole that should be dominated by leading business and professional people who alone are capable of understanding the intricate working of the metropolitan system and what it needs to function efficiently. At the same time, most have left the city's boundaries to enjoy homogeneous schools and tight suburban zoning. Within the city they wish the values of professionalism and expertise to prevail and hope for a corps of public servants committed to scientific rationality and sensitive to the needs of major businesses.[42]

Supporters of local autonomy and representation, on the other hand, view their neighborhoods and their own groups as the focal points of their lives and fear that a public policy directed toward the needs of downtown business means socialism for the wealthy and private enterprise for themselves. Even before Cleveland had a substantial black population, it was something of a divided city. In the late nineteenth and early twentieth centuries, Cleveland's business leadership came disproportionately from old stock Americans, many of them of New England origin and proud of it. For many years the Western Reserve Historical Society served as an institutional focal point for this group. As previously mentioned, in 1910, three-fourths of Cleveland's population was either born outside the United States or had at least one foreign-born parent. For much of the first half of the twentieth century, Cleveland could be described with considerable justification as a series of ethnic villages.[43]

As old stock descendants moved to the suburbs and new stock people came to the fore politically, the city's business and professional leadership differed substantially from the majority of its political officeholders. To a considerable degree such a split had existed even before 1910. In 1903, for example, the members of the council played baseball with one team consisting of "the Irish" and the other "the Germans." Insofar as surnames can be trusted, these designations did fit most of the players. The new immigrants and their offspring seemed even more removed from the cultural and social backgrounds of the private sector elite. Both groups did share a low tax ideology and a basic conservatism about the permissible extent of public activity. Where they differed was on whether government should be sensitive to neighborhood and ethnic group concerns or whether it should be universalistic and centralized.[44]

The combination of Ohio's financial limitations on cities, the distress Cleveland suffered during the Depression of the 1930s, the low tax mentality of the city, and the wariness with which business and political leadership viewed each other meant a series of administrations from the 1930s to the early 1960s best described as "caretaker." By the 1960s the trends of an increasing black presence in the city and a substantial loss of population and business to the suburbs had reached the point where the Cleveland metropolitan area fit the model posited by the Kerner Commission of a bifurcated society, separate and unequal, with an increasingly poor and black central city ringed by white suburbs of varying degrees of affluence. The election in 1967 of Carl Stokes as mayor of Cleveland was thought by some to herald a new day for the city.[45]

For a time at least it looked as if Stokes would be able to put together a coalition of downtown business and blacks that could arrest the decay of the city and perhaps promote its revitalization. Whatever prospect this scenario had came to a violent end the following year in the shoot-out at Glenville when seven people died in a gun battle between black militants and Cleveland police. In 1971 Stokes gave way to yet another caretaker, Republican Ralph Perk. Meanwhile, as the city's economic base eroded even more rapidly in the 1970s, a young self-styled urban populist, Dennis Kucinich, came to the fore as the enfant terrible of Cleveland City Council. Kucinich succeeded in winning the mayoralty in 1977 under the banner of a champion of the neighborhoods against downtown business. Kucinich was harshly critical of tax abatements and other inducements to the private sector to build or rebuild in Cleveland. In his view such concessions meant more costs than benefits for small taxpayers within the city who would in effect be subsidizing a higher rate of return for some businesses. Kucinich, only thirty-one when he was elected, coupled this by no means unreasonable position with an arrogant and confrontational style that was more than matched by many of his even younger aides. He barely survived a recall attempt after only one year in office, and there was general relief among the business community when his term ended and he was defeated by Republican George Voinovich in 1979.[46]

Cleveland's politics are much calmer under Voinovich and there seems to be a high level of cooperation between the public and the private sector to try to arrest the city's economic decline. In contrast to the heady days of Tom Johnson and Newton Baker when it seemed as if Cleveland's growth would continue indefinitely and that it had the opportunity to be a city on a hill, its leaders now concentrate on trying to keep the city afloat and maintaining basic services. ''Reform'' in a traditional sense now seems less important than survival, not the most exalted of aspirations but perhaps the most one can expect in this difficult time for older industrial cities.

DAVID D. VAN TASSEL
and
JOHN J. GRABOWSKI

Epilogue:
The Reform Tradition
Challenged, 1960–1980

Typical backyard in the lower Woodland Avenue neighborhood served by Hiram House social settlement, ca. 1905

We could not conclude this book about reform and its tradition in Cleveland without some mention of what has happened during the last two decades. While there are many opinions for these years, few are expert. Some writing exists, but little research, so what we offer here is an epilogue, an afterword—our observations based in part on experience, some our own, some that of others, as well as random reading in newspapers, documents and memoirs. There is much research and writing to be done before anyone fully understands the nature of the steady erosion of the promise of the era of Tom Johnson, moving ineluctably through the 1950s, coming to a heartening but temporary halt in the early 1960s, only to increase in pace, leading to destructive violence and bitterness, and leveling off into a slough of despond and finally bankruptcy default) in the 1970s. The tangible evidence of this erosion was nowhere more apparent or more dramatic than as one traveled over space and through time eastward from Public Square along Euclid Avenue.

During the late 1800s, Euclid Avenue was Cleveland's most fashionable street, comparable, said flattering foreign visitors and boasting guide books, to the Champs-Élysées or Unter den Linden. Many of the city's elite, both old-family and nouveau riche, maintained their residences on the avenue. Less than a century later, Euclid Avenue looked more like a back alley than a boulevard; the magnificent homes were gone, replaced by businesses—many of them abandoned—and by empty lots. The old families were also gone, having moved to suburban areas east of the city or out of the region altogether. A city of slogans, Cleveland now seemed to have only vitriolic messages crudely painted on billboards by Winston Willis, a black businessman. Waging verbal war with the city's white establishment, Willis's signs at East 105th and Euclid underlined the divisiveness in the city and appeared to be a sorry but inevitable epitaph to the glory that was once Euclid Avenue.

The street was a symbol of the general malady. Once the sixth largest city in America, Cleveland did not fall within even the top ten by 1980. Between 1950 and 1980, the city lost over three hundred thousand people. Those who remained included few, if any, "first families." Even the white immigrant tide had subsided. By 1980 almost half of the city's population was black, while substantial portions of the remainder were composed of Hispanic or Appalachian stock.

Industry, along with the people, departed the city. Faced with obsolete facilities and expensive union labor, many companies closed or moved to the sunbelt. Others moved to the interstate highway interchanges in the suburbs surrounding the city. Familiar and important names, such as Grabler, the American Stove Company, and W. S. Tyler disappeared.

The effect of these changes on the city's reform tradition seemed marked. Certainly, the failure of an efficient, ordered industrial economic system would have repercussions for any social or reform system based on its model.

Nowhere did this failure loom as enormous as in the area of race relations. Any promises perceived by the city's black community during the 1940s had vanished by the 1960s. While many white suburban areas prospered in the economic growth which accompanied the Vietnam era, inner-city blacks remained without jobs and, most importantly, without the reality of equality promised some twenty years earlier. Even public housing, the city's shining reform of the 1930s, had evolved into a series of crime-ridden miniature ghettos some three decades later. Despairing of white solutions and white role models, many blacks sought their own answers. A few Cleveland blacks followed radical nationalist leaders such as Fred Ahmed Evans, while others pursued change through more established bodies such as the Urban League and NAACP. Change did not come quickly enough and rioters savaged the city's Hough and Glenville neighborhoods in 1966 and 1968. Even the mayoralty of Carl Stokes, a black, could not prevent the troubles in Glenville.

If the black community inherited the city, it also inherited its schools. By the 1960s the vaunted Cleveland Public School system was in decline. Efforts to build new structures in the mid-1960s elicited protest from the black community which perceived the construction as an effort to strengthen a system of de facto segregation. Both black and white protestors staged sit-ins in the halls of the school board administration building and pickets attempted to block construction at several sites. In one instance a bulldozer accidentally backed over and killed a protestor, a white clergyman, Bruce Klunder. In 1979 the federal courts found the school system segregated and imposed bussing in an effort to alleviate the condition. The bussing was met by white flight from the public schools and administrative chaos at the board of education. Plagued by internal dissension, discipline problems, and recurrent teachers' strikes, the Cleveland schools were farther from becoming "the one best system" than they had been in several decades.

Cleveland's problems were shared by many other aging cities in the industrial East and Midwest. And Cleveland, like those cities. sought help from the state and federal governments. This was a far cry from the situation some fifty years earlier. During the 1920s, the city met all of its welfare needs from the private donations solicited by the Community Chest and distributed by the Welfare Federation. Overwhelmed by the Depression, the city sought nonlocal aid through various New Deal programs. By the time of the Great Society, Cleveland's fate seemed more in the hands of legislators in Columbus and Washington than in those of its own citizens and leaders. Federal and state monies assisted education, minority business ventures, neighborhood redevelopment, women's organizations, and other reform-oriented projects or agencies whose support was once strictly the purview of private, local initiative. In what appeared to be the ultimate irony, the state of Ohio took over the Euclid Avenue mansion of Samuel Mather as a part of the new Cleveland State University complex. Though Mather, the grand old man of Cleveland industry and philanthropy, had died some thirty years earlier, the action appeared to herald the end of a laissez-faire, evangelical tradition which dated back to Mather's colonial forebears.

To the casual observer, it seemed that the tradition of reform in Cleveland had been shattered by the exigencies of demographic change, industrial decline, and creeping federalism. A closer examination of the city would have revealed that though the dollars came from different sources, the plans and programs for the city's future and the necessary changes in its structure still emanated largely from a corps of old family and business elite. Residences may have been moved to Hunting Valley or Waite Hill, but the residents still retained an interest in and concern for the city.

In the field of education, it seemed to many that Governor James Rhodes's investment in Cleveland State University and the federal judiciary's interest in the public schools marked the cutting edge of educational change in the 1960s and the 1970s. However, the most significant changes in the educational system during this period emanated from the Commission on Higher Education. Chaired by Ralph M. Besse, head of the Cleveland Electric Illuminating Company, the commission laid the foundations for the community college movement in the Greater Cleveland area. Whereas Central High School may have been viewed as the foremost educational innovation of the 1850s, the two-year colleges may well be viewed in the same sense in years to come. Though these institutions, including Cuyahoga Community College, are publicly funded, their governing boards, as are the boards of major private institutions such as Case Western Reserve University, are still filled with dozens of the city's most prominent citizens. The names Otis and Mather may be missing, but they have been replaced by Haddens, Fords, and others who have always viewed community service as a duty.

While public monies, for welfare, day-care, and neighborhood centers poured in from Washington and Columbus, they were met, but not matched by a growing supply of private funds solicited by the city's United Way campaign. Descendant of the Community Chest, the United Way of Cleveland has continually elicited the highest per capita donation of any city in the United States. Annual campaigns have always been headed by a prominent businessman or woman and much of the promotional work in the campaigns has been undertaken by "loaned" business executives.

The social service agencies, health care organizations, and other community organizations which have received the United Way's largess, as well as that of the state and federal governments, have continued to be governed by local interests. It is at the board level that the tradition of reform is still most evident. While the boards of the Federation for Community Planning, Hiram House, and the Goodrich-Gannet Center have lost their exclusivity, they still have attracted and retained members from some of the city's most prominent families. For these board members service has been and is a social obligation. Their new peers who have often represented new money and the most promising members of a variety of racial and ethnic groups have tended to view their services somewhat differently. For them the duty is as much a social reward as it is an opportunity to chart the destiny of an organization or a cause. For the more traditional board members, the duties being performed may well have lost a direct psychic link to the Protes-

177

tant tradition—that connection having long since been blurred by an increasingly secular world—but the service is still more of an obligation than it is a reward.

The tradition of reform continued not only in older established organizations or movements, but penetrated and tamed newer ones. The Free Clinic of Cleveland, a product of the "dropout" and drug culture of the 1960s and 1970s grew to be an accepted community organization by the late 1970s, its respectability having been molded by wealthy donors and board members. The clinic, conceived in that era of acid rock, was by 1981 holding fund-raising marathons on the city's classical music radio station, WCLV.

Similar "radical" movements or organizations, including abortion rights, the alternative schools, and the women's movement have been boosted to respectability by the money and interest of the elite and well-to-do. Gwill York, a resident of the city's posh eastern suburbs, charted the course of the city's activities during the International Women's Year, assisted in her efforts by a variety of professional women as well as ardent feminists.

If reform is accepted generally as change and if the primary agent of change in the United States is conceded to be its political system, then it is the recent political history of Cleveland which must bear final witness to any continuation of a tradition of reform in the city. During the past three decades the city's mayors have seemed to reflect every hue of the racial and ethnic spectrum, except white Anglo-Saxon Protestant. Its city council has shown similar characteristics. Yet it is evident that the city's political life has been a coalition effort carried on by its elected representatives in concert with the leaders of the area's business and society. The presence and necessity of this coalition was proved by its absence during the administration of Mayor Dennis J. Kucinich.

Kucinich wished to model his mayoralty after that of Tom L. Johnson, the city's premier reform mayor. Like Johnson he appealed to the common man, traveling to neighborhoods and speaking before rallies attended by blue-collar workers and union officials. And like Johnson, he fought monopolistic practices and special interest groups. However, unlike Johnson, he seemed unable to comprehend that the city existed as a delicate balance of labor and business and order and change. Johnson, a millionaire turned reformer, realized that while he might joust with the business community and established interests in the city, he could not afford to alienate them entirely. Kucinich did not accept compromise and thus drove his adversaries to abandon him, and temporarily, the city he governed. The resulting chaos allowed the city to slip into default and eroded the mayor's populist support to the point where the citizenry almost succeeded in removing him from office through a recall petition.

All of this does not, of course, prove that a coterie of established interests governs the city's destiny with the same effectiveness it did some fifty years ago. It does, however, indicate that ordered change and a sense of service to humanity and society still bear upon the history of Cleveland, Ohio.

Notes

ABBREVIATIONS USED IN NOTES

Annals   U.S., Work Projects Administration, Ohio, *Annals of Cleveland* (Cleveland: WPA, 1936–38)
CWRU   Case Western Reserve University
DTD   *Daily True Democrat*
HG   *Cleveland Herald and Gazette*
Herald   *Cleveland Herald*
K & P   *Knight and Parson's Business Directory of the City of Cleveland* (Cleveland: E. G. Knight and Co., and Parsons and Co., 1853)
Leader   Cleveland Leader
PD   Cleveland Plain Dealer
WRHS   Western Reserve Historical Society
Whig   *Cleveland Whig and Herald*

Introduction: Cleveland and Reform

1. Lincoln Steffens, *The Struggle for Self-Government* (New York: McClure, Phillips & Co., 1906), 183. There is very little of either a general or specific nature in scholarly work on reform movements in Cleveland that is not already cited by the authors in various chapters of this book. However, one should mention Hoyt Landon Warner's *Progressivism in Ohio, 1897–1917* (Columbus: Ohio State Univ. Press, 1964), a basic, insightful and thorough study of the Progressive movement in this state. A splendid piece of scholarly research and interesting writing is Professor Robert A. Wheeler's monograph, *Pleasantly Situated on the West Side* (Cleveland: Western Reserve Historical Society, 1980). Produced for the catalog to the inaugural exhibition (Oct. 5, 1979, through Aug. 17, 1980) at the Nelson A. Sanford House of the Western Reserve Historical Society, the work consists of an introductory essay on the economic and social history of the Ohio City area. Wheeler does a great deal in a relatively short essay to illustrate early Cleveland's—or, more correctly, Ohio City's—attempts to meet the problems of a growing urban area, not only in terms of bridge building and communication, but also in health, police, and fire services. Kenneth Kusmer's *A Ghetto Takes*

NOTES

Shape: Black Cleveland, 1870–1930 (Urbana: Univ. of Illinois Press, 1976), and Josef Barton's *Peasants and Strangers: Italians, Rumanians, and Slovaks in an American City, 1870–1890* (Cambridge: Harvard Univ. Press, 1975), both deal essentially with the roots of ethnic and social problems which are central to the reformer. There are also many unpublished doctoral dissertations and master's theses in the libraries of Case Western Reserve University and Kent State University dealing with specific reforms and/or reformers. Many of these are cited in the essays in this work. Articles have appeared from time to time in *Ohio History* and the *Western Reserve Magazine* which deal with reform in Cleveland. There is much yet to be done in this area of research for the city of Cleveland; for example, there has been no thorough study of the administration of Cleveland mayor Tom L. Johnson that might be compared to Zane Miller's excellent book, *Boss Cox's Cincinnati: Urban Politics in the Progressive Era* (New York: Oxford Univ. Press, 1969).

2. All population statistics are taken from William Ganson Rose, *Cleveland: The Making of a City* (Cleveland: The World Publishing Co., 1950). Rose's book considers the city's history up to 1946 and is, as of this writing, the most recent general reference work for the history of Cleveland.

3. James Beaumont Whipple, "Cleveland in Conflict: A Study in Urban Adolescence, 1876–1900" (Ph.D. diss., Western Reserve University, 1951), provides an excellent overview of the changes that affected Cleveland in the late nineteenth century. Kusmer, *Ghetto*, is the definitive study of the major period of growth for the city's black community.

4. Ronald Walters, *American Reformers, 1815–1860* (New York: Hill and Wang, 1978), 12.

5. Frederick C. Howe, *The Confessions of a Reformer* (New York: Charles Scribner's Sons, 1925), 17.

6. Thomas A. Johnson, "Special Introduction," in Louis H. Masotti and Jerome R. Corsi, *Shoot-Out in Cleveland, Report to the National Commission on the Causes and Prevention of Violence* (New York: Bantam Books, 1969), vi.

7. The slogans quoted in this paragraph were popular from the 1950s to the 1970s and were used either by business and government to promote the city or by its detractors to make light of its problems.

Leading Men, True Women, Protestant Churches, and the Shape of Antebellum Benevolence

The author wishes to thank Kim Cahaus, Laura Darcy, Louise Boston Mayerik, Ed McNeeley, Janice Tobin, Jackie Warren, and Lorraine Zimmer for their help with data entry, record linkage, and computer programming.

1. *K & P*, 17; *Whig*, July 21, 1847, p. 1 (*Annals* 1847: 63).

2. *Forest City Democrat*, Jan. 26, 1854, p. 3 (*Annals* 1854: 46); *PD*, Jan. 24, 1857, p. 2.

3. For examples of individual and ad hoc benevolence throughout the antebellum years, see *PD*, Nov. 5, 1852, p. 3, Nov. 24, 1852, p. 2, Oct. 14, 1853, p. 3, Oct. 8, 1857, p. 3; *DTD*, May 28, 1853, p. 1 (*Annals* 1853: 537), Aug. 1, 1853, p. 2 (*Annals* 1853: 538); *Leader*, Sept. 18, 1855, p. 3 (*Annals* 1855: 680), Feb. 19, 1858, p. 3 (*Annals* 1858: 592), Oct. 28, 1858, p. 2 (*Annals* 1858: 594); and *Herald*, Dec. 20, 1842, p. 2 (*Annals* 1842: 445).

NOTES

Recent work in urban and local history has highlighted the public contribution to benevolence and the overlapping participation of local authorities and private societies: Priscilla Ferguson Clement, "The Response to Need, Welfare and Poverty in Philadelphia, 1800 to 1850" (Ph.D. diss., University of Pennsylvania, 1977), 21, 38–40, 98–99, 145–49, 193–95, 253; Irwin F. Flack, "Who Governed Cincinnati? A Comparative Analysis of Government and Social Structure in a Nineteenth Century River City: 1819–1860" (Ph.D. diss., University of Pittsburgh, 1978), 168, 186, 192, 198; Paul S. Boyer, *Urban Masses and Moral Order in America* (Cambridge: Harvard Univ. Press, 1978), 65, 132–37; Kathleen D. McCarthy, *Noblesse Oblige: Charity and Philanthropy in Chicago, 1849–1929* (Chicago: Univ. of Chicago Press, 1982), 3–96; and Raymond A. Mohl, *Poverty in New York, 1783–1825* (New York: Oxford Univ. Press, 1971).

4. *PD*, Dec. 2, 1856, p. 3, and Dec. 24, 1856, p. 3.

5. First Presbyterian Church, Record, 1837–49, First Presbyterian Church, Cleveland, July 19, 1837.

6. Cleveland Centennial Commission, *History of the Charities of Cleveland: 1796–1896* (Cleveland: Cleveland Centennial Commission, 1896), 15; *PD*, Nov. 9, 1847, p. 3. The "Martha Washington" of the society's name suggested it would be the counterpart of the Washington temperance societies then being formed in the East; the "Dorcas" was for the biblical woman who aided the sick and was "full of good works and charity." Dorcas, from the Greek, or Tabitha in the Aramaic, was a disciple at Joppa who was brought back to life by Peter (Acts 9:36–43) and who was known for making coats and garments. Thus female charitable and sewing societies took the name "Dorcas."

7. *PD*, Nov. 9, 1847, p. 3.

8. *DTD*, Dec. 4, 1850, p. 2 (*Annals* 1850: 464–65).

9. Catharine Lyon quoted by Mary Ingham, *Women of Cleveland and Their Work: Philanthropic, Educational, Literary, Medical and Artistic* (Cleveland, 1893), 105, 106–7, 111; *DTD*, Dec. 4, 1850, p. 2 (*Annals* 1850: 464–65); *PD*, Nov. 17, 1849, p. 3.

10. The quote of the Episcopal minister is from Thomas Starkey, *A Sermon in Behalf of Trinity Church Home, 1860, also The Annual Report of the Managers* (Cleveland: Nevins, Plain Dealer, 1860), 17, emphasis in original. See also *PD*, Jan. 20, 1855, p. 2, Dec. 16, 1857, p. 3, and Feb. 18, 1859, p. 3; *DTD*, Dec. 24, 1850, p. 2, and Dec. 20, 1850, p. 2 (*Annals* 1850: 465–66); *Leader*, Dec. 7, 1854, p. 3 (*Annals* 1854: 466); Rector [James A. Bolles], Trinity Episcopal Church, *Fourth Annual Report and Pastoral Letter* (Cleveland: Fairbanks, Benedict and Co., 1858), 9; Cleveland Orphan Asylum, *Ninth Annual Report of the Board of Managers* (Cleveland: Fairbanks, Benedict and Co., 1861), 6.

11. *DTD*, Dec. 28, 1850, p. 2 (*Annals* 1850: 466); *PD*, Dec. 20, 1851, p. 2, Dec. 16, 1851, p. 2, and Dec. 31, 1852, p. 3.

12. *PD*, June 19, 1857, p. 3. In the winter of 1858–59, the Sons of Malta distributed $2,000 in aid: *PD*, Sept. 22, 1859, p. 3, Feb. 3, 1859, p. 3, and Apr. 11, 1859, p. 3; Centennial Commission, *History of the Charities*, 78; *J. H. Williston and Co.'s Directory of the City of Cleveland* (Cleveland: J. H. Williston and Co., 1859–60), 28.

13. Euclid Street Presbyterian Church, Records, 1853–70, Church of the Covenant, Cleveland, Jan. 3, 1859, Jan. 14, 1859; Euclid Presbyterian, Missionary Record, 1859, Church of the Covenant, Cleveland.

14. H. C. Luce, "Report of January 1861," Euclid Presbyterian, Missionary Record.

15. Euclid Presbyterian, Missionary Record, Nov. 30, 1859; Luce, "Report."

16. *PD*, Dec. 31, 1852, p. 3, emphasis in original.

17. Luce, "Report." The paragraph which contained Luce's observation that those who were most able were not the most willing has "OMIT" written over it. Whether this represented second thoughts of Luce or a contemporary, or perhaps of a later church member, is not clear.

18. *DTD*, Dec. 20, 1850, p. 2 (*Annals* 1850: 465).

19. Cleveland, Ohio, Common (City) Council, "Act of Incorporation," Mar. 1836, Sec. 13 in *Charters of the Village of Cleveland, and the City of Cleveland, with Their Several Amendments: To Which Are Added the Laws and Ordinances of the City of Cleveland* (Cleveland: Sanford and Co., 1842), 33; Centennial Commission, *History of the Charities*, 9; Clara Anne Kaiser, "Organized Social Work in Cleveland, Its History and Setting" (Ph.D. diss., Ohio State University, 1936), 90; Samuel P. Orth, *A History of Cleveland, Ohio*, vol. 1 (Chicago and Cleveland: S. J. Clarke Publishing Co., 1910), 403; *HG*, June 4, 1838, p. 2 (*Annals* 1838: 356), Apr. 27, 1838, p. 2 (*Annals* 1838: 49), May 9, 1838, p. 2 (*Annals* 1838: 53), July 26, 1838, p. 2 (*Annals* 1838: 59); *Herald*, Mar. 31, 1841, p. 3 (*Annals* 1841: 255).

20. Kaiser, "Organized Social Work," 91, 403; Cleveland, Ohio, City Council, *Charters of the Village of Cleveland, and the City of Cleveland, with Their Several Amendments: To Which Are Added the Laws and Ordinances of the City of Cleveland* (Cleveland: Harris, Fairbanks and Co., 1851), 47; *PD*, Mar. 22, 1849, p. 2.

21. Cleveland, Ohio, City Council, *The Acts to Provide for the Organization of Cities and Villages, and the Revised Ordinances of the City of Cleveland* (Cleveland: Plain Dealer, 1862), Jan. 10, 1856, pp. 159, 160. A committee appointed by the city council in 1855 recommended changes to correct lack of coordination and loose management; *PD*, Mar. 9, 1855, p. 2.

22. *Leader*, June 12, 1856, p. 3 (*Annals* 1856: 27–28); *DTD*, Jan. 18, 1850, p. 2 (*Annals* 1850: 29). For other expressions of concern about abandoned and ill-disciplined children see *Annals* listings under "Juvenile Delinquency," including *Annals* 1855: 24–25; *Whig*, Sept. 29, 1847, p. 1 (*Annals* 1847: 99); and *Leader*, Jan. 16, 1855, p. 3 (*Annals* 1855: 24).

23. James Leiby, *A History of Social Welfare and Social Work in the United States* (New York: Columbia Univ. Press, 1978), uses the phrase "urban Huckleberry Finns." The Ragged School established by the First Methodist Church is not to be confused with the public elementary school often called the "ragged school" (see the essay by Edward M. Miggins in this collection).

24. For the Catholic orphan asylums, see George F. Houck, *A History of Catholicity in Northern Ohio and in the Diocese of Cleveland from 1749 to December 31, 1900* (Cleveland: J. B. Savage, 1903), vol. 1, pp. 60, 82, 740–44; Michael J. Hynes, *History of the Diocese of Cleveland: Origin and Growth (1847–1952)* (Cleveland: Diocese of Cleveland, 1953), 90–92; and John O'Grady, *Catholic Charities in the United States* (1931; rpt. New York: Arno Press, 1971), 86, 388. The founding of the Cleveland Orphan Asylum is described by Ingham, *Women of Cleveland*, 106, and Centennial Commission, *History of the Charities*, 35. The institution changed its name to the Cleveland Protestant Orphan Asylum in 1875. Cleveland Industrial School, *Annual Report of the Superintendent, 1858* (Cleveland: Fairbanks, Benedict and Co., 1859), 6, gives the account of the Ragged School's children. For the House of Correction, see

Leader, Mar. 1, 1855, p. 3 (*Annals* 1855: 216), and Robert M. Mennel, " 'The Family System of Common Farmers': The Early Years of Ohio's Reform Farm, 1858–1884," *Ohio History* 89 (Summer 1980): 281.

25. Cleveland Orphan Asylum, *Report of the Board of Managers* (Cleveland: Fairbanks, Benedict and Co., 1859), 9, and *Eighth Annual Report of the Board of Managers* (Cleveland: Fairbanks, Benedict and Co., 1860), 7; *PD*, Mar. 13, 1855, p. 2; *Leader*, Nov. 25, 1857, p. 3 (*Annals* 1857: 388); Cleveland Orphan Asylum, *Ninth Annual Report*, 6.

26. Centennial Commission, *History of the Charities*, 26–27; *PD*, Dec. 27, 1856, p. 3; *Leader*, Dec. 17, 1856, p. 3, Dec. 18, 1856, p. 3, Dec. 24, 1856, p. 3, Dec. 25, 1856, p. 1, all in *Annals* 1856: 532–33.

27. First Methodist Church, *First Methodist Episcopal Church of Cleveland, Ohio, 1827–1884* (Cleveland: J. B. Savage, 1884), 26–27; Orth, *History of Cleveland*, 403; Centennial Commission, *History of the Charities*, 26; *Annals* 1857: 387–88; Cleveland Industrial School and Children's Aid Society, *Annual Report of the Superintendent, 1859* (Cleveland: Fairbanks, Benedict and Co., 1860), 27; *PD*, May 31, 1858, p. 3; *Leader*, Oct. 31, 1860, p. 1, Apr. 4, 1860, p. 3, Sept. 14, 1860, p. 1, Oct. 12, 1860, p. 1, all in *Annals* 1860: 527–28. Foote's remark is in *Leader*, Jan. 21, 1858, p. 3 (*Annals* 1858: 595). Foote was a founder and long-term commissioner of Ohio's Reform Farm. He served in both houses of the state legislature and on Cleveland's city council.

28. Cleveland Industrial School, *Annual Report, 1858*, 13–17, 19–22, and *Annual Report, 1859*, 19–20, 24–25; *Leader*, June 8, 1857, p. 3 (*Annals* 1857: 387), and Oct. 29, 1857, p. 3 (*Annals* 1857: 388); *PD*, Oct. 31, 1857, p. 3; *Annals* 1858: 593, 596, 597; *PD*, Mar. 8, 1858, p. 3, Mar. 12, 1858, p. 3, Jan. 12, 1859, p. 1, Jan. 15, 1859, p. 3, and June 8, 1859, p. 3.

29. *DTD*, July 6, 1850, p. 2 (*Annals* 1850: 466).

30. *PD*, Sept. 22, 1852, p. 3. For examples of contributions by businesses: Cleveland Industrial School, *Annual Report, 1858*, 12–13; Cleveland Orphan Asylum, *Ninth Annual Report, 1861*, 8; *Fifth Annual Report* (Harris, Fairbanks and Co., 1857), 10; Ingham, *Women of Cleveland*, 107, 109–10; and *PD*, Dec. 10, 1858, p. 3.

31. The social functions of participation in voluntary organizations are discussed by Mary P. Ryan, *Womanhood in America from Colonial Times to the Present* (New York: New Viewpoints, 1979), 85–92, 105–7; Barbara J. Berg, *The Remembered Gate: Origins of American Feminism—the Woman and the City* (New York: Oxford Univ. Press, 1980), 142, 145, 221; Keith Melder, "Ladies Bountiful: Organized Women's Benevolence in Early 19th-Century America," *New York History* 48, no. 3(July 1967): 234, 242–43; Marlene Stein Wortman, "Domesticating the Nineteenth-Century American City," in *Prospects: An Annual of American Cultural Studies*, vol. 3, ed. Jack Salzman (New York: Burt Franklin and Co., 1977), 545; Female Baptist Sewing Society, Records, 1834–36, Jan. 2, 16, 30, Feb. 13, 27, 1834. Adella Prentiss Hughes Papers, WRHS; First Baptist Church, *History of the First Baptist Church of Cleveland, Ohio, 1883* (Cleveland: J. B. Savage, 1883), 65.

32. Ingham, *Women of Cleveland*, 109; *PD*, June 19, 1857, p. 3; *Williston Directory*, 28.

33. The information about the wealth of benevolent society officers and other Clevelanders is based on a letter sample from the 1850 census (2,460 names). Of the six benevolent society officers included in the 1850 census sample, four owned real property. The mean property-holding of the four was $3,925.00. Of the 707 men over eighteen in the sample, 115 held property, with a mean property-holding of $2,724.00. Two

women who were benevolent society officers were found in the census. Neither had any real property, but the head of household of one of them had $33,000.00 in real property. Of the 659 women over eighteen in the sample, 4 owned real property, with a mean of $4,250.00. In addition, 321 of the 659 had heads of household with property, and the mean for them was $1,765.20. See McTighe, "Embattled Establishment," 367–78, 578–79.

34. The membership lists include only an estimated three-fifths of all Protestant church joiners for the antebellum years. Cleveland's first "native" Protestant church—non-Catholic and non-German—was established in 1816. By 1860, thirty-five had been founded. Complete or substantial listings of those who joined were available for fourteen. These were all for churches of major denominations. Substantial records were found for two of the three Baptist churches, three of the five Episcopal, six of the ten Presbyterian and Congregational, and three of the six Methodist. In all, names of 13,096 church joiners were gathered. Based on a comparison of the membership totals of the churches for which records were available with totals for those whose records were not, it is probable that one-half to two-thirds of all those who joined non-Catholic and non-German churches in Cleveland before the Civil War are accounted for. Names of benevolent society officers, political party candidates, city government officeholders, school administrators and teachers, and officers of business, moral reform, and fraternal organizations (6,117 names) were gathered from newspapers, city histories, and the city directories of 1837, 1845, 1850, 1853, 1857, and 1860.

For a more extended discussion of the information and record linkage which form the basis of the portrait of Cleveland's benevolent reformers see Michael J. McTighe, "Embattled Establishment: Protestants and Power in Cleveland, 1836–60" (Ph.D. diss., University of Chicago, 1983), Appendix D, 575–82. For tables which break the totals down by church, see 362–66.

35. James A. Thome, *Address at the Ninth Annual Meeting of the Oberlin Agricultural Society* (Oberlin, Ohio: J. M. Fitch, 1847), 28; Second Presbyterian Church, "Self-Examination," in *Manual* (Cleveland: Harris and Fairbanks, 1854), 7; Female Baptist Sewing Society, Records, 1834–36, Jan. 2, 1834. Stephen B. Page, minister of Third Baptist, recommended "pure and disinterested benevolence": "We are therefore not only to trust, to have faith, but to do good." Cleveland, or Rocky River Baptist Association, *Minutes, 1852–60*, 1856, pp. 20–21. For another example, see R. Rouse to the Board of the Cleveland P. O. Asylum, Dec. 9, 1883, in Hughes Papers, WRHS. The pervasiveness of Protestant rhetoric and ideology in antebellum reform is described by Robert T. Handy, *A Christian America: Protestant Hopes and Historical Realities* (New York: Oxford Univ. Press, 1971), 27–64; James H. Moorhead, "Social Reform and the Divided Conscience of Antebellum Protestantism," *Church History* 48 (Dec. 1979): 416–30; William G. McLoughlin, *Revivals, Awakenings and Reform: An Essay on Religion and Social Change in America, 1607–1977* (Chicago: Univ. of Chicago Press, 1978), 112–13; Timothy L. Smith, *Revivalism and Social Reform: American Protestantism on the Eve of the Civil War* (New York: Harper and Row, 1965); Ronald Walters, *American Reformers, 1815–1860* (New York: Hill and Wang, 1978); Martin E. Marty, *Righteous Empire: The Protestant Experience in America* (New York: Dial, 1970), 89–99; and Sydney E. Ahlstrom, *A Religious History of the American People* (New Haven, Conn.: Yale Univ. Press, 1972), 637–47, 422–28.

36. Starkey, *Sermon*, 12; Ingham, *Women of Cleveland*, 77–81, 83; Harriet Taylor Upton, *History of the Western Reserve* (Chicago: Lewis Publishing, 1910), 518. For the

Western Seamen's Friend Society, see *The Boatmen's Magazine* 1 (Oct. 1834): 7; Centennial Commission, *History of the Charities*, 16; "1st Annual Report," in *Spirit of the Lakes, and Boatman's Magazine* 1 (Sept. 27, 1848): 3–10; "Third Annual Report," in *Spirit of the Lakes* 2 (Oct. 14, 1850): 173–81.

37. *PD*, Jan. 20, 1855, p. 2.

38. *PD*, Nov. 25, 1848, p. 3, Jan. 16, 1852, p. 3. See also *PD*, Dec. 20, 1854, p. 3. Catholic opposition to the Ragged School is discussed by Lucius Mellen in Early Settlers' Association of Cuyahoga County, *Annals of the Early Settlers' Association of Cuyahoga County, Ohio* 5, no. 4 (1906): 293.

39. *PD*, Feb. 2, 1853, p. 3. See also *Leader*, Nov. 28, 1857, p. 2 (*Annals* 1857: 39–40), and Dec. 16, 1857, p. 2 (*Annals* 1857: 41).

40. Such a description, in fact, describes Clevelander Truman P. Handy. Links between religion and leadership groups have also been found in other towns of the Western Reserve: James Herbert Stuckey, "The Formation of Leadership Groups in a Frontier Town: Canton, Ohio, 1805–1855" (Ph.D. diss., Case Western Reserve University, 1976), 266–68; Michael Allen McManis, "Range Ten, Town Four: A Social History of Hudson, Ohio, 1799–1840" (Ph.D. diss., Case Western Reserve University, 1976), 38–43, 143–48.

41. Suggestive analyses of the influence of Protestant and leadership elites are provided by Moorhead, "Social Reform and the Divided Conscience of Antebellum Protestantism"; Paul E. Johnson, *A Shopkeeper's Millenium: Society and Revivals in Rochester, New York, 1815–1837* (New York: Hill and Wang, 1978), 6, 8, 136–41; Anthony F. C. Wallace, *Rockdale: The Growth of an American Village in the Early Industrial Revolution* (New York: Knopf, 1978); Alan Dawley, *Class and Community: The Industrial Revolution in Lynn* (Cambridge: Harvard Univ. Press, 1976), 113–22; M. J. Heale, "From City Fathers to Social Critics: Humanitarianism and Government in New York, 1790–1860," *Journal of American History* 61 (June 1976): 21–41; McCarthy, *Noblesse Oblige*, 3–96; Mohl, *Poverty in New York*, 138, 152–54; Judith M. Wellman, "The Burned-Over District Revisited: Benevolent Reform and Abolitionism in Mexico, Paris, and Ithaca, New York, 1825–1842" (Ph.D. diss., University of Virginia, 1974), 418–41; Don Harrison Doyle, *The Social Order of a Frontier Community: Jacksonville, Illinois, 1825–1870* (Urbana: Univ. of Illinois Press, 1978), 179, 223–26; Mary P. Ryan, *Cradle of the Middle Class: The Family in Oneida County, New York, 1790–1865* (New York: Cambridge Univ. Press, 1981).

Social Reform and Philanthropic Order in Cleveland, 1896–1920

1. William Ganson Rose, *Cleveland: The Making of a City* (Cleveland: The World Publishing Co., 1950), 296, 500, 600.

2. Bath House Committee minutes, Dec. 17, 1901, Greater Cleveland Growth Association Records, WRHS, Container 5, Volume 13; Chamber of Commerce minutes, Dec. 13, 1903, Greater Cleveland Growth Association Records, WRHS, Container 5, Volume 13.

3. Rose, *Cleveland*, 500, 600.

4. For the history of the social gospel movement see Robert T. Handy, ed., *The Social Gospel in America* (New York: Oxford Univ. Press, 1966). See also the essay by Michael J. McTighe in this volume for an examination of the nature of religious involvement in benevolence in the antebellum period.

5. Rose, *Cleveland*, 490; Annual reports, 1859, 1870–1901, 1902–15, YMCA Records, WRHS, Container 15, Folders 1–6, Container 16, Folder 1; Annual reports, 1867, 1872, 1873, 1891–1913, YWCA Records, WRHS, Containers 8 and 9.

6. Shurtleff was, along with many settlement leaders, a member of the Cleveland Council of Sociology. See Cleveland Council of Sociology Records, WRHS.

7. Annual reports, YWCA Records.

8. Rose, *Cleveland*, 566–57.

9. Allen F. Davis, *Spearheads for Reform: The Social Settlements and the Progressive Movement, 1890–1914* (New York: Oxford Univ. Press, 1967).

10. Davis, *Spearheads*, 12. The other settlement in Cleveland in 1900 was the Central Friendly Inn, an outgrowth of a Woman's Christian Temperance Society mission.

11. "The Settlement Movement and the History of Hiram House," Hiram House Records (hereafter HHR), WRHS, Container 50, Volume 1.

12. *Hiram House, A Social Settlement* (Cleveland: Hiram House Settlement, 1896), in HHR, Container 50, Volume 1; Hiram House reports and publications, HHR, Container 50, Volume 1.

13. Judith A. Laughlin, "The History of Hiram House from 1896–1934: A Descriptive Study of the Stages in the Development of the Program, Physical Structure and Personnel of Hiram House, Cleveland, Ohio, from 1896–1934" (master's thesis, School of Applied Social Sciences, Western Reserve University, 1935), 18; John J. Grabowski, "A Social Settlement in a Neighborhood in Transition: Hiram House, Cleveland, Ohio, 1896–1926" (Ph.D. diss., Case Western Reserve University, 1977), 43–75.

14. George Bellamy, autobiographical notes, HHR, Container 45, Folder 1. Most general histories, such as Rose, *Cleveland*, consider Bellamy to have been the director of Hiram House from its inception. The settlement's records indicate that his initial work as solicitor was subordinate to that of H. Maud Thompson, the head resident of Hiram House in 1896–97. See *Hiram House* and Grabowski, "A Social Settlement," 16, 58.

15. Bellamy, autobiographical notes, and also essay dated Sept. 9, 1946, HHR, Container 39, Folder 2.

16. Bellamy, autobiographical notes.

17. Grabowski, "A Social Settlement," 57–58, and Appendix I, 319–20; Hiram House board minutes, 1899–1900, HHR, Container 45, Folder 1; Grabowski, "A Social Settlement," Appendix II, 328.

18. *Hiram House Life*, in HHR, Container 52, Volume 1; Grabowski, "A Social Settlement," 149–78.

19. Bellamy, autobiographical notes; Bath House Committee minutes, 1901, Greater Cleveland Growth Association Records, Container 5, Volume 13; and Housing Problem Committee minutes, 1903, ibid., Container 6, Volume 12.

20. Bellamy, "The Social Test of Theology," in HHR, Container 40, Folder 3.

21. *Tenth Annual Report of Hiram House* (Cleveland: Hiram House Settlement, 1906), in HHR, Container 50, Volume 1; Grabowski, "A Social Settlement," 83–86, 294–96.

22. Judith A. Trolander, *Settlement Houses and the Great Depression* (Detroit: Wayne State Univ. Press, 1975), 39–40; Henry E. Bourne, *The First Four Decades, Goodrich House* (Cleveland: Goodrich House, 1938), 1–9, in Goodrich Social Settlement Records, WRHS, Container 5, Folder 1.

23. Samuel Mather to Henry E. Bourne, Jan. 23, 1909, Goodrich Social Settlement Records, Container 5, Folder 2.

24. Correspondence from Flora Stone Mather to Henry E. Bourne, ibid; Bourne, *The First Four Decades.*

25. "Cadwallader," in Cleveland clipping file, Cleveland Public Library; *The Goodrich Social Settlement* (Cleveland: Goodrich Social Settlement, 1900), in Goodrich Social Settlement Records, Container 4, Folder 8.

26. Rose, *Cleveland,* 578–79. See also *Goodrich Social Settlement.*

27. *Goodrich Social Settlement.*

28. Ibid., 9. Also cited in Clara Anne Kaiser, "Organized Social Work in Cleveland, Its History and Setting" (Ph.D. diss., Ohio State University, 1936), 131.

29. Trolander, *Settlement Houses,* 40.

30. History files, Alta Social Settlement Records, WRHS, Container 4, Folder 6.

31. See Grace Goulder Izant, *Rockefeller, the Cleveland Years* (Cleveland: WRHS, 1975). Izant shows an extraordinarily strong bond between Rockefeller and religious charities, including those supported by his church, the Euclid Avenue Baptist Church.

32. History files, Alta Social Settlement Records, Container 4, Folder 6.

33. John D. Rockefeller to Mrs. M. E. Rawson, Feb. 20, 1900, Alta Social Settlement Records, Container 4, Folder 2; History files, ibid., Container 4, Folder 6.

34. History files, Alta Social Settlement Records, Container 4, Folder 6.

35. Carl J. Reifsnider, *Alta House* (Cleveland: Alta Social Settlement, 1953?).

36. Katherine Smith to Mrs. Campbell, Mar. 30, 1900, Alta Social Settlement Records, Container 4, Folder 2.

37. History files, ibid., Container 4, Folder 6.

38. Council of Jewish Women board minutes, 1897–98, Cleveland section, National Council of Jewish Women Records, WRHS, Container 1, Folder 1.

39. Lloyd P. Gartner, *History of the Jews of Cleveland* (New York and Cleveland: The Jewish Theological Seminary of America and WRHS, 1978), 221, 222, 152–59.

40. Grabowski, "A Social Settlement," 76–81.

41. Council of Jewish Women board minutes, 1897–98.

42. Council Educational Alliance board minutes, Nov. 9, Aug. 12, 1903, and Dec. 10, 1906, Jewish Community Center Records, WRHS; Gartner, *History of the Jews,* 222–26.

43. Kaiser, "Organized Social Work," 166; Committee on Benevolent Association minutes, June 29, 1900, Greater Cleveland Growth Association Records, Container 5, Volume 9.

44. Committee on Benevolent Association minutes, 1900–1901.

45. Ibid.; Historical files, Federation for Community Planning Records, WRHS, Container 9, Folder 204.

46. Kaiser, "Organized Social Work," 169.

47. Historical files, Federation for Community Planning Records, Container 9, Folder 204. This is taken from data Howard Strong compiled several decades after his service.

48. Kaiser, "Organized Social Work," 224–29.

49. Ibid., 227; Collection inventory, Whiting Williams Papers, WRHS.

50. Kaiser, "Organized Social Work," 228.

51. Ibid., 145.

52. Ibid., 174.

53. Ibid., 182–83.

54. Ibid., 231.

55. Ibid., 235. The current descendant organizations of the Welfare Federation of Cleveland and the Community Fund are the Federation for Community Planning, which directs welfare activities, and the United Way, which solicits and allocates funds.

56. Rose, *Cleveland*, 786 (this estimate is based on the city's population of 796,841 in 1920); Kaiser, "Organized Social Work," 233.

57. For information on the early history of University Neighborhood Centers, see Reports, 1926–47, University Settlement Records, WRHS, Container 15, Folders 1 and 2.

Temperance Reform in the "Providential Environment," Cleveland, 1830–1934

1. On the origins of the Cuyahoga County Total Abstinence Society, see William Ganson Rose, *Cleveland: The Making of a City* (Cleveland: The World Publishing Co., 1950), 121; the other groups are described in *K & P*, 62.

2. W. J. Rorabaugh, *The Alcoholic Republic: An American Tradition* (New York: Oxford Univ. Press, 1979), 239, 202–12.

3. *Annals* 1841:296.

4. American Temperance Society, Introduction to *Permanent Temperance Documents of the American Society*, vol. 1 (Boston, 1835); Cleveland City Temperance Society, "Report on Temperance" (Cleveland, n.d.) in "Temperance," Vertical file, WRHS, 3, 10.

5. *K & P*, 62.

6. Jed Dannenbaum, "Drink and Disorder: Temperance Reform in Cincinnati, 1841–1874" (Ph.D. diss., UCLA, 1978), 30–34; Ronald Walters, *American Reformers, 1815–1860* (New York: Hill and Wang, 1978), 130–34; Joseph Porketts, "The Good Samaritan: An Awful Warning to Professors of Religion and an Ark of Safety to All Who Have Embraced the Cause of Total Abstinence from Every Appearance of Evil" (Cleveland: 1844), 38–39, WRHS.

7. Elijah Peet, *Peet's General Business Directory of the City of Cleveland, 1846–1847* (Cleveland, 1846), 32; *Annals* 1844:792; *Annals* 1845:362; Mary Ingham, *Women of Cleveland and Their Work: Philanthropic, Educational, Literary, Medical and Artistic* (Cleveland, 1893), 101–7; *Annals* 1850:451.

8. John Allen Krout, *The Origins of Prohibition* (New York: Knopf, 1925), 107; Dannenbaum, "Drink and Disorder," 31.

9. Sons of Temperance, *Constitutions of the Order of the Sons of Temperance of North America* (Philadelphia, 1848), 156, 162; Rose, *Cleveland*, 221, and see examples of fraternal orders on pp. 184, 186, 254.

10. *Annals* 1852:466, and 1853:509, 518.

11. Joan Bland, *The Hibernian Crusade: The Story of the Catholic Total Abstinence Union* (Washington, D.C.: Catholic Univ. of American Press, 1951), 10–11; Michael J. Hynes, *History of the Diocese of Cleveland: Origin and Growth (1847–1952)* (Cleveland: Diocese of Cleveland, 1953), 104.

12. Catholic Total Abstinence Union of America, *Proceedings of the Catholic Total Abstinence Union of America* (Philadelphia, 1884), 8; Bland, *Hibernian Crusade*, 268.

13. Honorable Woodbury Davis, National Temperance Union, "Appendix to the National Temperance Convention to be held in Cleveland, July 20, 1868," pamphlet 961, pp. 1–5, WRHS; George L. Case, "The Prohibition Party: Its Origin, Purpose, and Growth," pamphlet (Cleveland, 1889), 4–5, WRHS.

14. Case, "The Prohibition Party," 8, 11.

15. David Leigh Colvin, *Prohibition in the United States* (New York: George H. Doran Co., 1926), 91–93, 124–25, 90.

16. Ernest H. Cherrington, ed., *Standard Encyclopedia of the Alcohol Problem*, vol. 5 (Westerville, Ohio: American Issue Publishing Co., 1929), 2052; quoted in *Annals* 1873:430; *PD*, Apr. 4, 1893, p. 2, and Apr. 2, 1895, p. 1.

17. This group's published annual reports and unpublished records are catalogued at the WRHS under "Woman's Christian Temperance Union of Cleveland," although the group had several designations, as this paper indicates. These documents are hereafter designated as WCTU, Nonpartisan, *Annual Reports* or Records. This citation, for example, is from the WCTU, Nonpartisan, *Annual Report* 1896:40.

18. *Annals* 1851:422.

19. Dannenbaum, "Drink and Disorder," 194; *Annals* 1875:750–52; Ingham, *Women of Cleveland*, 168–69.

20. W. H. Daniels, ed., *The Temperance Reform and Its Great Reformers* (Cincinnati: Hitchcock and Walden, 1878), 352.

21. WCTU, Nonpartisan, Records, Aug. 1, 1874, WRHS, MS. 3247, Container 1, Folder 1; F. M. Whitaker, "The Ohio WCTU and the Prohibition Amendment Campaign of 1883," *Ohio History* 83 (Spring 1974): 93–102.

22. Ruth Bordin, *Woman and Temperance: The Quest for Power and Liberty, 1873–1900* (Philadelphia: Temple Univ. Press, 1981), 129–30; WCTU, Nonpartisan, *Annual Report* 1896:45, and *Annual Report* 1880:21.

23. Bordin, *Woman and Temperance*, 129; WCTU, Nonpartisan, *Annual Report*, 1888, for example, lists Rockefeller as president of the Board of Trustees and a generous donor.

24. See Records of the Women's Philanthropic Union, 1928–51, in Container 3 of the WCTU, Nonpartisan, MS. 3247.

25. Bordin, *Woman and Temperance*, 3; Barbara Leslie Epstein, *The Politics of Domesticity: Women, Evangelism, and Temperance in Nineteenth-Century America* (Middletown, Conn.: Wesleyan Univ. Press, 1981), 1, 6, et passim; WCTU, Cuyahoga County, Quarterly Convention, Jan. 1890, Container 1, Folder 1; Directory 1911–12, Container 1, Folder 6; Directory 1917, Container 2, Folder 5, MS. 2271, WRHS.

26. WCTU, Cuyahoga County, Quarterly Convention, May 1894, Container 2, Folder 2; Dec. 8, 1887, Container 1, Folder 1; Sept. 1894, Container 1, Folder 2; Sept. 1905, Container 1, Folder 2; Sept. 1912, Container 2, Folder 2; Sept. 1918, Container 2, Folder 2.

27. E. H. Cherrington, *History of the Anti-Saloon League* (Westerville, Ohio: American Issue Publishing Co., 1913), 43; Jack S. Blocker, Jr., "The Modernity of Prohibitionists: An Analysis of Leadership Structure and Background," in Blocker, ed., *Alcohol, Reform, and Society: The Liquor Issue in Social Context* (Westport, Conn.: Greenwood Press, 1979), 149–67; Joseph Timberlake, *Prohibition and the Progressive Movement, 1900–1920* (Cambridge: Harvard Univ. Press, 1963), 122.

28. Jack S. Blocker, Jr., *Retreat from Reform: The Prohibition Movement in the United States, 1890–1913* (Westport, Conn.: Greenwood Press, 1976), 205; *Cleveland*

City Directory for the Year Ending July 1896, vol. 63 (Cleveland, n.d.), 1315; Ohio Anti-Saloon League, "The Church Temperance League in the Buckeye State: The Ohio Anti-Saloon League" (Columbus, n.d.), 4, in Ohio Anti-Saloon League materials, WRHS, Pamphlet 15, Folder 2; Ohio Anti-Saloon League, pamphlet (n.p., n.d.) in ibid.

29. Peter Odegard, *Pressure Politics: The Story of the Anti-Saloon League* (New York: Columbia Univ. Press, 1928), 75; E. H. Cherrington, ed., *Anti-Saloon League Yearbook, 1908* (Westerville, Ohio: American Issue Publishing Co., n.d.), 70; Cherrington, ed., *Anti-Saloon League Yearbook, 1910* (Westerville, Ohio, n.d.), 131.

30. Ohio Anti-Saloon League, "Bulletin," in Ohio Anti-Saloon League materials, Folder 1; Lloyd Sponholz, "The Politics of Temperance in Ohio, 1880–1912," *Ohio History* 85 (Winter 1976): 12; Leslie J. Stegh, "Wet and Dry Battles in the Cradle State of Prohibition: Robert J. Bulkley and the Repeal of Prohibition in Ohio" (Ph.D. diss., Kent State University, 1975), 47–48, 91.

31. David E. Kyvig, *Repealing National Prohibition* (Chicago: Univ. of Chicago Press, 1979), 10.

32. Quoted in Stegh, "Wet and Dry," 129; Kyvig, *Repealing Prohibition*, 24.

33. Odegard, *Pressure Politics*, 244–66; Sponholz, "The Politics of Temperance," 4–27; Kyvig, *Repealing Prohibition*, 45–46; Stegh, "Wet and Dry," 181; Kyvig, *Repealing Prohibition*, 2.

34. Grace C. Root, *Women and Repeal: The Story of the Women's Organization for Prohibition Reform* (New York: Harper and Bros., 1934), 9, 18, 16, 45; Kyvig, *Repealing Prohibition*, 126; Cleveland Crusaders, "Bulletin," in "Temperance," Vertical file, WRHS; Stegh, "Wet and Dry," 17.

35. Stegh, "Wet and Dry," 160.

36. Kirk H. Porter and Donald Bruce Johnson, *National Party Platforms, 1840–1956* (Urbana: Univ. of Illinois Press, 1956), 338–39.

37. E. H. Cherrington, ed., *Anti-Saloon League Yearbook, 1929* (Westerville, Ohio: American Issue Publishing Co., 1929), 18–19.

38. WCTU, Cuyahoga County, Directory 1923–24, Container 2, Folder 2, and Quarterly Convention, Dec. 1925, Container 2, Folder 2; Helen E. Tyler, *Where Prayer and Purpose Meet: The WCTU Story, 1874–1949* (Evanston, Ill.: Signal Press, 1949), 180, 200–201; WCTU, Cuyahoga County, Quarterly Convention, Oct. 1934, Container 3, Folder 2, and Quarterly Convention, June 1935, Container 3, Folder 2.

39. E. H. Cherrington, ed., *Anti-Saloon League Yearbook, 1925* (Westerville, Ohio: American Issue Publishing Co., 1925), 56; ibid., *1932–1933* (Westerville, Ohio: American Issue Publishing Co., 1934), 7–11.

40. Blocker, *Retreat from Reform*, 14; Mary Ryan, *Womanhood in America from Colonial Times to the Present* (New York: New Viewpoints, 1979), 118–50; Blocker, "The Modernity of Prohibitionists," 149–66.

41. Norman Clark, *Deliver Us from Evil: An Interpretation of American Prohibition* (New York: W. W. Norton, 1976), 171–75; Ryan, *Womanhood*, 151–82; Frederick Wayne Adrian, "The Political Significance of the Prohibition Party" (Ph.D. diss., Ohio State University, 1942), 147, 156.

42. Kyvig, *Repealing Prohibition*, 3.

43. Cleveland Directory Co., *Cleveland City Directory, 1934*, vol. 63 (Cleveland, n.d.), 33.

NOTES

The Women's Movement in Cleveland from 1850

1. William O'Neill first used the term "social feminism" in *Everyone Was Brave: The Rise and Fall of Feminism in America* (Chicago: Quadrangle, 1969). Social feminists were women whose interests in women's rights were subordinated to more broad-based social welfare reform concerns. Political, "hard-core," or egalitarian feminists focused on women's rights alone.

2. Michael J. McTighe, "The Protestant Benevolent Community and the Limits of the Female Sphere, 1836–1860" (Paper presented at New Harmony, Indiana, Oct. 9, 1981).

3. Elizabeth Cady Stanton, Susan B. Anthony, and Matilda Joslyn Gage, *History of Woman Suffrage*, vol. 1 (1848–61) (Rochester, 1881), 103–19; "In Behalf of Women's Rights . . . ," pamphlet, WRHS; *PD*, Oct. 7, 1853.

4. Eleanor Flexner, *Century of Struggle: The Women's Rights Movement in the United States* (Cambridge: Harvard Univ. Press, 1959), chap. 6.

5. Mary Clark Brayton and Ellen F. Terry, *Our Acre and Its Harvest: Historical Sketch of the Soldiers Aid Society of Northern Ohio* (Cleveland, 1869).

6. Stanton, et al., *History of Woman Suffrage*, vol. 2, 1861–76 (Rochester, 1881), 756–59. For a description of these developments on the national scene, see Ellen Carol DuBois, *Feminism and Suffrage: The Emergence of an Independent Women's Movement in America, 1848–1869* (Ithaca: Cornell Univ. Press, 1978).

7. *Leader*, Nov. 8, 1869, Dec. 2, 1869, Feb. 8 and 11, 1870.

8. *Leader*, Nov. 22, 23, and 24, 1870; Stanton, et al., *History of Woman Suffrage*, vol. 3 (1876–85): 505, 509.

9. Susan B. Anthony and Ida Husted Harper, eds., *History of Woman Suffrage*, vol. 4, 1883–1900 (Rochester, 1902), 137, 219, 240, 250, 257.

10. Minutes and pamphlets of the YWCA, in Young Woman's Christian Association of Cleveland collections, WRHS.

11. "A Civic Institution with a Christian Purpose, 1929," YWCA Collection, WRHS.

12. "First Annual Report of the Retreat of the Salvation Army, 1893," WRHS.

13. Mary Ingham, *Women of Cleveland and Their Work: Philanthropic, Educational, Literary, Medical and Artistic* (Cleveland, 1893), vi, 97.

14. Mrs. Gertrude Van Rensselaer Wickham, ed., *Memorial to the Pioneer Women of the Western Reserve*, 5 vols. (Cleveland: Women's Dept. of the Cleveland Centennial Commission, 1896–1924).

15. *PD*, July 28, 1897; Anthony and Harper, *History of Woman Suffrage* 4:879, 881–83.

16. Allen F. Davis, *Spearheads for Reform: The Social Settlement and the Progressive Movement, 1890–1914* (New York: Oxford Univ. Press, 1967); Gladys Haddad, "Flora Stone Mather" (Paper presented at Ohio-Indiana-Michigan chapters of the American Studies Association, CWRU, Oct. 3, 1981); Dennis Irven Harrison, "The Consumers' League of Ohio: Women and Reform 1909–1937" (Ph.D. diss., Case Western Reserve University, 1975). On social settlement houses, see the essay by John J. Grabowski in this collection.

17. Harrison, "Consumers' League," introduction, and chaps. 1 and 2.

18. Ida Husted Harper, *The History of Woman Suffrage*, vol. 6 (1900–20) (New York: National American Woman Suffrage Assoc., 1922), 508–9. Upton wrote the chapter on Ohio for this sixth and last volume.

NOTES

19. Virginia Clark Abbott, *The History of Woman Suffrage and the League of Women Voters in Cuyahoga County, 1911–1945* (Cleveland: The William Feather Co., 1949), 11–15.

20. Lois Scharf, "The Great Uprising in Cleveland: When Sisterhood Failed" in Joan M. Jensen and Sue Davidson, eds., *A Needle, A Bobbin, A Strike: Women Needleworkers in America* (Philadelphia: Temple Univ. Press, 1984). On worker-reformer conflicts as well as cooperation see Robin Jacoby, "The Women's Trade Union League and American Feminism," *Feminist Studies* 3 (Fall 1975): 126–40. On National Trade Union League President Margaret Robin's brief stop in Cleveland and inability to locate a Cleveland branch, see Mary E. Dreir, *Margaret Dreir Robins: Her Life, Letters, and Work* (New York: Island Press Cooperative, 1950), 70–82.

21. Abbott, *Woman Suffrage and LWV*, 18.

22. Ibid.

23. Harper, *History of Woman Suffrage* 6:509–11. Officers, committees of the Cleveland league around 1913, and foreign-language posters printed in 1912 are located in WRHS.

24. Harper, *History of Woman Suffrage* 6:509–19; Jeanette Tuve, "Florence Allen and the Ohio Suffrage Campaign" (unpublished paper, 1981); Abbott, *Woman Suffrage and LWV*, 23, 26–28, 30–31.

25. *Cleveland Women,* June 26, 1917, Dec. 22, 1917.

26. Ibid., Apr. 6, 1918.

27. Harrison, "Consumers' League of Ohio."

28. *PD,* Dec. 3 and 4, 1918; *Women Street Car Conductors and Ticket Agents,* Women's Bureau Report (Washington, D.C.: Government Printing Office, 1921).

29. *Women Street Car Conductors;* W. Jett Lauck to Florence E. Allen, Mar. 19, 1919, Florence E. Allen Collection, Container 6, WRHS.

30. *Cleveland Dial,* Feb.–Mar., 1920.

31. "Marie Remington Wing–One Woman's Memories of Cleveland and Mentor," MS, WRHS; Abbott, *Woman Suffrage and LWV*, 75.

32. Eleanor Farnham, interview with author, June 18, 1980.

33. Abbott, *Woman Suffrage and LWV*, 74, 93–115, 120. On the National League of Women Voters in the 1920s, see J. Stantly Lemons, *The Woman Citizen: Social Feminism in the 1920s* (Urbana: Univ. of Illinois Press, 1972); in the 1930s, see Lois Scharf, *To Work and To Wed: Female Employment, Feminism, and the Great Depression* (Westport, Conn: Greenwood Press, 1980). The League of Women Voters Collections at the WRHS document the post–World War II period more fully.

34. "Marie Wing Memories"; Abbott, *Woman Suffrage and LWV*, 83–92.

35. Abbott, *Woman Suffrage and LWV*, 103, 121. Diminished appeal to women was obvious by the end of the 1920s. Cuyahoga County had twelve league chapters with a total membership of 2,205.

36. Harrison, "Consumers' League"; Lois Scharf, "Public Careers, Private Lives, and Feminism after 1920: The Case of Elizabeth Magee" (Paper presented at the Ohio-Indiana-Michigan chapters of American Studies Association, CWRU, Oct. 3, 1981).

37. Scharf, "Elizabeth Magee."

38. Louise Stitt to Elizabeth Magee, June 14, 1970, Elizabeth Magee Collection, Container 1, WRHS.

39. *PD,* Sept. 17, 1984.

NOTES

Abolition and Antislavery in Hudson and Cleveland:
Contrasts in Reform Styles

1. On Cincinnati, see Leonard J. Richards, *"Gentlemen of Property and Standing": Anti-Abolition Mobs in Jacksonian America* (New York: Oxford Univ. Press, 1970), esp. 92−100, 122−29, 134−50. But see two alternative analyses, Fred G. Gosman, "Opposition to Abolition in Cincinnati, 1835−1844" (master's thesis, Kent State University, 1972), and Patrick A. Folk, " 'The Queen City of Mobs': Riots and Community Reactions in Cincinnati, 1788−1848" (Ph.D. diss., University of Toledo, 1978). On Marius Robinson, see Dwight L. Dumond, ed., *Letters of James Gillespie Birney, 1831−1857* (hereafter cited as *Birney Letters*), 2 vols. (1938; rpt. Gloucester, Mass.: Peter Smith, 1966), 1:38n. 2, and Theodore Dwight Weld to Birney, June 26, 1837, 1:387−88; Russel B. Nye, "Marius Robinson: A Forgotten Abolitionist Leader," *Ohio State Archeological and Historical Quarterly* (hereafter *OH*), 55 (Jan.−Mar. 1946): 138−54; Emily Robinson, Reminiscences, n.d., Marius Robinson MSS, WRHS; Bertram Wyatt-Brown, "Reform and Anti-Reform in Garfield's Ohio," *Hayes Historical Journal* 3 (Spring 1982): 63−78.

2. *Herald,* Oct. 26, 1833.

3. Gilbert H. Barnes, *The Antislavery Impulse, 1830−1844* (1933; rpt. New York: Harcourt, Brace & World, 1964); Anne C. Loveland, "Evangelicalism and 'Immediate Emancipation' in American Antislavery Thought," *Journal of Southern History* 32 (May 1966): 172−88; James Brewer Stewart, *Holy Warriors: The Abolitionists and American Slavery* (New York: Hill and Wang, 1976).

4. David French, "Elizur Wright, Jr., and the Emergence of Anti-Colonizationist Sentiments on the Connecticut Reserve," *OH* 85 (Winter 1976), 56−57, sees *"proslavery sentiment"* developing as a result of moderate antislavery activity on the Reserve.

5. David Hudson to R. R. Gurley, July 23, 1832, American Colonization Society MSS, Library of Congress (hereafter ACS); James Brewer Stewart, *Joshua R. Giddings and the Tactics of Radical Politics* (Cleveland: Case Western Reserve Univ. Press, 1970), 8. 30.

6. *Herald,* Jan. 26, 1827, and Dec. 21, 1827; Isham quoted in Edward C. Reilley, "The Early Slavery Controversy in the Western Reserve" (Ph.D. diss., Western Reserve University, 1940), 9; James H. Kennedy, *A History of the City of Cleveland, Its Settlement, Rise, and Progress, 1796−1896* (Cleveland: Imperial Press, 1896), 224; Allan Peskin, ed., *North into Freedom: The Autobiography of John Malvin, Free Negro, 1795−1880* (Cleveland: Press of Western Reserve Univ., 1966), 55−56n. 1.

7. See French, "Elizur Wright, Jr.," 49−66. See also Bertram Wyatt-Brown, *Lewis Tappan and the Evangelical War Against Slavery* (Cleveland: Case Western Reserve Univ. Press, 1969), 51, 84−87; Lawrence J. Friedman, *Gregarious Saints: Self and Community in American Abolitionism, 1830−1870* (New York: Cambridge Univ. Press, 1982), 13−14.

8. Isaac Israel Bigelow to Carroll Cutler, undated but c. June 1876, Carroll Cutler MSS, Archives, CWRU (hereafter cited as Cutler MSS).

9. Elizur Wright, Jr., to the Rev. R. M. Walker, Dec. 5, 1875, copy, in Cutler MSS. See also President J. H. Fairchild, "Early Congregationalism on the Western Reserve," in Delavan L. Leonard, ed., *Papers of the Ohio Church History Society* (Oberlin, 1894), 18−20, on the New School and Old School division. See also, Lawrence B.

Goodheart, "Abolitionists as Academics: The Controversy at Western Reserve College, 1832–1833," *History of Education Quarterly* 22 (Winter 1982): 421–33.

10. Charles Backus Storrs, "Inaugural Address," Feb. 9, 1831, Charles Backus Storrs MSS, Archives, CWRU. See also Paul E. Johnson, *A Shopkeeper's Millennium: Society and Revivals in Rochester, New York, 1815–1837* (New York: Hill and Wang, 1978), 136–41; Paul S. Boyer, *Urban Masses and Moral Order in America, 1820–1920* (Cambridge: Harvard Univ. Press, 1978), pt. 1.

11. S. A. Whittlesey to Cutler, Nov. 6, 1875, Cutler MSS. On a western sense of inferiority, see Page Smith, *As a City upon a Hill: The Town in American History* (New York: Knopf, 1966), and David French, "Puritan Conservatism and the Frontier: The Elizur Wright Family on the Connecticut Western Reserve," *The Old Northwest* 1 (Mar. 1975): 85–95.

12. Wyatt-Brown, *Lewis Tappan*, 47, 62, 75n. 30; Bertram Wyatt-Brown, "Prelude to Abolitionism: Sabbatarian Politics and the Rise of the Second Party System," *Journal of American History* 58 (Sept. 1971): 316–41. Quotation from Stewart, *Giddings*, 14. See also Joshua R. Giddings to Elisha Whittlesey, Jan. 26, Feb. 7, 1828; Aug. 2, 24, 27, Sept. 2, 17, Nov. 22, 1831; all in Elisha Whittlesey MSS, WRHS. See also Goodheart, "Abolitionists as Academics."

13. *Hudson Observer and Telegraph*, Sept. 6, 1832, and other issues, from July 13 to Nov. 22, 1832. Clark's criticisms appear in Oct. 11, Nov. 1 and 22, 1832.

14. Frederick C. Waite, *Western Reserve University: The Hudson Era* (Cleveland: Western Reserve Univ. Press, 1943), 83–111, offers a hostile portrait of abolitionists. For a more sympathetic reading, see Carroll Cutler, *A History of Western Reserve College, during its First Half Century, 1826–1876* (Cleveland: Crocker's Pub. Co., 1876); and Clarence Henley Cramer, *Case Western Reserve University: A History of the University, 1826–1976* (Boston: Little, Brown, 1976), 15–26. Michael A. McManis, "Range Ten, Town Four: A Social History of Hudson, Ohio, 1799–1840" (Ph.D. diss., CWRU, 1976), 146, sees no economic differences between the two factions, but students and professors, owing to youth and occupation, seldom have wealth equal to college trustees. Green's sermons were later published as *Four Sermons, Preached in the Chapel of the Western Reserve College, on Lord's Days, November 18th and 25th, and December 2nd and 9th, 1832* (Cleveland: Office of the *Herald*, 1833).

15. Horace Taylor and David O. Hudson to R. R. Gurley, Oct. 29, 1832, ACS. On Nutting, see Waite, *Western Reserve*, 33–39, 61, 487.

16. O. N. Chapin to Cutler, Feb. 29, 1876; A. V. Hawley to Cutler, Oct. 8, 1875; Lyman U. Hall to Cutler, Nov. 15, 1875; Wright to Cutler, Jan. 12, 1876; Bigelow to Cutler, June 1875; all in Cutler MSS.

17. Philip J. Staudenraus, *The African Colonization Movement, 1816–1865* (New York: Columbia Univ. Press, 1961), 201, 210–11; Waite, *Western Reserve*, 120, 209, 211, 214–15, chronicles Arthur Tappan's benefactions for and break with the college. See also Wyatt-Brown *Lewis Tappan*, 100, 101 (on Storrs), and on Tappan's western concerns, 49–52. See also Storrs, journal entry for Jan. 16, 1833, and other entries for the winter, 1832–33, Storrs MSS; Elizur Wright, Jr., and Beriah Green to Theodore D. Weld, Feb. 1, 1833, in Gilbert H. Barnes and Dwight L. Dumond, eds., *Letters of Theodore Dwight Weld, Angelina Grimké Weld, and Sarah Grimké, 1822–1844* (hereafter cited as *Weld-Grimké Letters*), 2 vols. (1934; rpt. Gloucester, Mass.: Peter Smith, 1965), 1:101–5 (quotation, 103). On Wright's tour, see *Boston Liberator*, June 29, 1833, and David French, "Elizur Wright" (Ph.D. diss., CWRU, 1970), 159.

NOTES

18. Quoted in French, "Puritan Conservatism," 92. See also Elizur Wright, Sr., to Wright, Jan. 29, Oct. 11, 1833, as well as earlier correspondence, Elizur Wright, Jr., MSS, Archives, CWRU. Wright's replies are in the Elizur Wright MSS, Boston Public Library. See also, French, "Elizur Wright" (Ph.D. diss.), 13–37.

19. See Lewis Perry, *Radical Abolitionism: Anarchy and the Government of God in Antislavery Thought* (Ithaca: Cornell Univ. Press, 1973), 13–17, 105–6; Peter Walker, *Moral Choices: Memory, Desire, and Imagination in Nineteenth-Century Abolition* (Baton Rouge: Louisiana State Univ. Press, 1978). Quotation from Reilley, "Early Slavery Controversy," 12.

20. Edwards A. Park, "A Sermon Delivered September 17, 1833, at the Interment of Rev. Charles Backus Storrs . . ."; Richard Salter Storrs to Henry Storrs, Dec. 15, 1853; note by F. C. Waite, Oct. 3, 1933, on Storr's life and character, in Storrs MSS. "The *axe*," Green italicized, *"has always been my favorite instrument"*; Beriah Green, Western Reserve College, Oct. 1832, testimonial to Weld, in Theodore D. Weld, *The First Annual Report of the Society for Promoting Manual Labor in Literary Institutions, includng the Report of Their General Agent, Theodore D. Weld, January 28, 1833* (New York: S. W. Benedict & Co., 1833), 111–12.

21. See Robert M. Abzug, *Passionate Liberator: Theodore Dwight Weld and the Dilemma of Reform* (New York: Oxford Univ. Press, 1980), esp. 86–87; Weld to Wright, Jan. 10, 1833, in Barnes and Dumond, *Weld-Grimké Letters* 1:99. As late as Sept. 1832, before his arrival at Hudson, Weld was still a colonizationist. See Weld to Birney, Sept. 27, 1832, Dumond, *Birney Letters* 1:27. On career problems in antebellum reform, see Lois W. Banner, "Religion and Reform in the Early Republic: The Role of Youth," *American Quarterly* 22 (Dec. 1971): 677–95; Bertram Wyatt-Brown, "Conscience and Career: Young Abolitionists and Missionaries," in Seymour M. Drescher and Christine Bolt, eds., *Anti-Slavery, Religion and Reform: Essays in Memory of Roger Anstey* (Folkstone, Eng.: Wm. Dawson, 1980), 183–206, first presented at the Armington Seminar on Values in Children, CWRU, Sept. 1978.

22. "Records, Trustees, Western Reserve College," June 26, 1833, Archives, CWRU. Wright arranged a student performance that satirized the colonizationists and he scandalized the assembly by escorting a black abolitionist in the procession. Quotation from Wright to Storrs, Aug. 31, 1833, Wright MSS, CWRU. On Storrs's death, see *Boston Liberator*, Sept. 21, 1833; John G. Whittier, *Complete Poetical Works* (Boston: Riverside Press, 1894), 170.

23. Waite, *Western Reserve*, 160, 168–69; Cramer, *Case Western Reserve University*, 28–38.

24. *Herald*, Apr. 23, 1833; *Ravenna Ohio Star*, May 2, 1833; *HG*, June 30, July 13, 1837; Kennedy, *History of the City of Cleveland*, 292, 294.

25. *Whig*, Aug. 26, 1835. The reception is all the more remarkable because August 1835 was the season of more antiabolitionist mobs than almost any other throughout the country, owing to the national society's vigorous pamphlet campaign. See Bertram Wyatt-Brown, "The Abolitionists' Postal Campaign of 1835," *Journal of Negro History* 50 (Oct. 1965): 227–38.

26. *Whig*, Sept. 15, 1847; *HG*, July 13, 1837.

27. Larry Gara, *The Liberty Line: The Legend of the Underground Railroad* (Lexington: Univ. of Kentucky Press, 1961), 148–49, and also, 138, 180–81. See also on St. John's Episcopal Church and antislavery, MS. 2787, WRHS. On nonradical involvement in fugitive slave cases, see conservative lawyer Thomas Bolton's handling of a

case in 1841 in Kennedy, *History of the City of Cleveland*, 387–89 and 388–89n. 9; *Herald*, Nov. 5, 1845. On the blacks in Cleveland, see Benjamin Quarles, *Allies for Freedom: Blacks and John Brown* (New York: Oxford Univ. Press, 1974), 151.

28. *Leader*, Nov. 8, 1855; see also Jan. 13 and May 21, 1857, and other issues easily accessible through *Annals*.

29. These brief remarks do injustice to the complex development of Ohio political abolitionism, a program which began at the Ohio Anti-Slavery Society convention in Cleveland, 1839. See Betty Fladeland, *James Gillespie Birney: Slaveholder to Abolitionist* (Ithaca: Cornell Univ. Press, 1955), 181. Stewart, *Giddings*, 95, 202–5; Giddings to Ephraim Brown, Nov. 21, 1838, Brown to Giddings, Dec. 19, 1838, Vertical file, WRHS; see especially, Harold W. Davis, "The Social and Economic Basis of the Whig Party in Ohio, 1828–1840" (Ph.D. diss., WRU, 1932). Giddings supported Harrison rather than Birney, the Liberty candidate. See Richard E. Sewell, *Ballots for Freedom: Antislavery Politics in the United States, 1837–1860* (New York: Oxford Univ. Press, 1976), 64, 76, 77. On Backus, see Peskin, *North into Freedom*, 67.

30. M. W. Holtslauder to [?], Sept. 22, 1852, Vertical file, WRHS. Edward Wade should be not confused with his brother Benjamin, Giddings's rival. There is no biography of Benjamin Tappan nor of Thomas Morris, and a satisfactory one of Salmon P. Chase has yet to appear. See also, Sewell, *Ballots for Freedom*, 206–11.

31. Citizens of Cleveland to Charles G. Finney, July 15, 1835, Charles G. Finney MSS, microfilm, Mudd Learning Center, Oberlin College; Elbert Jay Benton, *Cultural Story of an American City: Part II, Cleveland During the Canal Days, 1825–1850* (Cleveland: WRHS, 1943), 53–55.

32. See Robert S. Fletcher, *A History of Oberlin College: From Its Foundation through the Civil War*, 2 vols. (Oberlin: Oberlin College, 1943), 1:472–88.

33. *Whig*, Sept. 15, 1847. For a typical *Plain Dealer* editorial on the subject, see *PD*, Nov. 18, 1859. See Frederick Douglass, *The Claim of the Negro Ethnologically Considered, An Address before the Literary Societies of Western Reserve College, at Commencement, July 12, 1854* (Rochester: Lee, Mann, & Co., 1854).

34. Stewart, *Giddings*, 41–43, 89–90, 185, 192n. 56; Rev. A. B. Cristy, *Cleveland Congregationalists, 1875: Historical Sketches of Our Twenty-Five Churches and Missions* (Cleveland: Williams, 1896), 71–73; "Plymouth Church of Shaker Heights, 1916-23," Vertical file, WRHS; Roy E. Bowers, *Ohio Congregational Christian Story* (Cleveland: privately printed, 1952), 75; William Ganson Rose, *Cleveland: The Making of a City* (Cleveland: The World Publishing Co., 1950), 232, 265; *HG*, Dec. 23, 1837, and Jan. 8, 1839; *Herald*, Nov. 29, 1845; Aiken quoted in Benton, *Cultural Story*, pt. 3, 52; Rev. David McMillan, "Samuel C. Aiken—Living with a Dying Calvinism," unpublished paper, n.d., prepared for Fairmount Presbyterian Church, Cleveland Heights, kindly supplied by the author. Malvin quoted in Peskin, *North into Freedom*, 84, and see also 83–84n. 4.

35. Thome to Weld, July 16, 1836, in Barnes and Dumond, *Weld-Grimké Letters* 1:313; Rev. Sidney Strong, "The Exodus of Students from Lane Seminary to Oberlin in 1834," in Delavan I. Leonard, *Papers of Ohio Church History Society* 3 (1893): 1–16; Abzug, *Passionate Liberator*, 91–92, 117, 119, 139–40, 156–57, 200, 214–15, 278; Thome to Finney, June 3, 1837, in John A. Auping, S. J., *The Relative Efficiency of Evangelical Non-Violence: The Influence of a Revival of Religion on the Abolition of Slavery in North America, 1740–1865* (Rome: Pontificae Universitatis Gregorianae, 1977), 216–18 (quotation, 218).

36. Henry M. Tenney, "The History of the First Congregational Church of Cleveland," in Frank H. Foster, ed., *Papers of the Ohio Church History Society* 2 (1892): 26–43. On immersions in Lake Erie, see *Leader*, May 3, 1858.

37. *In Memoriam Rev. J. A. Thome . . . Funeral Services at Cleveland, Ohio, March 10, 1873* (Cleveland: Nevin Brothers, 1873); Tenney, "History of the First Congregational Church of Cleveland," 42.

38. *Leader*, Mar. 21, 22, Apr. 6, 1859.

39. Cleveland blacks did not join Brown's efforts as he expected, but they were very much his admirers after Harpers Ferry. See Quarles, *Allies for Freedom*, 61–62, 72, 80, 147; on Brown's stay in Cleveland, see Stephen B. Oates, *To Purge This Land with Blood: A Biography of John Brown* (New York: Harper & Row, 1970), 266–70.

40. *Leader*, Dec. 3, 10, 1859; Rose, *Cleveland*, 295.

At the Leading Edge: The Movement for Black Civil Rights in Cleveland 1830–1969

1. Kenneth Kusmer's work develops this thesis for the years 1870–1930. Kenneth Kusmer, *A Ghetto Takes Shape: Black Cleveland, 1870–1930* (Urbana: Univ. of Illinois Press, 1976). This essay supports Kusmer's argument and extends it through the Depression and war years.

2. Kusmer, *Ghetto*, 10. There are no statistics available to indicate the number of blacks in Cleveland through the first half of the nineteenth century. In 1850 the first year for which data are available, there were 200 blacks in a total city population of 17,034. By 1870 there were 1,293 blacks in a total city population of 92,829.

3. A. G. Riddle, "Rise of Anti-Slavery Sentiment on the Western Reserve," *Magazine of Western History* 6 (1887): 54; *Herald*, Nov. 14, 1820.

4. Russell H. Davis, *Memorable Negroes in Cleveland's Past* (Cleveland: WRHS, 1969), 6–8.

5. Riddle, "Anti-Slavery Sentiment," 145–46; Karl Geiser, "The Western Reserve in the Anti-Slavery Movement, 1840–1860," Mississippi Valley Historical Society, *Proceedings* 5 (1811–1912): 73–98; *Herald*, Nov. 14, 1820, and Oct. 5, 1839; and *HG*, Sept. 23, 1838.

6. Davis, *Memorable Negroes*, 11; and Benjamin Quarles, *Black Abolitionists* (New York: Oxford Univ. Press, 1969), 153.

7. *Herald*, Apr. 9, 1846. The brief quotation is reported in Kusmer, *Ghetto*, 28.

8. Benjamin Quarles, *The Negro in the Civil War* (Boston: Little, Brown & Co., 1953).

9. Harry E. Davis, "Early Colored Residents in Cleveland," *Phylon* 4 (July 1943): 235–36.

10. Kusmer, *Ghetto*, 28. The quotation is in Davis, *Memorable Negroes*, 47.

11. John Hope Franklin, *From Slavery to Freedom* (New York: Knopf, 1967), 439–41.

12. *U.S. Census Reports, 1890–1930*. For a discussion of the factors related to the World War I migrations see Kusmer, *Ghetto*, 157–60.

13. Christopher G. Wye, "Midwest Ghetto: Patterns of Change and Continuity in the Black Social Structure, 1930–1945" (Ph.D. diss., Kent State University, 1974), 2; Kusmer, *Ghetto*.

14. Kusmer, *Ghetto*, 113–54.

NOTES

15. Wye, "Midwest Ghetto," 9–14.

16. Kusmer, *Ghetto*, 114; John P. Green, *Fact Stranger than Friction: Seventy-Five Years of a Busy Life with Reminiscences of Many Great and Good Men and Women* (Cleveland: Riehl Printing Co., 1920).

17. Green, *Fact Stranger than Friction*. The quotation is from the *Leader*, Oct. 30, 1902.

18. William J. Simmons, *Men of Mark: Eminent, Progressive, and Rising* (Cleveland, 1887), 194–97.

19. *Cleveland Gazette*, Nov. 15 and 22, 1930, Mar. 7 and May 9, 1931; Davis *Memorable Negroes*, 32–43.

20. Kusmer, *Ghetto*, 260; Charles W. White to Walter White, Feb. 25, 1927, "Cleveland Branch NAACP, Annual Report," Nov. 21, 1929, and David H. Pierce to Herbert T. Seligman, Oct. 25, 1930, in NAACP Branch Files, WRHS; Dudley S. Blossom to Charles W. White, Oct. 24, 1928, in George A. Myers MSS, Ohio Historical Society; *Cleveland Gazette*, July 6 and Dec. 23, 1929, and May 10, 1930; and interview with author, Aug. 4, 1972.

21. Davis, *Memorable Negroes*, 45.

22. *Cleveland Journal*, Mar. 25, 1904; *Cleveland Gazette*, Apr. 22, 1905, Nov. 27, 1909.

23. *Cleveland Journal*, Apr. 8, 1905; *Cleveland Gazette*, Jan. 1, 1910.

24. *Cleveland Journal*, Apr. 11, 1903, Apr. 16 and 23, 1910.

25. *Cleveland Gazette*, Mar. 10 and Nov. 17, 1917, May 25, 1918; Interview, Jan. 18, 1972; Board of Trustees Meeting, minutes, Mar. 8, 1928, and Mar. 27, 1930, Cleveland Urban League MSS, WRHS.

26. Wye, "Midwest Ghetto," chaps. 1 and 9.

27. *Cleveland Gazette*, Dec. 19, 1931, Feb. 21, 1941; *Cleveland Eagle*, Apr. 17, 1936.

28. Interviews, Oct. 2 and 17, 1969, and Jan. 18, 1972; *Cleveland Call and Post*, Sept. 22, 1934; *Cleveland Gazette*, Oct. 17, 1931.

29. Interviews, Oct. 2, 1969, Feb. 19, 1972.

30. *Cleveland Gazette*, Jan. 24, 1931; David H. Pierce to Walter White, Apr. 1, 1933, and David H. Pierce to Herbert T. Seligman, Oct. 25, 1930, NAACP Branch Files, Library of Congress.

31. *Cleveland Call and Post*, May 15, 1935, Feb. 27 and May 28, 1936; *Cleveland Gazette*, Apr. 25, 1936; *Cleveland Eagle*, Apr. 24, Oct. 17, and Nov. 6, 1936; *Cleveland Union Leader*, Sept. 30, 1937.

32. Charles H. Loeb, *The Future is Yours: The History of the Future Outlook League, 1935–1946* (Cleveland: The Future Outlook League, Inc., 1947), 15–18, 22–24; Interviews, Oct. 19, 1969, May 16 and 26, 1972; *Cleveland Call and Post*, May 5, 1938; John O. Holly to William O. Walker, Sept. 12, 1935, Future Outlook League MSS, WRHS.

33. *Cleveland Gazette*, June 22, 1935; *Cleveland Call and Post*, May 11, Aug. 8, Sept. 19, 1935, June 4, Aug. 15, 1936; John O. Holly to Joseph Soloman, Sept. 10, 1935, Future Outlook League MSS.

34. For Urban League see Board of Trustees Meeting minutes, June 17, 1938, and Apr. 16, 1941, Cleveland Urban League MSS. For the NAACP see *Cleveland Call and Post*, Mar. 24, 1938, May 17 and 24, and June 14, 1941.

35. This interpretation of the generational, class, and career imperatives underlying black leadership patterns is developed in Wye, "Midwest Ghetto," chap. 9.

36. Cleveland Welfare Federation, *Central Area Study*, 1943, p. 125, on file at Cleveland Public Library.

37. Ibid.

38. *Cleveland Press*, Sept. 23, 1943; *PD*, Sept. 23, 1942.

39. Wye, "Midwest Ghetto," 81, 82, 91.

40. Russell H. Davis, *Black Americans in Cleveland: From George Peake to Carl B. Stokes, 1796–1969* (Cleveland: The Associated Publishers, 1972), 271–304.

41. Wye, "Midwest Ghetto," 1–30; 66–110.

42. Interview, Jan. 1972; Davis, *Black Americans*, 377–85.

43. Davis, *Black Americans*, 353, 376, 377–85.

44. Interview, Feb. 19, 1972; Davis, *Black Americans*, 351.

45. "Escape Burning," *Saturday Evening Post*, July 29, 1967, 38–42; "You Can't Stop the Riot from Coming," *Look*, May 30, 1967, p. 96.

46. Davis, *Black Americans*, 407–13; and "Stokes Elected," *Newsweek*, Nov. 17, 1969, p. 36.

The Search for the One Best System:
Cleveland Public Schools and Educational Reform, 1836–1920

1. Kenneth Lottich, *New England Transplanted* (Dallas: Royal Publishing Co., 1964), 9; Andrew Freese, *Early History of the Cleveland Public Schools* (Cleveland: Robison, Savage and Co., 1876), 7.

2. Lottich, *New England*, 77; Frederick Binder, *The Age of the Common School, 1830–1865* (New York: John Wiley & Sons, Inc., 1974), 19; John W. Willey quoted in Elbert Jay Benton, *Cultural Story of an American City: Part II, Cleveland During the Canal Days, 1825–1850* (Cleveland: WRHS, 1943), 45–46; Freese, *Early History*, 10–11; William Akers, *Cleveland Schools in the Nineteenth Century* (Cleveland: The W. M. Bayne Printing House, 1901), 9; Harry N. Irwin, "Dual Administrative Control in City School Systems: A Case Study of Its Origin and Development," *The Elementary School Journal* 22 (Apr. 1923): 573–85.

3. Akers, *Cleveland Schools*, 21. Bradburn was a member of the school board for the years 1842–48, 1852–54, 1857–60. In 1848 and 1851 he ran for city council to influence the passage of legislation in support of the public schools.

4. Stella Welty, "The Establishment of a Free Public High School System in Cleveland" (master's thesis, Western Reserve University, 1931), 35; Freese, *Early History*, 32.

5. Lottich, *New England*, 206–7.

6. David B. Tyack, *The One Best System: A History of American Education* (Cambridge: Harvard Univ. Press, 1974), 39–59; David Nasaw, *Schooled to Order: A Social History of Public Schooling in America* (New York: Oxford Univ. Press, 1979), 105–13; Patricia Graham, *Community and Class in Modern America, 1865–1918* (New York: John Wiley & Sons, Inc., 1974), 6–7.

7. Cleveland Board of Education, *Annual Report* 1866:33. All annual reports cited herein are those of the Cleveland Board of Education. These and other primary sources cited can be found in either the WRHS or the social science department of the Cleveland Public Library.

8. Tyack, *The One Best System*, 44–45; *Annual Report* 1868:41.

9. *Annual Report* 1871:78–79.

10. *Annual Report* 1874:57–60; Nasaw, *Schooled to Order,* 61–63; *Annual Report* 1872:109–27.

11. *Annual Report* 1878:61; *Leader,* June 17, 1871.

12. *Annual Report* 1876:109–27; Akers, *Cleveland Schools,* 88.

13. Ann M. Giblin, "Factors Influencing Nineteenth Century Architecture in Cleveland School Buildings," *The Journal of the Cuyahoga County Archives* 1 (1981): 36; *Annual Report* 1878:114.

14. *Annual Report* 1878:17–19; Herbert A. Miller, *The School and the Immigrant* (Cleveland: The Survey Committee of the Cleveland Foundation, 1916), 85.

15. Harold E. Davis, *Hinsdale of Hiram: The Life of Burke Aaron Hinsdale* (Washington, D.C.: The University Press of America, 1971), 113; Burke A. Hinsdale, *Our Common School Education* (Cleveland: J. B. Savage, 1877), 21; Andrew Rickoff, *Past and Present of Our Common School Education* (Cleveland, 1877), 75; and Samuel P. Orth, *A History of Cleveland, Ohio,* vol. 1 (Cleveland: S. J. Clark Publishing Co., 1910), 530.

16. Burke A. Hinsdale, "President Eliot on Popular Education," Clipping file, WRHS; *Annual Report* 1886:37.

17. *Annual Report* 1885:97–99.

18. *Annual Report* 1886:17 and 1885:91.

19. Davis, *Hinsdale of Hiram,* 139; Burke A. Hinsdale, "The Relation of School Boards to Schools," Clipping file, WRHS.

20. "Manual Training in Public Schools Got Start Here in 1884—with Barn as Lab," *Cleveland News,* Sept. 9, 1940; *Annual Report* 1887:55.

21. Akers, *Cleveland Schools,* 223; *Annual Report* 1887:62; *Annual Report* 1889: 107–8; *Annual Report* 1891:95–96. The school board hired George E. Goodrich, former principal of Berea Schools and a detective on the Cleveland Police Force, as the first truant officer.

22. Ronald M. Johnson, "Politics and Pedagogy: The 1892 Cleveland School Reform," *Ohio History* 84 (Autumn 1975): 198. See also Samuel P. Hays, "The Politics of Reform in Municipal Government in the Progressive Era," *Pacific Northwest Quarterly* 55 (Oct. 1964): 157–69. For a description of the Federal Plan, see Cleveland Board of Education, *School Board Proceedings* 1894:4–6; further references to these proceedings will be to those of the Cleveland Board of Education. Edwin B. Pandin, a former judge in the common pleas court, contacted Edwin Cowles, the publisher of the *Cleveland Leader,* about revising the city charter. This led to a discussion of the Federal Plan before the Board of Trade.

23. Ronald Johnson, "Captain of Education: An Intellectual Biography of Andrew S. Draper, 1848–1913" (Ph.D. diss., University of Illinois, 1970), 122; *School Board Proceedings* 1894:26, 69. See also Cleveland Board of Education, *The Special Schools and Curriculum Centers* (Cleveland: The Cleveland Board of Education, 1931), 52.

24. *Annual Report* 1894:10.

25. *Annual Report* 1894:49, 1900:54–55, and 1896:14.

26. *Annual Report* 1900:47–48.

27. *Annual Report* 1901:35, and 1895:95; Elroy M. Avery, *A History of Cleveland and Its Environs* (Chicago: Lewis Publishing, 1918), 377. Avery, the principal of the normal school and founder of the Logan Republican Club, personally appealed the

dismissal to Superintendent Jones, but the latter curtly remarked that it must be accepted as a "closed incident."

28. *Annual Report* 1901:48.

29. *Annual Report* 1886:78–79.

30. Robert Wiebe, *The Search for Order, 1877–1920* (New York: Hill and Wang, 1967), 111–13.

31. Marvin Lazerson, *Origins of the Urban School* (Cambridge: Harvard Univ. Press, 1971), 34–35; Michael Katz, "Education and Social Development in the Nineteenth Century," in Paul Nash, ed., *History and Education: The Educational Uses of the Past* (New York: Random House, 1970), 83–113.

32. *Annual Report* 1900:32.

33. Edward A. Krug, *The Shaping of the American High School* (New York: Harper & Row, Publishers, 1964), 249–83. See also Lawrence Cremin, *Transformation of the School: Progressivism in American Education, 1876–1957* (New York: Vintage Books, 1964), 127–76.

34. Justin Galford, "The Foreign Born and Urban Growth in Cleveland" (Ph.D. diss., New York University, 1966), 14.

35. Prudence Randall, "The Meaning of Progressivism in Urban School Reform, 1901–1909" (Ph.D. diss., Case Western Reserve University, 1971).

36. Irwin, "Dual Administrative Control," 672–73; Orth, *History of Cleveland* 1:534; *Report of the Education Commission* (Cleveland: The Board of Education, 1906), 113–20. Among the members of the commission were the following: J. G. W. Cowles, one of the founders of Cleveland Trust Company; Francis Prentiss, president of Hiram House and Cleveland Twist Drill Company; Charles F. Thwing, President of Western Reserve University, and E. M. Baker, a broker and the secretary of the Jewish Federation of Charities.

37. *Annual Report* 1907:29, 51. See also William P. Elson, "The Technical High School in Cleveland," *The School Review* 16 (June 1908): 353–59, and Sol Cohen, "The Industrial Education Movement, 1906–1917," *American Quarterly* 20 (Spring 1968): 95–110.

38. Andrew S. Draper, "The Adaption of the Schools to Industry and Efficiency," *National Education Association* 46 (1908): 69; Randall, "The Meaning of Progressivism," 221; *Annual Report* 1908:65–66, 1909:95, and 1903:33–34. Only fifty-one students out of an original enrollment of 426 graduated in 1904.

39. *Annual Report* 1909:48; Orth, *History of Cleveland*, 536; *Annual Report* 1910:59–62; Merritt Wight, "The Outhwaite School for the Slow Learning and Socially Maladjusted Pupil" (Ph.D. diss., Western Reserve University, 1944), 24. The course for girls included cooking, laundering, sewing and garment making, the care of the sickroom and home. The industrial course for boys included mechanical and freehand drawing, woodwork, pattern making, design, and craft. One half of the day was devoted to English, mathematics, geography, history, and hygiene.

40. *Annual Report* 1903:33–34. In 1895 the Ladies Aid Society of Old Stone Church opened summer vacation schools. The Day Nursery and Free Kindergarten Association opened playgrounds in 1903. The Home Gardening Association, headquartered in the Goodrich Settlement House, was the sponsor of the gardening program. See the *Annual Report* 1909:51–52.

41. *Annual Report* 1910:66, 1911:36, 1907:56.

42. *Annual Report* 1910:33, 1909:110, 119.

43. *Cleveland Press*, Oct. 5, 1937; *Municipal Bulletin* 15 (Sept. 1911): 24; Edward M. Miggins, "Businessmen, Pedagogues and Progressive Reform: The Cleveland Foundation's 1915 School Survey" (Ph.D. diss., Case Western Reserve University, 1975).

44. Letters of Allen T. Burns to Leonard Ayres, Mar. 16, 1915, and Leonard Ayres to Allen T. Burns, Mar. 19, 1915, in Cleveland Foundation Papers, Manuscript Collection of the WRHS. In 1909 Ayres had published *Laggards in Our Schools* (New York: Charities and Publication Committee, 1909), a critique of the public schools' inability to adjust to the needs of immigrant children.

45. Leonard Ayres, *Child Accounting in the Public Schools* (Cleveland: The Survey Committee of the Cleveland Foundation, 1915).

46. Frank E. Spaulding, "The Application of the Principles of Scientific Management," *National Education Association: Addresses and Proceedings* 1913:259–79; *School Superintendent in Action in Five Cities* (Rindge, N.H.: Richard R. Smith Publishers, Inc., 1955); *Civic Affairs*, no. 10 (Nov. 1917).

47. Glenn C. Altschuler, *Race, Ethnicity and Class in American Social Thought, 1865–1919* (Arlington Heights, Ill.: Harlan Division, Inc., 1982), 48; Cleveland Board of Education, "Division of Reference and Research," no. 39 (Board of Education, Oct. 1, 1924). Schools with a concentration of immigrants had a nonpromotion rate of 39.5 percent—higher than what the school survey had reported earlier. See Raymond Moley, *A Review of the Surveys of the Cleveland Foundation* (Cleveland: The Cleveland Foundation, 1923), 8–13.

48. Lazerson, *Origins*, 257.

49. Lawrence Cremin, *The American Common School* (New York: Teachers College Press, 1951), 58–59; Josef Barton, *Peasants and Strangers: Italians, Rumanians, and Slovaks in an American City, 1870–1890* (Cambridge: Harvard Univ. Press, 1975). The author claims that Cleveland's Rumanian immigrants were able to "sponsor" or retain their children in the schools longer than the other two groups and this factor helps to partially explain their higher economic and social mobility.

50. Andrew Draper, "Plans of Organization for School Purposes in Large Cities," *Educational Review* 6 (June 1983): 299–300.

51. Nasaw, *Schooled to Order*, 154; *Annual Report* 1868:54.

52. Colin Greer, *The Great School Legend: A Revisionist Interpretation of American Public Education* (New York: The Viking Press, 1973); Clarence Karrier, et al., *Roots of Crisis: American Education in the Twentieth Century* (Chicago: Rand McNally & Co., 1973); Michael Katz, *Class, Bureaucracy and Schools: The Illusion of Educational Change in America* (New York: Praeger Publishers, 1971). See also John A. Morford, et al., *Alternative Schools in Greater Cleveland: A Descriptive Study* (Cleveland: The Martha Holden Jennings Foundation, 1973), and Ivan Illich, *Deschooling Society* (New York: Harper and Row, Publishers, 1970).

Political Reform in Cleveland

The research for this essay was supported by generous grants from the National Endowment for the Humanities and the University of Akron Faculty Research Committee.

1. The literature on reform in the early twentieth century, the Progressive Era, is

vast. For useful statements of particular points of view see Peter G. Filene, "An Obituary for 'The Progressive Movement,' " *American Quarterly* 22 (Spring 1970): 20–34; Samuel P. Hays, "The Politics of Reform in Municipal Government in the Progressive Era," *Pacific Northwest Quarterly* 55 (Oct. 1964): 157–69; Martin Schiesl, *The Politics of Efficiency* (Berkeley: Univ. of California Press, 1977); Gabriel Kolko, *The Triumph of Conservatism* (New York: The Free Press, 1963).

2. *PD*, Aug. 8, 1900; Chamber of Commerce minutes, 1901–2, Chamber Meeting, Dec. 17, 1901, Greater Cleveland Growth Association Records, WRHS.

3. *PD*, June 27, Aug. 26, Oct. 22, 1902; *Ohio Laws* 95 (1902): 20–106; Max B. May, "The New Ohio Municipal Code," *Annals of the American Academy of Political and Social Science* 21 (Jan. 1903): 125–28; Tom L. Johnson, *My Story* (Seattle: Univ. of Washington Press, 1970), 185–87.

4. Mayo Fesler, "Home Rule for Ohio Cities," *National Municipal Review* 1 (Oct. 1912): 714–15; Hoyt Landon Warner, *Progressivism in Ohio, 1897–1917* (Columbus: Ohio State Univ. Press, 1964), 440–42; Chamber of Commerce minutes, 1912–13, vol. 1, Committee on Legislation, Feb. 24, Apr. 4, 1913; Newton D. Baker to E. W. Harley, Apr. 25, 1913, Baker Papers WRHS, noted that there was no sentiment in favor of either a commission or city manager form. Cleveland did adopt a city manager charter amendment in 1921.

5. This conclusion rests upon the newspaper reports of Johnson and Baker's campaign appearances. The level of information and respect for the intelligence of the audience was much higher then than now.

6. Chamber of Commerce minutes, 1909–10, vol. 1, Board of Directors, Mar. 19, 1910, pp. 1–4; *Ohio Laws* 101 (1910): 430–35. *PD*, Feb. 4, May 21, June 10, 1911; *Ohio Laws* 102 (1911): 268–69.

7. Chamber of Commerce minutes, 1918–19, vol. 1, Board of Directors, Oct. 29, 1918, pp. 14–18; "Issues Submitted to the Voters," *Civic Affairs* (Oct. 1920): 6–7; *PD*, Nov. 3, 7, 1920.

8. Johnson, *My Story*, 125–31.

9. The long and tangled street railway story can be followed in the *Street Railway Journal* and the *Electric Railway Journal*, trade publications favorable to the private companies, in Johnson's memoirs, and in the Johnson and Baker papers at the WRHS.

10. *Electric Railway Journal* 41 (Jan. 25, 1913): 141; 41 (Mar. 8, 1913): 438–39. I am indebted to my colleague, Douglas V. Shaw, on this point about the jitneys.

11. Johnson, *My Story*, 125–31.

12. This conclusion rests upon the Chamber of Commerce minutes, for the years from 1900 to 1930.

13. *PD*, May 28, 1923, on the changes of name of the organization. Its publications, *Municipal Bulletin*, *Civic Affairs*, and later *Greater Cleveland* are important for their information and for the organization's point of view.

14. *City Record* 22 (Dec. 31, 1935): 1357. For a useful sketch of Fesler, see Thomas F. Campbell, *Freedom's Form* (Cleveland: The City Club, 1963), 95–96.

15. *Cleveland Press*, Oct. 2, Nov. 2, 1916.

16. Schiesl, *Politics of Efficiency*, 172–88.

17. Ibid.

18. Chester C. Maxey, "The Cleveland Election and the New Charter," *American Political Science Review* 16 (Feb. 1922): 83–86; Chester C. Maxey, "An Analysis of Cleveland's New Charter," *National Municipal Review* 12 (Jan. 1923): 29–35; Cleve-

land Committee of Fifteen to Investigate the Desirability of a City Manager Plan, *Cleveland Engineering* 3 (Nov. 6, 1919): 1–8; *PD*, Jan. 8, 1922, Annual Review Section; Maurice Maschke, "Memoirs of Maschke," chap. 22, Cleveland Public Library.

19. Cleveland, Committee of 100. City Manager Plan, *The Meaning of the City Manager Plan* (1921), pamphlet, Cleveland Public Library.

20. Philip W. Porter, *Cleveland: Confused City on a Seesaw* (Columbus: Ohio State Univ. Press, 1976).

21. Citizens League of Cleveland, "Five Years of City Managers Government in Cleveland," *National Municipal Review Supplement* 18 (Mar. 1929): 203–20; Mayo Fesler, "Cleveland Again Defeats Attack on City Manager Charter," *National Municipal Review* 18 (Oct. 1929): 601–3.

22. Randolph O. Huus, "Cleveland Council Removes City Manager Hopkins," *National Municipal Review* 19 (Mar. 1930): 155–57; "A Disgraceful Proceeding," *Greater Cleveland* 5 (Jan. 16, 1930): 79–80; *Cleveland City Record*, Jan. 22, 1930, pp. 43–49; "Cleveland's First City Manager Removed," *Greater Cleveland* 5 (Jan. 23, 1930): 94; "Political Parties in City Government," *Greater Cleveland* 5 (Feb. 27, 1930): 115–18; Jack Raper, *The Soviet Table* (Cleveland: Public Affairs Committee, 1935), 15; Thomas F. Campbell, *Daniel E. Morgan, 1877–1949: The Good Citizen in Politics* (Cleveland: Western Reserve Univ. Press, 1966).

23. Raper, *Soviet Table*, 41–42; Maschke, "Memoirs," chap. 36; Porter, *Cleveland*, 85–88.

24. Jon Teaford, *City and Suburb: The Political Fragmentation of Metropolitan America, 1850–1970* (Baltimore: Johns Hopkins Univ. Press, 1979); Chamber of Commerce, *Annexation* (Cleveland: Chamber of Commerce, 1916), pamphlet, Cleveland Public Library; "City and County Consolidation," *Civic Affairs* (Jan. 1917): 1–3; *Cleveland City Record*, Dec. 26, 1918, pp. 1046–47.

25. "County Home Rule," *Greater Cleveland* 2 (Feb. 10, 1925): 3; Chamber of Commerce minutes, 1924–25, vol. 1, Board of Directors, Dec. 17, 1924, p. 37; vol. 2, Board of Directors, Apr. 8, 1925, pp. 4–27.

26. *PD*, Jan. 17, Feb. 24, Oct. 18, 1924.

27. "County Home Rule in Ohio," *Greater Cleveland* 2 (Dec. 22, 1926): 71–78, 2 (Feb. 9, 1927): 104.

28. Teaford, *City and Suburb*, 127–28.

29. Haskell P. Short, "Robert Alphonso Taft: His Eight Years in the Ohio General Assembly" (master's thesis, Ohio State University, 1951), 97–98; Teaford, *City and Suburb*, 142–48, 157–61.

30. Teaford, *City and Surburb*, 159–61; Raper, *Soviet Table*, 43–44; Robert Rawson, *Inside Local Government* (Cleveland: Public Affairs Committee, 1948), 102–10.

31. Teaford, *City and Suburb*, 165.

32. See for example, Robert Wood, *1400 Governments* (Garden City, N.Y.: Anchor Books, 1964); Raymond Vernon, *The Myth and Reality of Our Urban Problems* (Cambridge: Harvard Univ. Press, 1966).

33. Teaford, *City and Suburb*, 177; Richard A. Watson and John Romano, "Metropolitan Government for Metropolitan Cleveland: An Analysis of the Voting Record," *Midwest Journal of Political Science* 5 (Nov. 1961): 367–71.

34. John J. Harrigan, *Political Change in the Metropolis* (Boston: Little, Brown, 1981), 304–5.

35. David C. Rogers, *The Management of Big Cities* (Beverly Hills: Sage Publishing Co., 1971).

36. *Press,* June 19, 23, 24, 29, July 1, 1981.

37. *Press,* July 1, 1981; *New York Times,* Jan. 3, 1979.

38. Kenneth Kusmer, *A Ghetto Takes Shape: Black Cleveland, 1870–1930* (Urbana: Univ. of Illinois Press, 1976); Christopher G. Wye, "The New Deal and the Negro Community: Toward a Broader Conceptualization," *Journal of American History* 59 (Dec. 1972): 621–39; Carl B. Stokes, *Promises of Power: A Political Autobiography* (New York: Simon and Schuster, 1973), 140–45.

39. Stokes, *Promises of Power,* 140–45.

40. *Press,* June 12, 24, 25, 1981.

41. *Press,* Oct. 12, 1980.

42. Schiesl, *Politics of Efficiency,* 149–51, 171–88; Samuel P. Hays, "The Changing Political Structure of the City in Industrial America," *Journal of Urban History* 1 (Nov. 1974): 6–38.

43. John N. Ingham, "The American Urban Upper Class: Cosmopolitans or Locals?" *Journal of Urban History* 2 (Nov. 1975): 81–85; Josef Barton, *Peasants and Strangers: Italians, Rumanians, and Slovaks in an American City 1870–1890* (Cambridge: Harvard Univ. Press, 1975).

44. George E. Condon, *Cleveland: The Best Kept Secret* (Garden City: Doubleday, 1967), 321–30.

45. Porter, *Cleveland,* 126, 175–80, 227–28; Rogers, *Management,* 119–24, For Stokes' apologia see his *Promises of Power;* for a much more critical view see Porter, *Cleveland,* 238–54.

46. Louis Masotti and Jerome R. Corsi, *Shootout in Cleveland: Black Militants and the Police* (New York: Frederick A. Praeger, 1969); Stokes, *Promises of Power;* Porter, *Cleveland; New York Times,* Nov. 9, 1977, Aug. 18, 1978, Mar. 7, 1979, Nov. 7, 1979.

Index

INDEX

Contributors and Editors

JOHN J. GRABOWSKI, curator of manuscripts at the Western Reserve Historical Society, is editor of the *Ohio Archivist* and has taught at Cuyahoga Community College and Kent State University. He has published numerous articles and is currently managing editor of the *Encyclopedia of Cleveland History*, forthcoming.

MICHAEL J. McTIGHE teaches history of American religion at Cleveland State University. He has also taught at Baldwin Wallace College, Hiram College, John Carroll University, and Oberlin College. He is working on a book on religion and society in Cleveland from 1836 to 1860.

MARIAN J. MORTON is professor of history at John Carroll University. Her publications include *The Terrors of Ideological Politics: Liberal Historians In A Conservative Mood* and numerous articles, many on Cleveland, the most recent of which is, "Seduced and Abandoned in an American City: Cleveland and Its Fallen Women, 1869–1936," *Journal of Urban History* (1985).

EDWARD M. MIGGINS, associate professor of history at Cuyahoga Community College, was a National Endowment for the Humanities Fellow at Columbia University and served as research director of the Cleveland Library's Cleveland Heritage Program. His publications include *A Guide to Studying Neighborhoods and Resources on Cleveland* and *The Birth of Modern Cleveland, 1865–1929*, forthcoming.

JAMES F. RICHARDSON is professor of history and urban studies at the University of Akron and author of *The New York Police: Colonial Times to 1901*, editor of *The American City: Historical Studies*, and co-editor of and contributor to *The Urban Experience: Themes in American History*.

LOIS SCHARF, executive director of National History Day, teaches American history at Case Western Reserve University. She is author of *To Work and To Wed: Female Employment, Feminism, and the Great Depression*, and co-editor of and contributor to *Decades of Discontent: The Women's Movement, 1920–1940*.

DAVID D. VAN TASSEL, Elbert J. Benton Professor of History at Case Western Reserve University, is president of National History Day Inc. He is author of *Recording America's Past: An Interpretation of the Development of Historical Studies in America 1607–1884*, co-editor of and contributor to *Science and Society in the United States*, editor of *American Thought in the Twentieth Century*, of *Aging, Death and the Completion of Being*, and of the *Encyclopedia of Cleveland History*, forthcoming.

BERTRAM WYATT-BROWN is Milbauer Professor of History at the University of

Florida and formerly a member of the Department of History at Case Western Reserve University. He is author of *Lewis Tappan and the Evangelical War Against Slavery*, *Southern Honor: Ethics and Behavior in the Old South*, and *Yankee Saints and Southern Sinners*, and editor of *The American People in the Ante-Bellum South*.

CHRISTOPHER WYE is the director of the Office of Policy Analysis and Evaluation in the Office of Community Planning and Development at the U.S. Department of Housing and Urban Development in Washington, D.C. He has published a number of articles on the black experience in Cleveland, and his book *Midwest Ghetto: Change and Continuity in the Cleveland Black Community, 1929–1945* will be published by Holmes and Meier.